THE COLOUR
OF INJUSTICE

Also by Lee Lawrence

The Louder I Will Sing

THE COLOUR OF INJUSTICE

LEE LAWRENCE

abacus
books

ABACUS

First published in Great Britain in 2025 by Abacus

1 3 5 7 9 10 8 6 4 2

A CIP catalogue record for this book
is available from the British Library.

ISBN 978-0-349-14670-6

Typeset in Bembo by M Rules
Printed and bound in Great Britain by Clays Ltd, Elcograf S.p.A.

Papers used by Abacus are from well-managed forests
and other responsible sources.

Abacus
An imprint of
Little, Brown Book Group
Carmelite House
50 Victoria Embankment
London EC4Y 0DZ

The authorised representative
in the EEA is
Hachette Ireland
8 Castlecourt Centre
Dublin 15, D15 XTP3, Ireland
(email: info@hbgi.ie)

An Hachette UK Company
www.hachette.co.uk

www.littlebrown.co.uk

I dedicate this book to those whose lives have been sacrificed and to their loved ones who have been affected. They turned their trauma into triumph and pain into purpose, benefiting us all.

Contents

Introduction

I was just eleven years old when, shortly after 7 a.m. on the morning of Saturday, 28 September 1985, I was awoken by the sound of what I would later learn was the front door of our family home being kicked in.

I was in the downstairs bedroom, sharing with my parents and my thirteen-year-old sister Sharon, and quickly drifted back to sleep, vaguely aware that my mum Cherry had got out of bed to investigate.

A few seconds later there was a loud BANG and I jumped up and saw my mum lying on the floor, blood pooling around her. There was a man leaning over her with a revolver in his hand, bellowing at her: 'Where's Michael Groce, where's Michael Groce?'

When my mum spoke back, her voice was weak, as if she were a long way away. 'I can't breathe. I can't feel my legs. I think I'm going to die.'

Instincts took over and a red mist descended. I began screaming, over and over: 'What the fuck have you done? You shot Mum! You shoot my mum again and I'm going to kill you.'

The man with the gun in his hand turned and pointed his weapon directly at me. 'Somebody better shut this fucking kid up,' he said.

I froze, and it was only at this moment that I became aware

that the gunman was not the only stranger in the house. There were dozens more, some with guns of their own, others with dogs straining at their leashes, and everyone seemed to be shouting.

The reality of the situation quickly dawned: the man who had shot my mum wasn't some random street thug or wannabe assassin: he was a police officer. He was meant to be one of the good guys.

Something else struck me at the same time. It was obvious that my mother could not have been a threat to him in any way. There could be no justification for shooting her at all, but nothing in the man's demeanour showed any sign of remorse, any indication that he knew he'd made a terrible mistake. Nothing about his attitude told me he was sorry about what he had done.

It would be decades before we learned the truth – that the police raid was a debacle, based on incorrect and out of date information. It should never have taken place. And it was decades before I came to understand that the main reason my mother had been shot at all was simply because of the colour of her skin.

Racial inequality has been part and parcel of policing and the wider criminal justice system since at least the start of the twentieth century. Decades before the arrival of HMT *Empire Windrush* in 1948 there are multiple instances of members of the Black community being under-protected as victims, over-policed as suspects and suffering as a result.

Many of the attitudes and biases that existed appear to have been shaped directly by the British Empire, but now many people seem to conveniently ignore the connection.

Sathnam Sanghera, author of *Empireland*, summed it up brilliantly: 'The amnesia comes from the fact we mostly identify as the nation that won World War Two, not as the nation which had the greatest empire in human history. That helps us forget that there was at least a century where we were quite massively white supremacist and sometimes genocidal.'

Despite multiple acts of Parliament, public inquiries, independent reports, political promises, mass protests, violent uprisings and more, the needle has moved relatively little. Yes, progress has been made but there is still a long, long way to go and the rights of Black citizens in the UK continue to be ignored.

I had little interest in politics and history at the time my mum was shot – I was just too young. I became her primary care giver for the twenty-six years that followed before she finally succumbed to injuries that resulted directly from the bullet fragments that had torn into her flesh.

I spent much of that time fighting for justice, trying to get the police to accept that they should bear responsibility. Along the way I discovered that my case was far from an isolated one. The more I looked, the more cases of racial injustice I found and the more I realised that the issues being faced are not the result of one or two isolated bad apples within police forces and the judiciary.

Instead, what we are fighting against are deep-seated prejudices and biases that have resulted in a culture of racism that is so widely accepted and so deeply ingrained that far too many people just assume it is the norm.

Justice is about fairness. And if my family had been treated fairly in the beginning, we wouldn't have gone through what we did and my mother would still be here today. We didn't receive justice, we achieved justice because we had to fight for it.

In the decades-long struggle my family and I faced, it was the power of the collective voice of our community which really made a difference. The stories in this book and my exploration of the historical context of the issues we all face will, I hope, show you how much strength is to be gained from those like me and my family who endured similar struggles in the past.

Numerous laws have been introduced to safeguard people of colour in the UK, yet there have been many cases where the rights of Black individuals have been overlooked or violated, and this continues today. In the ten years from 2011 to 2021, there were fifty-two deaths of Black individuals in situations involving police custody or contact. This is a mortality rate four times higher than the demographic representation of Black people in the general population.

According to the National Police Chiefs' Council: 'Black people are seven times more likely to be stopped and searched than white people and five times more likely to be subjected to the use of force ... 10 per cent of our recorded searches, 27 per cent of use-of-force incidents and 35 per cent of Taser incidents involved someone from a Black ethnic group. The latest estimates suggest that only 3.5 per cent of the population is Black.'

The murder of George Floyd in the spring of 2020 may have taken place in the United States but it brought a fresh focus to the issues of the excessive use of force by police officers in relation to the Black community, as well as a wider debate about racism around the world.

I had been hopeful that the protests that followed Floyd's death would usher in a cosmic shift in police relations with the Black community. But still the problems continue.

In January 2023, the United Nations Working Group of Experts on People of African Descent published a statement following the ten-day fact-finding mission to the UK that they had conducted the previous year. Their damning conclusions led them to call for prosecutors to immediately end all use of joint enterprise due to concerns it was leading to a disproportionate number of Black teenagers being sent to prison. They also called for an immediate moratorium on the use of strip searches during stop and searches by police: 'We have serious concerns about impunity and the failure to address racial disparities in the criminal justice system, deaths in police custody, "joint enterprise" convictions and the dehumanising nature of the stop and (strip) search.'

The introduction of austerity measures had led to the

intensification of racism and racial discrimination for Black people and this had negatively impacted their basic rights. 'Racialised acts targeting people of African descent have remained steadfast, and the experience is similar across different parts of the UK. They are victimised and have no assurance of effective redress from authorities or the justice system.'

One UN group member, Dominique Day, said: 'I've never visited a country before where there is a culture of fear pervading Black communities – relating to a range of asylum, residency, policing issues. An entire community experiences constant and ongoing human rights violations as a routine and normalised part of daily life.'

The working group acknowledged the ongoing repercussions of the *Windrush* scandal, which had 'caused irreparable harm to many and has left a deep vein of disaffection and disappointment within the community ... The emotional trauma of this generation cannot be quantified.'

Group chair Catherine Namakula said that the findings related to joint enterprise had especially surprised the investigators. 'There are many Black boys in detention not because they have committed offences but because they are associated with people who have committed offences. The legal system has inappropriately cast expressions of Black culture, including drill or rap music ... as markers of criminality.'

The working group also examined issues related to education, including the unequal expulsion rates of young Black male students from schools and academies. It was noted that policing within the school environment seemed to be 'directly linked to the presence of Black students and a practice that intimidates, stigmatises, and criminalises Black children and young people'.

They were repeatedly told that, while groups of Black teenagers were always seen as gangs, white teenagers who gathered together were seen primarily as a friendship group.

The UN team had visited London, Birmingham, Manchester

and Bristol, meeting government ministers, local council representatives, police officials and hundreds of individuals. They also
engaged in discussions with families who had lost loved ones while
in police custody and gained insight into the profound effects of
racial bias within the family court system.

The names of many of the people and places at the heart of the
landmark racial injustice cases that will be featured in this book
are well known, but just as many have been all but forgotten. Yet
in all cases, they have had a lasting impact on policing, the judicial
system and even society as a whole.

The reason we have a court of criminal appeal is because of
racial injustice; the reason police interviews are now recorded
rather than simply being written out by the interviewing officer is
because of racial injustice. The reason the law of double jeopardy
was partly abolished after eight hundred years on the statute books
was because of racial injustice. It's also the reason police vans and
custody units are now fitted with cameras.

It took thirty-one years to get some level of justice for what happened to my mum. We received an apology from the Metropolitan
Police and some accountability through the restorative justice
process. Some of the cases you will read about here waited even
longer and for some, the battle continues to this day.

In an effort to find out why the pursuit of justice has proved so
elusive, I looked back to the past to see if I could understand how
things ended up the way they did.

It's often said that history repeats itself but until I began work on
this book, I hadn't realised quite how true that statement could be.
Going back in time and examining past incidents provides a deep
insight into how we have ended up where we are today.

And that is the purpose of this book. It goes back to uncover
the origins of racial bias and injustice and the impact it has had on
the Black community in the decades leading up to the shooting of

my mum and in the decades that have passed since. We can learn from the past and effectively apply those lessons to build a better future and create positive change.

It's encouraging to see how far we have come and good to know that the work done up to now will hopefully mean fewer families and loved ones will have to wait decades for justice to be done the way that I did. But at the same time there is still so much further to go.

Nowadays I sit on police advisory boards and help them find ways to improve their practices. I've been able to begin my own healing process and, by learning to mediate and by training in restorative justice, I'm ready to try to inspire and encourage others.

In the anti-racism training which I offer to officers, I take them back to the history of the force and examine some of the most seminal incidents in policing, relating to the Black community. This book does the same, showing how countless human stories have accumulated to emphasise the need for radical change.

What you are about to read is a selection of key episodes of racial injustice. It is by no means a comprehensive list – and I admit we are only scratching the surface. There are literally thousands more incidents that never achieve the same level of public attention, let alone ever see the inside of a courtroom.

There is a huge difference between what some will consider an injustice and what actually ends up in a court of law. Yet all too many of these low-profile, little-known cases will have every bit as much impact on the individuals and families involved as the murder of Stephen Lawrence, the incarceration of the Cardiff Three or the death of Dalian Atkinson.

Racism is the word used to describe the unfair treatment and biased attitudes directed towards individuals due to their racial or ethnic backgrounds and it therefore has the potential to impact any member of society, but I want to be clear that within this book, the focus is very much on the impact racism and racial injustice has upon Britain's Black community.

Issues of race are often seen under the umbrella term of BAME (Black, Asian and Minority Ethnic) but this can sometimes dilute the issues faced by specific groups. For example, while BAME men and women make up 14 per cent of the overall population, they make up 25 per cent of the prison population, according to the Lammy Review.

But when you look at Black people alone, the picture changes. Despite making up just 4 per cent of the population, they account for 12 per cent of adult prisoners. While other groups are also found to be overrepresented it is to a much lesser degree, and in the case of Asians, the proportion of individuals in prison is currently lower than the percentage of the general population.

A 2020 report by the Independent Office for Police Conduct (which replaced the Independent Police Complaints Commission in 2018) found that since 2015, there had been eighty-six deaths in or following police custody, of which twenty involved people from a BAME background. Of that twenty, fourteen were Black, four were Asian and the remaining two 'mixed and other'.

Not surprisingly, this disparity is reflected in the make-up of the police themselves and speaks volumes about how reluctant members of the Black community are to join the ranks.

As of 2024, Asian officers make up 3.8 per cent of forces in England and Wales and mixed-race officers 2.6 per cent. Black officers make up just 1.3 per cent of the total.

If the police are a force – and let's face it, you can't realistically look at them in any other way – then they should be a force for good. I want to help that happen.

Justice is supposed to be fair because justice is supposed to be impartial. But it turns out this is just a myth. The next time you're in central London, take a wander down to the Central Criminal Court, a building better known by the name of the street on which it stands: Old Bailey.

Look up to the top of the dome and you'll see a golden statue of Lady Justice, a figure recognisable in courthouses across the world and dating back to ancient Greek and Egyptian times. She holds a set of scales in one hand to represent the fact that she always seeks to balance out the evidence before her. She also holds a sword to represent authority, along with the idea that justice is swift and final.

And, of course, she wears a blindfold to show that she is impartial and that her judgments are not influenced by race, colour or creed, age, gender or sexual orientation.

But if you look a little closer, you'll see there is no blindfold on the statue at the Old Bailey. Although many people assume that justice has always been 'blind', this particular detail was only introduced in the mid-sixteenth century and can be found on only a minority of statues.

As we shall see, the judiciary, along with the policing system that supports it, have failed to show impartiality for hundreds of years. The reality is that Lady Justice sees everything, including the fact that those most likely to suffer from the racism and disparity are Black.

Origins

1

Origins

My mum, Dorothy 'Cherry' Groce, was born in the parish of Portland on the Caribbean island of Jamaica in September 1948.

Earlier that same year, on 22 June, a former troopship had docked at the port of Tilbury in Essex, carrying 1,027 passengers. Of these, 539 gave their last country of residence as Jamaica and a further 263 named other Caribbean islands including Bermuda and Trinidad. In total, 693 of those on board said they intended to settle in the United Kingdom.

That ship was HMT *Empire Windrush* and its arrival has since become a watershed moment in the history of Black migration to the UK.

Five weeks later, a new piece of government legislation, the British Nationality Act, passed into law. One of its key provisions was to award citizenship to all those born under the flag of the British Empire. It meant that anyone from the Caribbean, India,

Africa and many other countries was entitled to the same rights and privileges as British citizens living in the UK.

Between 1948 and 1971, when a new set of immigration laws were introduced to curtail such movement, some six hundred thousand people journeyed from the Caribbean and other parts of the Commonwealth to set up home in what many referred to as 'the mother country'.

These migrants became known as the *Windrush* generation and included my maternal grandmother, who made the journey during the 1950s, and the eldest of her eight children, my mum, who left the rest of the family behind to join her in the early 1960s at the age of fourteen.

But while 1948 is seen as a milestone in the history of migration to Britain, it would be a mistake to think that there was no significant Black presence in the UK prior to that date.

In fact, Black people have been living in this country since Roman times, when a unit of up to five hundred soldiers was garrisoned in a fort near Burgh-by-Sands, close to the western end of Hadrian's Wall. A fourth-century inscription refers to the unit as 'Aurelian Moors' suggesting they came from the area now known as Morocco.

In the year 668, the abbot of St Augustine's Abbey in Canterbury was an African-born man named Hadrian. A few hundred years later, a drawing of a Black Briton appears in the Domesday Book and in 1507 the court of King Henry VII records the appearance of a Black trumpeter.

The number of Black people in Britain increased dramatically as the result of the country's deep involvement in the slave trade. By the 1760s around twenty thousand Blacks were in the country, three-quarters of them in London.

Not all of them were slaves in the traditional sense – at the time, a Black servant working as a page, footman or handmaid was seen as a status symbol. Their treatment varied enormously with some earning fair wages and given significant freedoms but others forced to wear brass collars engraved with the names of their owners.

There were also significant numbers of Black seamen, traders and other merchants in cities that were home to major international ports. But regardless of their position the vast majority would likely have experienced some kind of racism or prejudice as a result of the colour of their skin.

Between the years 1720 and 1841, 420 individuals of African heritage appeared at the Old Bailey. Of these thirty-one were witnesses, forty-nine were victims and 161 were mentioned in passing. The remaining 179 appeared as defendants.

Underlying racial prejudice was a significant issue with many of the Black defendants questioned about their understanding of right and wrong or asked to confirm whether or not they had been baptised. White defendants were rarely asked such questions.

In some cases, skin colour formed the entire basis of a prosecution. In 1737, when Anne Godfrey reported the theft of some washing from her home in Hackney, witnesses reported that three men were responsible, two of them white and one Black.

Having been identified as the only Black man in Hackney at the time, George Scipio was dragged before the courts and prosecuted on this basis alone. The two white men were never identified and remained free.

The African-born population swelled again when hundreds of Black soldiers and seamen settled in Britain after fighting in the Napoleonic Wars. Royal Navy records show that during the 1805 Battle of Trafalgar, eighteen men aboard all the ships involved in the day's fighting were listed as having been born in Africa, including at least one on HMS *Victory* itself. That man, twenty-three-year-old George Ryan, is immortalised in a bronze panel on the base of Nelson's Column that was installed more than 175 years ago.

By the late eighteenth century, the Black community in London was large and prosperous enough for exclusive Black-only parties to take place on a regular basis, sometimes with hundreds of guests at a time.

The early nineteenth century saw laws introduced which made it illegal to import slaves into Britain and then in 1833, slavery was abolished completely. But with only a few thousand slaves among a population of millions, most Britons had never seen a Black person in the flesh or were even aware that there were significant numbers living in the UK.

The result was an alarming creation: human zoos where native Africans were placed on display inside glorified cattle enclosures that mimicked their 'natural habitat' and made to perform. An 1895 exhibition at London's Crystal Palace saw eighty Somalis shipped in. Wearing only traditional animal skins despite the cold weather, they were made to perform native dances, cook food on open fires and set up and take down their accommodation so that people could see how they lived.

They also took part in mock battles, first against opposing tribes and finally against European settlers who were, of course, always victorious. All this only reinforced the idea that Black people were closer to animals than they were to white people, a myth that had always been wholly necessary to justify slavery in the first place.

After abolition, Britain could claim to hold the moral high ground in relation to slavery, but the racism and prejudice that had underpinned the trade continued to grow as the British Empire spread into further corners of the world.

Concerns about the poor treatment of those living in the parts of Africa and the Caribbean that were under British control prompted discussions among leading Black academics of the time. This in turn led to the first Pan-African Conference, which took place in Westminster in July 1900.

The themes included anti-racism and self-governance. American clergyman and civil rights leader Bishop Alexander Walters said in his opening address that 'for the first time in history Black people had gathered from all parts of the globe to discuss and improve the condition of their race, to assert their rights and organize so that they might take an equal place among nations'.

It was fitting that the first such event should take place in London, where even those Black migrants who very clearly defied such racist stereotypes by being well spoken, highly educated and in many ways, thanks to their colonial education, more British than the British themselves, faced an uphill struggle.

Take, for example, the case of Harold Moody. Born in Kingston, Jamaica, in 1882, he was the eldest son of a modestly wealthy, devoutly Christian family and became interested in healthcare from an early age after being inspired by his father, who ran a successful pharmacy.

In 1904, he sailed to England and enrolled at King's College, London, to study medicine and immediately found himself up against the so-called colour bar – the informal term given to the practice of denying goods, services and even employment to non-whites. Although Britain never introduced laws to legally segregate races, legislation to outlaw such practices would not be introduced until 1965.

On his very first day in London, Moody was given a list of potential lodging houses by the local YMCA, but every single one turned him away because of the colour of his skin. He eventually managed to find a small attic room to live in.

At university, most of the other students refused to speak to him, but despite this he excelled academically and won a number of prestigious prizes during the course of his medical training, eventually qualifying as a doctor in 1910.

Moody sought employment at King's College but was turned down because the matron refused to accept the idea of having a man of colour working as a doctor in the hospital. He then applied for the post of medical officer for the Camberwell Board of Guardians but was told that, despite him having the best qualifications of all the candidates, people would not accept being treated by a Black man so he could not be offered the job. Moody applied for multiple positions over the next three years but was denied them all. In February 1913, frustrated with his inability to practise his chosen profession, he opened up his own practice in Peckham, south-east London, and slowly started making a living while gaining a reputation for excellence.

That same year, John Archer, the Liverpool-born son of a ship steward from Barbados and an Irish mother, was elected mayor of Battersea. Prejudice and racism had hung over him like a cloud throughout his campaign with some newspapers expressing surprise that he was able to speak English so fluently. Others questioned whether he was truly a British citizen at all. A letter written to the editor of a newspaper commented: 'It is not meet that the white man should be governed and controlled by a man of colour. It has always been that the white man ruled, and it must always be so. If not, goodbye to the prestige of Great Britain.'

Speaking after his victory, Archer said: 'My election tonight means a new era. You have made history tonight. For the first time in the history of the English nation a man of colour has been elected as mayor of an English borough. That will go forth to the coloured nations of the world and they will look to Battersea and say Battersea has done many things in the past, but the greatest thing it has done has been to show that it has no racial prejudice and that it recognises a man for the work he has done.'

(Archer was likely not aware that another Black man, Allan Minns, who was born in the Bahamas, had been elected mayor of the small Norfolk town of Thetford almost a decade earlier.)

For a country that has seen the issue of immigration regularly dominate the social and political agenda, it's something of a surprise to learn that, just four decades before the arrival of the *Windrush*, controls on immigration to Britain simply didn't exist.

By the start of the century, the British Empire had grown to be the most expansive empire in history, governing almost a quarter of the world's population. In theory, every single one of those subjects was a British citizen with as much right to work and reside in the country as someone who had been born here.

Up until 1905, Britain had an open-door policy towards immigration, meaning that anyone from anywhere in the world who wanted to settle there was able to do so. Although there was a legal distinction between British subjects (which included anyone born within the British Empire) and 'aliens' – everyone who was not a British subject – both groups were equally able to enjoy freedom of movement into and out of the country.

The seeds of change were sown in the 1880s when thousands of Jews fleeing from Russia and Poland arrived in the country, sparking concerns over competition for housing and work, as well as the fear that an 'invasion' of migrants would undermine British culture.

The eventual solution was the passing of the 1905 Aliens Act which denied entry to Britain by anyone found to be an 'undesirable immigrant'. The wording of the act was vague, and it was only intended to be applied to Jewish and Eastern European immigrants. Subjects of the British Empire were still able to enjoy free movement. It was the first piece of legislation the country ever introduced with a view to controlling the movement of people across its borders. It would not be the last.

While some wealthy families from the far-flung corners of the world sent their children to Britain in order to get a first-class education or relocated in order to experience first hand all that the 'mother country' had to offer – Harold Moody is a good example – there had never been an open invitation. These people could not be called immigrants as they already had legal right of residence. However, in reality, no one ever expected more than a few hundred to set up shop here in any one year.

All this changed with the outbreak of the First World War in 1914. As casualties mounted up, a call was put out across the

Empire for volunteers to come and fight. Many individuals from the Caribbean followed this path, frequently inspired by activist leaders such as Marcus Garvey, who told them that doing so would be an excellent way of demonstrating allegiance to the king. This, in turn, would prove they were entitled to be treated the same as all other citizens of the Empire.

Despite the influx of volunteers, the government initially remained adamant that Black British individuals should not be allowed to enlist. However, over time, King George V's encouragement, along with the urgent need for more and more soldiers to replace those who had been killed or wounded, meant the policy of exclusion was scrapped.

In 1915 the British established the West Indies Regiment, which brought together volunteers from across the Caribbean. More than 15,600 men served across its twelve battalions, supporting the Allied forces. Those in command were, however, always white, and regulations were put in place so that no Black soldier was able to rise above the rank of sergeant.

While Black units were deployed against non-white combatants in Africa and the Middle East, they were not permitted to engage in combat on the Western Front. This restriction was due to concerns that having colonial soldiers fight alongside or against white Europeans might weaken British authority. The fear was that, once the war was over, such soldiers might demand equality or even independence, and because of their combat experience, would know exactly how to fight for it.

Instead, West Indian soldiers worked as labourers – tasked with filthy, physically demanding and often highly dangerous duties such as loading ammunition, setting up telephone lines and excavating trenches – or guarded prisoners of war. The vast majority were never even issued with guns and those that were had to make do with decades-old rifles that performed badly compared to more modern weapons.

Many died, some because of shells and bombs but far more from disease and an inability to withstand the harsh conditions in which they found themselves.

There were changes on the home front, too. Before the war, Black workers had been prevented from taking all but the filthiest, least desirable jobs that inevitably paid the lowest wages. But once war broke out, the situation became different.

With so many men heading to the front, there was well-paid work available for Black men everywhere from the munitions and chemical factories to the flour mills and sugar refineries, work that had previously been denied to them. At the same time, Black sailors found themselves able to take a variety of roles within the merchant navy as the majority of eligible white seamen were being drafted into the Royal Navy.

Even before the war Black communities in Britain's port cities had begun to expand rapidly as a result of the switch from sail to steam. The latter required a very different skill set but a factor that deterred many British sailors from adopting the new roles was that work in the engine rooms was also extremely harsh.

Shipping companies of the day held firmly to the pseudo-scientific belief that those hailing from Africa or the Caribbean were more suited to high temperatures and therefore better able to withstand the work. An additional factor was that workers who were taken on from non-British ports were paid significantly less, boosting profits even further.

Firemen, also known as stokers, fed the boilers with a constant supply of coal while 'trimmers' on a deck above were required to constantly feed coal into hoppers so that it fell within easy reach of the firemen, allowing them to continue shovelling without having to stray too far from the open mouths of the boilers.

It was hard, physical work with long hours and constant filth but often the only option available to Black sailors. The combination of lower costs and a perceived aptitude for such work led many shipping companies to switch to all-Black crews below decks, though the captains and officers were always white.

When war came, the work became even more dangerous. Feeding the boilers meant working at the waterline, the exact spot where a torpedo strike would occur, giving zero chance of escape in the event of a hit. Hundreds of firemen lost their lives as a result.

The Empire had been built upon the idea that Black people were somehow inferior to whites. The Black soldiers who played their part in the conflict had hoped that their bravery and sacrifice might change this view. They were about to be sorely disappointed.

2

Charles Wotten

Of all the communities with large numbers of Black people, none compared to Cardiff's Tiger Bay, which had a mixed community dating back more than two hundred years.

By the early nineteenth century, Cardiff had become one of the biggest docks in the world, exporting huge quantities of iron and coal with a vast number of ships entering and leaving on a daily basis for destinations across the globe.

The influx of foreign sailors brought with them much more than just cargo. They came with their own cultural preferences when it came to music, food and more. Pubs, gambling dens and brothels sprang up to service their needs. Bars with names like the Bucket of Blood and the Snakepit became notorious for the tough, hard-drinking men who gathered there and brawls reminiscent of the old Wild West were a common feature.

During the daytime, sailors could nurse their hangovers in any of the Basque, Somali or Italian cafés that were interspersed between clubs and drinking dens.

No matter how hard you worked, no one seemed to earn enough to do much more than barely survive, but this brought the community together and developed a sense of racial harmony.

Tiger Bay was where the first mosque in Wales was built and was also home to the first curry restaurant in the UK. Children attended schools where thirty or forty different languages would be spoken and boasted of grandparents from the four corners of the world.

With so much mixing going on, many Black seamen found themselves forming relationships and having families with local white women. A key reason for this was that, unlike many other countries in the world at the time, Britain had no anti-miscegenation laws. Such legislative prohibitions, which criminalised inter-racial marriage, had existed in the United States since the 1860s and were also on the statutes of countries such as Australia, South Africa, China and India.

However, the spread of such relationships opened up the first cracks in the city's inter-racial relations. In July 1918, the city's chief constable, David Williams, opposed a multi-racial cricket league, as the mere sight of Black men in their kit would simply prove too alluring for local women to resist: 'White flannels are more revealing than corduroys and make Black men more attractive to white girls. Young Cardiff girls should not be allowed to admire such beasts.'

Regardless of how much racial harmony existed within the community as a whole, the fact that the man in charge of the local police force held such views would soon be reflected in the way his officers acquitted themselves in the months to come.

The First World War finally ended in November 1918 and in the months that followed, hundreds of thousands of British soldiers were demobilised and returned home, hoping to pick up their lives exactly where they had left off.

They expected to be appreciated for the sacrifices they had made and to return to 'a land fit for heroes'. Instead they came back to a very different place where homes were scarce (many had been destroyed and house building had virtually ground to a halt during the conflict) and where the jobs they had previously relied on were now being carried out by others.

Austerity measures during the war meant the Black workers were usually being paid less than the white workers had received prior to the conflict. So, the Black workers became the scapegoat for the wrath of the white workers and it became almost inevitable that it would not end well.

The fact that the majority of Black sailors and soldiers who had fought in the conflict, along with the other Black workers who had replaced their white counterparts in factories and mills, had the exact same rights of citizenship made no difference. Tensions rapidly rose as the white workers demanded their jobs back and insisted they should be given preference over and above any Black workers.

The situation declined rapidly when 120 Black employees working in Liverpool refineries – where demobilisation had seen the Black population rise to as many as five thousand – were dismissed over the course of a single week because white workers would not work with them. Black workers were evicted from their lodgings, to free up space for white residents, forcing them to crowd into the few boarding houses remaining open to them.

In May 1919, the secretary of the Liverpool Ethiopian Association met with the Lord Mayor of Liverpool and informed him that there were at least six hundred Black men, the vast majority former soldiers and sailors and many wounded or disabled, who were unable to find work in the city purely on account of their race.

That same month, the Lord Mayor also met with representatives of five thousand unemployed white ex-servicemen, who complained that Black men in work were proving to be an impediment to their own employment opportunities.

As tensions mounted, the Colonial Office suggested that many of the Black workers be repatriated to their country of origin, but the amounts being offered to support such a move were woefully inadequate, barely covering the cost of a ticket on a ship. In any case, many of those workers and former servicemen now considered Britain to be their home. A significant number had children that had been born here. Despite widespread publicity around the scheme, there was little interest.

And then came another insult. The government arranged a huge victory march in London to celebrate the achievements of its soldiers, including those from across the Commonwealth such as Canadians, Australians and South Africans. Black soldiers from Africa and the Caribbean were not invited to attend.

The anger quickly grew on both sides of the racial divide. The tinder had been set – the smallest of sparks would set it all off.

On 4 June, a West Indian man named John Johnson was making his way through the docks of Liverpool when he was approached by two Scandinavian sailors and asked for a cigar. When he refused, one of the men stabbed him in the face. News of the attack quickly spread throughout the tight-knit community and a few nights later, a group of Johnson's friends went out hunting for the men responsible. At some point, a glass of beer was thrown over a group of Scandinavians by a Black man in naval uniform.

More Blacks then joined the affray, armed with knives, iron bars, sticks and razors. A group of nearby police officers tried to intervene but one of them was knocked out cold. When the scuffle was over, five of the Scandinavians required hospital treatment, though their injuries were mostly minor.

Eager to stop any further outbreaks of trouble, the police decided to raid boarding houses used by Black seamen, ostensibly to take them into custody as a protective measure as the word on the street was that major reprisals were being planned.

But the Black residents trusted the police even less than they trusted the white sailors and refused to leave their homes. When the police tried to remove them by force, more fighting broke out. At least two officers were shot in the process of trying to enter the boarding houses, one in the mouth and another in the neck, possibly by the same bullet. A further two received serious injuries including a slashed face and broken wrists.

A white mob quickly formed and began attacking the boarding houses where Black sailors were known to live. In Upper Pitt Street, they attacked a boarding house at number eighteen, but one man managed to escape out of the back of the property.

Twenty-four-year-old Charles Wotten from Bermuda had been a ship's fireman in the merchant navy but was discharged earlier that year. If he thought that he had escaped all the danger by slipping out of the house, he was badly mistaken. A mob of at least three hundred people spotted him and began to give chase, all the while throwing missiles at him.

Charles ran for his life all the way to the edge of Queens Dock, more than a mile away from his boarding house. A couple of police officers managed to get hold of him. But it wasn't for long: members of the mob descended and tore Charles out of their grasp.

What happened next is unclear but somehow, Charles ended up in the water. He may have jumped in due to his desperation to get away but it's also possible he was thrown in by the crowd.

At that, the fury of the braying mob only grew stronger and he was pelted with rocks and stones as he tried to keep his head above the murky water. People were heard chanting, 'Let him drown.' An officer descended the ladder by the side of the dock and reached out to pull Charles back in, but just then one of the rocks that was being thrown struck him on the top of the head, knocking him unconscious. He sank and never returned to the surface.

Later that evening, Wotten's body was recovered from the dock. Despite the heavy police presence, no arrests were made. No one was even questioned about the incident. The murder remains unsolved to this day.

An inquest into the death of Charles Wotten opened and closed in a single day one week after his death. By now rumours were circulating that Charles had been armed and had fired a shot at the police in an attempt to escape lawful arrest. Detectives reported that the stone that hit him had come from somewhere within the crowd, making it impossible to identify a suspect. They insisted an officer had tried to rescue him shortly before this occurred.

The jury returned a verdict of death by drowning without even considering the fact he had clearly been unlawfully killed.

In the days that followed crowds of whites, sometimes several thousand strong, kept up their attacks on homes and hostels occupied by Black workers. The buildings were vandalised with all the furniture smashed or stolen, and several were set alight. Black seamen did their best to protect themselves, barricading themselves inside their homes. The police locked up more than seven hundred Black residents for their own safety.

On 10 June, a Black delegation delivered a statement at the offices of the *Liverpool Echo*, in which they set out their plight and called for justice. The secretary of the Ethiopian Association stated:

The coloured men have mostly served in the Forces, Navy and transport. They are largely British subjects, and are proud to have been able to have done what they have done for the Empire. [...]

On May 13 I visited the Lord Mayor with a view to the repatriation of some coloured men and to find if it was possible for a bounty to be given to these men through the Colonial Office, as the majority of them have pawned their clothes in order to obtain food. This was due to their being unable to obtain work as seafarers. Our goods and our houses have been broken and taken away from us.

Some of us have been wounded, and lost limbs and eyes fighting for the Empire to which we have the honour to belong.

At present between forty and forty-three coloured men report themselves daily for repatriation. [...]

We ask for British justice, to be treated as true and loyal sons of Great Britain. We must remind the public that in Africa there are white men, and last week 180 Europeans came home on leave from the West Coast. The Liverpool public must reflect on these points.

Police reports claimed the blame lay squarely at the feet of the Black community. Rather than taking into account the incident involving John Johnson which led to his friends seeking to avenge him, the police portrayed the attack on the group of Scandinavians who were thought to be responsible as an unprovoked attack by a group of West Indians.

The same reports describe the Black crowds as being full of men armed with a range of weapons while the white crowds are described as being made up of women and children. When they were asked to disperse, they did so quietly while the Black crowds resisted arrest and assaulted the officers at every opportunity.

The specific tensions that led to the violence were not unique to Liverpool. Similar disturbances had been seen in Glasgow in January of that year when mobs attacked groups of Black sailors. Once again, the catalyst was the return of demobilised soldiers from the battlefields of France who had expected a hero's welcome but found only unemployment and deprivation waiting for them.

Unions decided to call for the working week to be lowered from forty-seven hours to forty hours in order to free up more jobs, but with the Black sailor willing to work for lower rates of pay, many felt this would not be enough to address the difficulties.

The final straw came when a full-blown brawl broke out between sailors seeking employment at the Merchant Marine Office.

Hopelessly outnumbered, some thirty Black sailors made a run for it, eventually seeking refuge in a boarding house on the Broomielaw, a major thoroughfare in the city. The group pursuing them grew larger as other local men joined in the chase. Soon a

mob several hundred strong had gathered outside and began systematically attempting to break their way inside. By now three
people had sustained serious injuries.

Fifty police officers arrived at the scene and, in what would later
become a familiar pattern, took all thirty Black sailors into what
they insisted was protective custody. All those in the white mob
were allowed to disperse freely with no arrests. By contrast, all the
Black men were later charged with riot and weapons offences. The
lawyer who defended them during the subsequent trial noted that
no white people had been arrested and that the evidence presented
by the police had been weak.

It was, in many ways, the first recorded instance of what would
come to be known as institutional racism in British policing.

The next month, trouble flared in South Shields.

In the weeks that followed more clashes were reported in
Salford and parts of London, but the most serious violence was
that which took place in Cardiff, right in the heart of Tiger Bay.

Despite its reputation as a place of racial harmony, tensions
were also rising across the Welsh capital. What finally broke the
levee holding back the growing waves of fury was the sight of a
horse-drawn carriage pulling into the centre of Cardiff Bay with
a mixture of Black men and white women on board.

They were witnessed by a large group of unemployed soldiers
who deeply resented not only the fact that the Black men were
clearly capable of paying for such a conveyance, but also that they
were fraternising with local women. Once again, a small scuffle
broke out and quickly developed into a full-scale riot.

In 1977 the historian Richard Pankhurst published extracts
from a first-hand account of the events in an Italian academic
journal. The passages were taken from an unpublished autobiography, written in 1928, of a Somali seaman named Ibrahim Ismaa'il
who was present when the violence broke out. After spending
many years working on merchant ships travelling to port cities all
around the world, from Buenos Aires to Karachi, he arrived in

London in the early summer of 1919 and immediately made his way to Cardiff, aware that a substantial Somali community had been established there. To his great misfortune, he arrived just as things were reaching their peak: 'In Millicent Street, the fight started at about 7.30 p.m. and lasted a fairly long time. Seven or eight Warsangeli [members of a Somali clan] defended the house and most of them got badly wounded.'

He went on to describe in terrifying detail how a white mob managed to occupy the first floor of the building and set it alight, forcing the Somalis to flee through a neighbouring house until the police arrived and arrested them.

At its height, the mob numbered in excess of two thousand people, roaming around Cardiff attacking anyone they could get their hands on. Even a Somali clergyman was set upon, and the *South Wales News* reported BLACKS HUNTED BY A FURIOUS MOB. Another newspaper recounted one such attack: 'A black man was spotted – he was first insulted and then attacked by three whites, one of whom blew a whistle. This seemed to be the expected signal, because hundreds of persons rushed up from the neighbouring street, including many women and girls – who had sticks and stones, and flung them at the unfortunate coloured man as they chased him along the street.'

Three people were killed, but the death toll would likely have been far higher had it not been for the geographic advantage of Tiger Bay. Separated from the rest of Cardiff by a single road under the railway bridge, members of the community were able to barricade themselves in and hold off their attackers at the boundary of the district. They did so for three days and nights.

Following the events in Cardiff, the British authorities ramped up a repatriation initiative, resulting in the removal of approximately three thousand Black and Arab sailors and their families from Britain between 1919 and 1921.

*

By 1919 Harold Moody's medical practice had taken off. Having made only a single pound during its first year of operation, the years that followed saw rapid growth as word of his reputation as a caring and considerate doctor began to spread. He and his wife would go on to have six children and as his achievements grew, he became increasingly influential and sought out by Black politicians from around the world whenever they visited London.

Aware of the growing levels of poverty and disillusionment that had in part led to the unrest, he was eager to help out whenever he could, offering his home as refuge to any Black person who needed it. He also began lecturing on the notion of community harmony, using his own unique vision that was the result of his childhood experiences and expectations.

In 1931, realising an organisation could do more than he could ever achieve as an individual, he set up the League of Coloured Peoples. There were four key aims: '1) to promote and protect the social, educational, economic and political interests of its members; 2) to interest members in the welfare of coloured peoples in all parts of the world; 3) to improve relations between the races and 4) to co-operate and affiliate with organizations sympathetic to coloured people.'

The LCP published a journal called *The Keys* – a name inspired by the idea of the black and white keys of a piano being in harmony – which reproduced the four key aims on its inside front cover. The magazine featured articles that supported the campaign against racist ideologies. But ultimately, Dr Moody saw the LCP as having a Christian purpose, rather than a political one, and as a result he was often seen as being ineffective. But that did not stop him stepping in to help what would become one of the most high-profile cases of racial injustice of the pre-*Windrush* era.

3

Next Generation

Many of those who boarded the *Windrush* in 1948 and the ships that arrived in the UK the previous year had expected a warm welcome and were eager to make a good impression. But a few had been paying close attention and had seen the warning signs that gave a better idea of the true nature of the reception that would be awaiting them.

Learie Constantine was born into a relatively prosperous family on Trinidad in 1901 and from an early age demonstrated that he had picked up his father's talent for cricket. As a teenager he quickly progressed from local competitions to regional and national ones. It was during this time he had his first experiences of racism.

Only white players were allowed to captain the West Indian team. Black players were permitted to bowl and field, but the belief at the time was that only white players were capable of mastering the skills of both batting and captaincy. Constantine's exceptional talents on the field began to challenge this but ultimately the pace of change would be slow. He joined a number of West Indies teams that toured England and elsewhere during the 1920s and, seeing greater opportunities to advance his career here rather than back home, he eventually moved to Lancashire, setting up home in the small town of Nelson.

Known as the 'coloured catapult', he proved a hugely popular player with hundreds of eager fans turning out to see him play. In addition, in a part of the country where few Black faces were ever seen, he was a great ambassador for his race, highly respected for his polite, educated and softly spoken demeanour.

He remained in England throughout the 1930s and was still there when the Second World War started. Eager to do as much as possible to help, he joined the Ministry of Labour as a welfare officer, supervising the living conditions of the many West Indian workers who had travelled to Britain to fill the wartime labour shortage. But he also continued to play cricket whenever the opportunity presented itself.

In July 1943 he was invited to take part in a number of matches at Lord's to raise money for various charities. Wanting to make the most of the trip to London, Constantine decided to take a short break beforehand with his wife and daughter and duly booked rooms at the Imperial Hotel in Russell Square for four nights.

Well aware of the fact that racial prejudice was simply 'an unpleasant part of daily life in Britain' at the time, even for someone with the level of celebrity status he enjoyed, Constantine decided to take precautions. He had once been refused a room he had booked at a hotel in Brighton simply because of the colour of his skin and was keen not to repeat the experience. While booking at the Imperial, he made sure to inform the staff that he and his family were Black and asked whether this would be an issue. They were reassured that it would not. He duly sent a deposit for the rooms by cheque and thought no more about it. But on arrival, it immediately became clear that there was a problem.

Speaking to the manageress, Margaret O'Sullivan, Constantine was told: 'You can stop tonight but not any longer.' When he tried to explain that he had booked for four nights he was told that this would no longer be possible and that he would have to find somewhere else for the remainder of his time in London.

Arnold Watson, one of Constantine's colleagues at the Ministry of Labour, was with him, and he decided to speak to the manageress himself.

'He can stay tonight but he has to leave tomorrow morning and if he doesn't his luggage will be put outside and his door locked,' Watson was told. 'We are not going to have these niggers in our hotel.'

As Constantine waited in the reception area while Watson spoke to the management, he heard a passing guest comment: 'The Imperial is coming to something if you are going to take niggers in.'

Watson asked O'Sullivan to explain herself and she said the presence of a number of US servicemen in the hotel at the time was a concern because some would take offence at the presence of a Black family. Like much of America in the 1940s, the US Army was strictly segregated. So-called Jim Crow laws (named after a derogatory term for an African American) had been in place since the 1880s and controlled virtually every aspect of life from how people travelled and where they ate their meals to where they went to school and where they were allowed to sit in the cinema.

Eventually the hotel management offered to put up Constantine and his family at the Bedford Hotel, just a short distance away. Worried that the situation might get out of hand, Watson persuaded his colleague to move hotels.

Rather than simply accepting the situation, Constantine decided to take action. He had spoken out many times about the institutional racism that prevented a Black player from being captain of the West Indies (this only changed in 1960 with the appointment of Frank Worrell) and the irony of a being a first-class cricketer with thousands of adoring fans while living in a country that continued to treat him as a third-class citizen. He hoped that by making a stand, he might be able to do something to bring all the different races, religions and cultures together.

He hired a top barrister and announced that he would be suing the hotel company. His dramatic move was supported by Harold Moody's League of Coloured Peoples. Public awareness of the pending case increased dramatically in September that year when it became the subject of a brief debate in Parliament. A number of MPs asked the then Home Secretary, Herbert Morrison, if he would comment.

By that time, the legal proceedings were well underway, so Mr Morrison said he was unable to comment. He did say, however, that there was 'a responsibility on all members of the community to avoid discrimination against any British subject on grounds of race or colour'.

The case came to court in June 1944 and took place over two days. At the time there was no legislation in Britain which outlawed racial discrimination of this kind, so instead the case was about a breach of contract. Constantine had been denied pre-arranged accommodation despite the fact that he had paid a deposit and the hotel had plenty of rooms available. The fact that the denial was purely based on the colour of his skin had no bearing on the case.

Giving his evidence, the managing director of the hotel repeatedly denied that any racist terms had been used at any time during the conversation between Miss O'Sullivan and Constantine, even though they had been heard by many witnesses.

The defence also argued that, because the family had accepted the offer of rooms at an alternative hotel, just a few minutes' walk away from the Imperial, they had fulfilled their contractual obligation to provide accommodation. But the judge rejected this, pointing out that rooms had been available at the Imperial the whole time and that nothing in the manner in which Constantine had behaved could have given the hotel any reason to refuse him.

After a period of deliberation, the judge, Mr Justice Birkett, decided in favour of Constantine and made a point of saying he was satisfied that Miss O'Sullivan had indeed used 'deeply offensive' language, and had been 'a lamentable figure in the witness-box . . . she was not speaking the truth'. By contrast, he said that in court, 'Mr Constantine bore himself with modesty and dignity, dealt with all questions with intelligence and truth. He was not concerned to be malicious or vindictive, but was obviously affected by the indignity and humiliation that had been put upon him and caused him distress and inconvenience which he justifiably resented.'

In his judgment, Birkett said the prosecution had put in a request for exemplary damages 'because of the distress and humiliation Mr Constantine unjustifiably suffered', but explained that he was unable to grant this because there was no such law in place. Instead, Constantine received the sum of five guineas in damages due to the hotel breaching its contract.

'Had I been inclined to do so, I could probably have succeeded in a further action for defamation,' Constantine later wrote in his autobiography, *Cricket in the Sun*. 'But I was content to have drawn the particular nature of the affront before the wider judgment of the British public in the hope that its sense of fair play might help protect the people of my colour in England in future. From the tone of the hundreds of letters of congratulation I received from all over the country, I think my object was attained.'

Despite this optimism, Constantine's victory did nothing to end racial discrimination in Britain's boarding houses, hotels and restaurants, who were still free to refuse to serve Black people if they wished to do so. But what changed was that people became aware that victims of such treatment now knew they had a case for damages on the grounds of the distress they felt in response to such a refusal.

The case also highlighted the fact that the legislation to prevent such discrimination did not exist, ultimately becoming a legal milestone on the way to the 1965 Race Relations Act. But that would not come into force for another two decades and in the meantime, Black people across the country were still at the mercy of racial injustice in almost all aspects of their lives.

It is simply not possible to write a book about the history of the Black experience of the UK's criminal justice system without using words that many people find highly offensive.

One term in particular always elicits an especially strong reaction. When it came up in evidence during the 1995 murder trial of O. J, Simpson, prosecutor Christopher Darden, himself an African American, refused to say out loud what he said was 'the filthiest, dirtiest, nastiest word in the English language'.

This view is shared by the *Oxford English Dictionary* which warns that the word is: 'liable to be considered offensive or taboo in almost all contexts'. Indeed, when it was used during a July 2020 BBC News report that described it being shouted at a victim immediately prior to a racially aggravated attack, the corporation received almost twenty thousand complaints within the space of a few days.

We are, of course, talking about the n-word and in the pages that follow you will find it written out in full on several occasions.

Derived from 'niger', the Latin word for the colour black, the term did not originate as a racial slur but took on those connotations over time and became strongly associated with the transatlantic slave trade.

In an essay written in 1837, Black American minister Hosea Easton wrote that the term was 'employed to impose contempt upon [Blacks] as an inferior race' and noted that white adults often reprimanded their children for being 'worse than niggers' or 'ignorant as niggers'. For many children, a common punishment was being made to sit on the 'nigger seat', a forerunner of the naughty step.

But things were very different in the UK where, despite a history of colonialism and racism, the term didn't carry the same immediate and direct historical baggage related to slavery and segregation as it did in the States.

The word was in common use in Britain during the nineteenth century but almost always in the context of its original meaning – a term for a shade of black or very dark brown. The British Colour Council, established to introduce consistent colours for use throughout the British Empire, included 'Nigger Brown' – BCC 20 – in its first catalogue in 1930 and it remained there for the next few decades.

Another sign of just how popular the term was during the first half of the twentieth century is that it appears in the lyrics of the original 1932 version of the music hall song 'The Sun Has Got His Hat On'. (In 2014, a presenter on BBC Radio Devon unwittingly played this version and was forced to resign after a listener complained.)

Further evidence of the different ways the n-word was viewed on either side of the Atlantic came with the 1939 publication of a novel by Agatha Christie. The UK title was *Ten Little Niggers*, after an old minstrel song. In the US, the book was published a few weeks later under the title *And Then There Were None*. (Surprisingly, UK editions of the book continued to use the original title as late as 1985.)

It wasn't until 1963 that using the n-word in association with the colour was banned by a range of men's and women's clothes manufacturers when they finally realised how much offence it caused to their Black workers.

One of the lessons I've learned from looking at the early history of the Black community in the UK is that racist attitudes have always existed.

As I write this book, issues around immigration remain at the top of political and news agendas. The rhetoric is all too familiar: people are coming to Britain from elsewhere in the world and taking over jobs and using valuable resources.

Just the other day I picked up my daughter from school and she told me about an incident that had taken place there. All the girls who got questioned about it were Black. No white girls were spoken to at all. My daughter felt she and her friends were singled out because they are loud Black girls and their cultural expressions are associated with bad behaviour.

But you get all kinds of people in all kinds of races. Some are louder than others. With Black girls, that kind of behaviour is far too often seen negatively and that can be very damaging to the way they see themselves and their place in society.

And it only becomes worse when all these ideas are perpetuated by books and songs and TV shows that reinforce the stereotypes. You can end up viewing yourself through that lens and become conditioned to believe that this is the way things are.

The whole time when white people were using dubious science to prove they were superior to Black people, there were large numbers of Black people who absolutely believed this was the case. Many Black American slaves felt betrayed when they were granted their freedom and absolutely refused to leave their masters – they couldn't see beyond the rhetoric they had been brought up with their entire lives.

There are so many myths attached to Black people, for example about them being loud or scary or intimidating, and they help to form people's opinions. And after all, police officers are just members of society and are influenced in their actions the same way as everyone else. But they are also members of an organisation that gives them the power to act out their biases and prejudices if they choose to do so.

My daughter and I had a long conversation about all this as I drove her home that day. Schools sometimes don't realise how big a part they play in the early indoctrination of young people in terms of who is good and who is bad, and this means some can leave with a sense of themselves heavily influenced by the view of others.

It's why we owe so much respect to the likes of Dr Harold Moody and Learie Constantine – along with countless others – who had the guts to stand up and challenge the status quo. Their stories, along with the death of Charles Wotten, are the start of a pattern that you'll see repeated over and over again, often resulting in anger flaring up into periodic uprisings that provide an outlet for the frustration and resentment that has built up over the years.

But such incidents do nothing to resolve the underlying issues that lead to the clashes in the first place and even less to address the toxic mindset that sees skin colour and criminality as two sides of the same coin.

4

Mahmood Mattan

Like Charles Wotten before him, Mahmood Mattan first arrived in Britain aboard a merchant shipping vessel. He was born in the early 1920s in what was then known as British Somaliland, a crown colony and protectorate of the United Kingdom. The youngest of four brothers, he had little in the way of formal education and never learned to read or write. He spent much of his childhood helping out in the small grocery store that his father ran.

At the age of around sixteen or seventeen (he likely lied about his age to get work) and keen to remove the limits on his future prospects, he went to sea, starting out at the lowest possible position of pantry boy in the steward's department of a cargo ship. He quickly worked his way up, becoming a second steward, then a trimmer and finally a fireman.

In November 1946, at the end of a year-long voyage on the SS *Fort Ellice*, he found himself on British soil for the very first time. He landed in Middlesbrough without a passport but his status as a subject of the Empire was enough to allow him to pass through immigration without any trouble.

Eager to take advantage of the higher wages available to those starting their voyages from the UK, he moved to Newport in Wales and joined the merchant navy. In the twelve months that followed he went to sea on four separate occasions for around nine months in total before relocating to Bute Street in Cardiff's Tiger Bay, home to many fellow Somalis.

It was the same area where, just days after the death of Charles Wotten in June 1919, more unrest had broken out, leading to the death of twenty-one-year-old Mohammed Abdullah, after three nights of violence.

Tiger Bay was also where Mattan first met an eighteen-year-old local girl named Laura Williams who worked in a paper factory. His command of English was relatively poor, but it was enough to break the ice. 'I think you nice girl,' he told her, before asking whether she would go to the pictures with him.

Laura turned him down, explaining that her parents didn't allow her to have boyfriends. In reality, she knew their only objection would be because of the colour of his skin.

Mattan persisted and the pair eventually began dating. Many of Laura's friends stopped speaking to her and, according to an interview she later gave to *The Times*, some residents even 'threw buckets of water at Laura, calling her a "black man's whore"'. Despite this, the couple persevered and Mattan's charms even won over her family. In December 1947, just three months after meeting, the pair were married.

There would be no honeymoon. The very next day Mattan returned to sea on a journey lasting ten months. By the time he returned his first son, David, had been born. More voyages and a second son followed in the year after that, leading Mattan to leave the merchant navy and try to find more local work, in order to spend more time with his family.

They briefly moved to Hull to try to establish themselves there but within a year the couple had separated with Laura claiming Mattan was making 'excessive sexual demands' on her. She returned to her parents' house in Cardiff and Mattan moved into nearby lodgings. Despite the split, the pair remained on friendly terms and Mattan – who had been ordered to pay to support both his wife and children – had high hopes they might be able to reconcile.

He worked a number of casual jobs, labouring or helping out in local cafés but soon began to struggle financially, especially when a third son appeared on the scene, having been conceived shortly before the separation. His money troubles were made all the worse by a growing gambling habit and it was as a direct result of this that Mattan found himself in trouble with the police for the first time.

In April 1951, while visiting London, he won some money after betting on the dogs. To stop him spending it all right away, Mattan gave half of his winnings to a friend, Ahmed, who ran a café in Stepney, but when he returned to collect the money a few days later, Ahmed said he did not have it.

Furious, Mattan allegedly produced a razor, grabbed Ahmed by his jacket and threatened to cut his throat. A man living in the basement of the café heard the commotion and rushed up to help, giving Ahmed time to break away, lock himself in a room and call out for the assistance of a passing police officer.

Mattan was charged with demanding money with menaces but was acquitted at the Old Bailey the following month with the jury seemingly believing that the potential theft of the winnings was a greater crime than the use of force to try to recover them.

Mattan was in trouble again at the end of the year, this time accused of stealing £80 and a suit from the cabin of a Somali seaman whose ship was anchored at Cardiff docks. Mattan denied the charges and the case was dismissed.

Around the same time, he was also accused of stealing money from a local mosque. On this occasion, his luck finally ran out and he was found guilty of larceny, though not guilty of breaking and entering, which would have been a more serious charge. He was ordered to pay costs as well as restitution and placed on probation for three years.

The following February, Mattan got into an argument with a man who accused him of stealing a valuable wristwatch. During the scuffle that followed, Mattan once more produced a cutthroat razor and began waving it about, eventually cutting the man's thumb. The police were informed but took no action, most likely because witnesses suggested that the man brandishing the razor had been acting in self-defence.

For Mattan, his multiple acquittals were proof that the police were simply out to get him, constantly accusing him of crimes in which he had played no part. From the point of view of local officers, Mattan appeared to be taunting them about their inability to make the charges stick.

However, the fact that Mattan now had form for theft and was known to carry a razor at all times, along with the fact that he spoke openly about his distrust of and dislike for the police, was enough to ensure his name was near the top of the list of potential suspects when, a few weeks later, a brutal murder took place.

By the spring of 1952, forty-one-year-old Lily Volpert had been successfully running the general store she had inherited from her father for more than twenty-five years. Trading simply as Volpert's, it was located at 203/204 Bute Street, just a short walk from where Mattan had his lodgings. The shop sold a wide variety of clothes and shoes but also stationery, sports equipment, cigarettes, batteries and other goods.

A hugely popular figure throughout the tight-knit Tiger Bay community, Lily lived on the premises with her widowed sister, Doris, and niece Ruth. Their mother Fanny also dropped by most nights.

Although Lily liked to shut up shop around 8 p.m., she often opened after hours for those she knew. She also allowed regulars to purchase items on credit and cashed advance notes for merchant seamen, usually on the understanding that at least some of the money paid out would then be spent in the shop itself.

The business had long proved extremely profitable and the first few months of 1952 had been especially lucrative. Around the town it was well known that cash was taken to the bank only once a week, meaning large amounts could accumulate on the premises. Shortly before Christmas there had been a couple of attempted burglaries, both of which were unsuccessful but reported to the police nevertheless.

On the evening of 6 March, after closing the shop at around 8.05 p.m. and drawing a curtain across the glass-panelled front door, Lily finally sat down to have supper with her family in the back room. She had barely begun to eat when the doorbell rang. With a heavy sigh, she got back up and went to answer it.

Looking across to the front room and out into the street through the gap at the side of the curtain on the front door, both Ruth and Doris saw a dark-skinned Black man standing outside the shop. As Lily dealt with the customer, the rest of the family continued eating without her.

About ten minutes later, Doris looked over to the front room and could not see her sister, but assumed she was in another part of the shop, dealing with the customer.

Shortly after this, a local man named William Archbold arrived, hoping to buy some cigarette papers. Finding the door slightly ajar and the lights on, he spent a minute or two tapping the glass, hoping to attract Lily's attention. When there was no answer, he stepped inside, stamped his feet and looked around.

That was when he finally spotted her. Lying face down on the floor to his right. Surrounded by a deep pool of blood. Her throat slit from ear to ear.

The local police station was located a little further up Bute Street and William ran there, alerting the duty sergeant who immediately made his way back to the shop along with a constable.

After establishing that Lily was dead the officers were astonished to find the rest of her family still sitting in the back room, having only just finished their meal. With a thick door between the front and rear of the shop, they had not heard anything and were completely unaware of the deadly attack that had taken place just a few feet away. The two women and the young girl were quickly ushered upstairs before the terrible news was delivered.

More officers were summoned to the scene, along with Detective Chief Inspector Harry Power who would take charge of the investigation.

As the search for clues got underway it quickly became clear that the killer must have been a regular at Volpert's as Lily would only reopen the shop for those she knew once 8 p.m. had passed. Once the person was inside, she would bolt the door behind her to ensure no further customers could enter.

Detectives surmised that the customer had probably asked to buy a pair of shoes, meaning he would have followed her into the stockroom where neither her family nor anyone in the street could see what was happening. As she bent down to get some shoes off a shelf, he attacked, putting his knee into the small of her back, pulling back her head and drawing a sharp blade – most likely a razor – across her throat. A cut on her left hand showed she had tried to defend herself.

But Lily's body was not found in the stockroom. Despite her horrific injuries, she somehow had managed to crawl a few feet back into the main shop. Seeing this, the killer apparently panicked and left the door slightly ajar on his way out.

Blood stains from gloved hands showed the killer had first tried to open the safe then opened the drawer where she kept her float for cashing advance notes from local merchant seamen. Just over £100 had been stolen – around £3,000 in today's money. They had not attempted to open the till, probably due to having been disturbed.

Doris, Lily's sister, told detectives about the man she had seen earlier, explaining that he was Black and appeared to be either Somali or West African. He wore a dark suit with no hat, and had a very full face and bushy hair.

The officer in charge of the investigation quickly made the decision to focus attention on members of the local Somali community, especially those with links to previous criminal activity.

Aware that in the past, many crimes had gone unsolved because the perpetrators had simply sailed away, the officers knew they had to move fast and virtually the entire detective division of the force was immediately brought in to assist.

Within just an hour and a half of the murder, detectives had visited the lodging houses of at least thirty-nine Somali seamen, boarded all the ships in the city's four docks and interviewed all the crew members that were present, even searching their cabins.

At around 10.30 p.m. that evening, two detectives working their way down the list of suspects assigned to them reached the home of Mahmood Mattan, who was asleep in his room and answered the door wearing only a vest and underpants.

Without explaining why they were there, the two officers began questioning Mattan about his movements earlier that evening. Mattan explained that he'd been in the cinema on his own and had not left until 7.30 p.m., when he had headed directly home, not stopping to speak to anyone on the way. He was also asked if he carried a knife and said that he did not.

The officers searched Mattan's room and quickly found a razor in the pocket of a jacket hanging on a chair, but it was clearly broken and had not been used for some time.

Mattan was asked once again to confirm what he had been up to earlier in the evening and at that moment his patience ran out, especially when he learned no search warrant had been issued for the property. He demanded to know why the officers were harassing him when he had not done anything wrong.

One of the detectives explained that a woman had been murdered and that the suspect was a Black man. 'I don't talk to you,' snorted Mattan. 'Why a coloured man? You lie. All police officers are liars.'

The two detectives continued their search but found nothing suspicious – no bloodstained clothing, no gloves, no sign of the murder weapon or the stolen money. In fact, no evidence of anything linking Mattan to the murder at all.

The two officers crossed his name off their list and moved on to their next call.

As word of the murder and the police inquiry began to spread throughout the local community, some of those who knew their names would be likely to appear on the list of usual suspects decided to take a more proactive approach to clearing themselves.

Harold Cover was a thirty-one-year-old Jamaican who had arrived in England as a stowaway and then joined the merchant navy for many years. At the time of Lily's murder, he was working as a carpenter but had racked up a number of convictions in previous years for crimes including common assault, larceny and gaming.

A year earlier he had been charged with malicious wounding after getting into a fight with a man and slashing him repeatedly with a razor (though Cover insisted he had used a broken bottle and no other weapon was ever found). Although his victim had almost died from his injuries and required a blood transfusion, Cover had been acquitted of all charges in court with the jury choosing to believe he had not been the aggressor.

Aware that he may have been spotted in the vicinity of Volpert's around the time of the murder, he presented himself at the police station the following day to give his own account of his movements.

He explained that he had been on his way to a local club in Bute Street and that somewhere around 8 p.m., he had seen two Somalis at Volpert's shop, one coming out of the porch and the other standing beside the window, close to the doorway. He added that he recognised at least one of the men, having seen him around town, and that if he saw him again, he would easily be able to identify him. The detailed description Cover went on to provide sounded very much like the man Doris had seen ringing on the doorbell that evening but did little to bring the police any closer to actually naming a suspect.

Detectives continued their enquiries over the next few days, often working twelve- or fourteen-hour shifts as DCI Power became increasingly frustrated about the lack of progress. At one point it seemed there had been a breakthrough when a pile of bloody clothing was spotted in the vicinity of the shop, but it turned out to have been the result of a drunken brawl between a father and son and unconnected to the murder.

On Sunday, 9 March, hundreds of people gathered along the streets of Tiger Bay to watch Lily Volpert's funeral procession make its way along Bute Street and in its aftermath, members of her family discussed what they might be able to do to assist with bringing her killer to justice.

They decided to offer a reward of £200 to anyone able to provide information that would lead to a conviction. The development was announced in the local papers the following day and on Wednesday, 12 March, detectives turned their attention back to Mattan.

Having taken follow-up statements from his landlord and fellow lodger, detectives learned that Mattan had not returned home at 7.30 p.m. as he had claimed but rather at 8.30 p.m. This meant he could no longer account for his movements at the time of the murder. It didn't prove he was guilty, of course, but it gave the police plenty of justification for making further enquiries.

DCI Power ordered him to be brought in for more formal questions and it quickly emerged that he had lied about going straight home from the cinema as he had stopped, among other places, at Laura's house to ask her mother if she wanted him to go and buy cigarettes for her. They had heard this directly from Laura herself, but Mattan insisted it was untrue and that he had not done so.

Hugely mistrustful of the police, Mattan chose to give as little information as possible and even threw in a few fabrications of his own. So far as he was concerned, he hadn't done anything wrong and there was no evidence to suggest otherwise. If he wanted to keep the details of his day-to-day life and his movements to himself, there would be no harm in it. It was a piece of flawed logic that would soon come back to haunt him.

That evening, Mattan reluctantly agreed to appear in an identification parade. In those days there was no such thing as a two-way mirror. Witnesses were required to be in the same room as the suspects, walk up and down the line and then place their hand on the shoulder of the person they recognised.

Key witnesses included Lily's sister, mother and niece, but none of them were able to pick him out from the line-up of ten Somali men. One witness, a local shopkeeper, did identify him but only to say he had seen him in the area in the days leading up to the murder – something which Mattan had denied – rather than definitively putting him at the scene at the time the crime was committed. It was yet another foolish and unnecessary lie.

The detectives let him return home after the interrogation, but he was now the number one suspect for the murder of Lily Volpert, despite there being only the flimsiest of circumstantial evidence against him.

It was soon after this that another shopkeeper, May Gray, came forward with compelling evidence that seemed to point directly at Mattan. She told officers that sometime between 8.30 p.m. and 9 p.m. on the night of the murder, he had entered her premises in a breathless, excited manner.

Eager to close for the evening, Ms Gray had told him to come back the following day. Aware of his precarious financial situation, she also remarked that it was unlikely he had any money with which to purchase anything. In response, Mattan pulled a leather wallet out of his inside coat pocket and pointed to the thick roll of notes. She estimated there was between £80 and £100 inside. Mattan then abruptly left the shop and headed off in the direction of his home.

The story she told seemed a little too convenient, especially in terms of its timing just after the offer of a reward. In addition, her description of Mattan's clothing on the night of the murder failed to match those of others who had seen him, or any clothes he had in his possession.

And then, at last, a far more convincing witness had come forward. Mary Tolley, along with her friend Margaret Bush, had been the last customers Lily had served just before heading to the back room for supper. They had both been interviewed a number of times and given little of interest but now Mary suddenly and dramatically changed her statement.

She told detectives that while Lily was serving her, a Somali man came in and asked for cigarettes. Lily refused to serve him, saying she was already closed for the evening. The man flew into a temper and made some abusive comments about Jews before storming off. Mary did not see him actually leave the shop, but assumed he had. When officers showed her a photograph of Mattan, she identified him as the man she had seen.

There were huge problems with this version of events. For one, Lily was known to bolt the door behind her when serving customers to prevent anyone else coming in, so no one could have entered at the time. In addition, Margaret said she had not seen anything of the sort. Another problem was that this version of events simply didn't tally with her earlier statements or those of Doris and Fanny who had seen a man outside the shop ring the doorbell in an attempt to be served. If Lily had already turned the man away, why would she agree to serve him just a few minutes later? Finally, Mattan was very different in appearance from the man Doris and Fanny had seen. Doris had said the man was 'full faced' while Mattan was slender with a thin face. Fanny had said the man's head nearly touched the doorframe, making him close to six feet tall. Mattan was around five feet eight inches.

Today, one of the most crucial aspects of any criminal proceedings is the rule of disclosure. This, in essence, states that the prosecution must provide the defence with all materials that are capable of undermining the prosecution case or assisting the defence of the suspect. For example, if someone confesses to a crime and the police charge them, but later change their minds and file charges against someone else, the defence must be given all the details of the original suspect.

No such rules existed in the 1950s. This meant the police were able to pick and choose what evidence would be presented to the court and what would be left out. The end result of this was that anything that cast doubt on Mattan's guilt, anything that supported his alibi or pointed towards someone else being guilty of the crime was kept suppressed.

The police then began showing potential witnesses pictures of Mattan to see if they could place him at the scene – a practice that today would make any such identification inadmissible in court and was frowned on even then.

All these enquiries led to Mattan being arrested for the alleged theft of a raincoat – a charge that, with the benefit of hindsight, appears to have been a ruse to get Mattan into custody where he would be unable to intimidate witnesses or tamper with evidence. The arrest occurred just a few days after the murder and, hinting that he might be responsible for a far more serious matter, the police convinced magistrates to deny him bail.

For the police, it became less about finding the truth or keeping a dangerous killer off the streets and far more about finding someone they could pin the whole thing on, someone that a jury would be comfortable to convict. It would need to be someone who had form for theft and violence involving a razor. Someone with sufficient arrogance and hatred of the police to make all their denials appear hollow. Someone unable to account for their whereabouts on the night of the murder and with a reputation for violence.

That man was Mattan.

Under growing pressure from magistrates to make a decision one way or another, they decided to follow through on their hunches. At around 5.30 p.m. on Sunday, 16 March 1952, Mahmood Hussein Mattan was charged with the murder of Lily Volpert. The next morning, he made a brief appearance in the local magistrates' court. Asked if he wanted a solicitor to defend him, he replied, 'Defend me for what? I don't want anything, and I don't care anything. You can't get me for what I have not done.'

Taken to Cardiff prison, Mattan was denied bail on five separate occasions and would remain incarcerated for the next four weeks.

Prior to 2013, no case could proceed to the Crown Court until the evidence had been 'tested' in the magistrates' court through what were known as committal proceedings. The basic idea was that a hearing would be held in order for the magistrate to work out if there was enough evidence of a serious crime to justify a trial by jury. Such proceedings were, in essence, a miniature version of the trial but with only evidence for the prosecution heard. (Committal proceedings have since been abolished.)

Mattan's committal began at Cardiff Magistrates' Court on 16 April. Almost immediately, it seemed as though the case for the prosecution was going to collapse as their key witness changed her mind about what she had seen.

Mary Tolley now said Mattan was not the man who had come into the shop after all. This all but destroyed the elaborate scenario which the police had built up around the idea of Mattan entering the premises, hiding while the women had left and then attacking Lily as she was sorting out some shoes in the stockroom.

But the police case was saved when another witness also changed their statement. Previously Harold Cover, the Jamaican carpenter who had pre-empted a visit from the police by giving a voluntary statement soon after the murder, had spoken of seeing two Somali men close to the shop some time around 8 p.m. on the night of the murder. As he was being questioned, he now stated that the first of these two men had actually been Mattan himself.

As if the odds were not already stacked against him, Mahmood spoke very little English and was unable to read or write, meaning he could not comprehend much of the evidence that was being laid against him. His own statements were written down and read back to him so he could sign them, but he had no way of knowing exactly what the final versions of these statements said. The police persuaded prosecutors that Mahmood was lying and was fully literate, meaning he was not offered an interpreter.

The murder trial of Mahmood Hussein Mattan opened at the Glamorgan Assizes in Swansea on 22 July 1952 before Mr Justice Ormerod. The key witness for the prosecution was Harold Cover, who testified that he had seen Mattan leaving Volpert's shop around the time of the murder. Mary Tolley also provided testimony against Mattan – but it transpired she was one of the few witnesses who claimed to be able to identify him. The jury were never told that others were unable to do so. Mattan's shoes allegedly also revealed microscopic blood specks. But then it turned out he had retrieved them himself from a rubbish dump and there was no scientific proof linking the blood to the crime.

For much of his evidence, Mattan simply denied everything, believing that so long as he did so, the police would be unable to prove anything. But he soon became caught up in so many other lies, it did not take much for the jury to believe that he was lying about his inability to read as well; reading and writing, especially in the legal language of the court, would have been beyond his capabilities.

Caught up in his own web of deceit, he even denied some

suggestions that would have provided him with an alibi. When asked if his mother-in-law had been wrong to say he had been at her house at around 8 p.m., he said yes, she was wrong, he had been there much earlier.

He left the dock having made a terrible impression. He had insisted that every prosecution witness was lying, even on unimportant matters or ones that would actually count in his favour. He had been a fool unto himself. The last few questions asked of him were whether he had killed Lily Volpert and stolen the £100. He denied both, of course, but having denied so much before, it just made him look guilty.

For his closing speech, Edmund Davies, the prosecuting counsel, chose to quote part of Harold Cover's cross examination. Asked whether he might have been mistaken about seeing Mattan emerge from the shop porch, Cover replied: 'If I was not positive I do not think I would be here. I have no right to doubt it or to say anything or come here at all if I was not sure of the man I have seen.'

Davies then asked the jury whether, having heard the evidence from Cover, they believed he spoke 'with the tongue of truth'. If they did, he explained, then that was the end of the case.

Mattan's barrister, Thomas Rhys-Roberts, began his concluding speech:

> You have to ask yourselves this question when you saw him. What is he? Half child of nature, half semi-civilised savage? A man who is caught up in the web of circumstance. Who has come under the suspicion of the police and because he knows he is suspected has childishly tried to lie his way out of it. That is how he comes before you today.

Many, including Mattan's own family, could not understand why Rhys-Roberts would choose to use such words to describe a man whose life he was supposedly trying to save.

Mattan was found guilty of the murder of Lily Volpert, leaving the judge with no other option than to impose the death penalty.

Having held on to his belief in British justice and that it would simply not be possible for a man to be convicted of a crime he did not commit, Mattan was convinced he would be released before his execution. It was only in his final hours that the truth began to dawn, and he dictated a letter. It showed he was in no doubt that racism had played a major role in his conviction.

If it is good for the government that the killer is walking around and that I'm going to get hanged for nothing, good luck to the government and I'm very glad to be hanged for nothing. [. . .]

If you find the killer after I get hanged, I don't want him to get hanged at all. I can't tell you who he is because I don't know nothing about it. Only one thing I can say. It can't be two lives for one. [. . .]

I doesn't interfere with anybody else, and I don't tell one word lie in my case. I was true all the way . . . And if I am true, I hope my God to save me, that's all.

Despite the letter, Mattan remained convinced the authorities would eventually realise their mistake. He told anyone who would listen: 'I kill no woman.' He spoke excitedly about the fact that he would be entitled to compensation for his false arrest. His confidence proved infectious: in the weeks that followed his conviction, Laura believed that every knock at the door was her husband returning home.

In the USA, one of the few countries to retain the use of capital punishment for ordinary crimes, the average time spent on death row is now twenty-two years. In 1950s Britain, the wheels of justice moved far more swiftly.

Following a sentence of death, murderers would be allowed 'three clear Sundays' to make their peace with God. This meant

Mattan was set to be executed on 12 August. This date was postponed, however, when, a few days after the end of the trial, Mattan's lawyer filed an appeal. This was quickly rejected, chiefly due to the strength of the testimony of Harold Cover along with the presence of the spots of blood on the brown suede shoes.

The date of the execution was moved to 3 September. Now Mattan's only hope of avoiding the noose was a last-minute re-prieve direct from the Home Secretary himself. This was denied at the end of August. And yet Mattan remained confident, contin-uing to believe that British justice would prevail. Two days before he was due to go to the gallows, he told Laura: 'Don't worry. I'll be with you soon. They won't kill me.'

Her visit had been followed by one from a local imam, who told Mattan that if he had anything to confess or if he wanted to make peace with God, now was the time to say so. 'I have no peace to make. My conscience is clear,' was the reply.

Laura went to the prison on the morning of the execution, hoping to see her husband for one final time. But before she was admitted, an official attached a notice to the gate. The notice announced that Mahmood Hussein Mattan had been executed at 8 a.m., and that the execution had 'gone without a hitch'.

Mahmood Mattan was the last man to be hanged in Wales and his body was buried within the prison grounds, meaning she didn't even have a place to go to lay flowers or pay her respects.

In April 1969, eighteen-year-old Elaina Smith was having yet an-other argument with her father. She had started to show the first signs of interest in men, and he did not like it at all.

Things had become so bad she had sought safety in a nearby police station and then spent the night with her boyfriend. The following day she returned to the Tiger Bay home of her parents in order to collect her things with a view to moving out permanently.

Another argument ensued and when Elaina went up to pack her

bags, her father joined her in her bedroom. As she sat on the bed, he stood behind her, one hand on her shoulder, the other inside his jacket pocket. Without warning he gripped her hair and pulled her neck back while producing a cutthroat razor.

Elaina raised her hands to try to protect herself and the blade sliced into her finger. 'Don't be silly,' she gasped as her father flashed the blade again and drew it across her throat.

As Elaina shut her eyes and played dead, he laid her back on the bed, crossing her arms across her chest as if she were in a coffin. She heard him return downstairs and then her mother asking whether she had gone. 'No,' her father replied. 'She's upstairs dead on the bed.'

The man wielding the razor was none other than Harold Cover, the key prosecution witness in Mattan's murder trial some seventeen years earlier.

Elaina survived the attack and Cover was charged with attempted murder. Ironically, the man defending him at his trial the following month was Thomas Rhys-Roberts, the same man who had unsuccessfully defended Mattan.

Cover was found guilty of the charge and sentenced to life imprisonment.

As details of the attack emerged, they became big news across Tiger Bay. It turned out that Laura was not the only one to doubt her husband's guilt and the similarities with the attack on Lily Volpert made people question whether the right person had gone to the gallows.

Two journalists from the *People* newspaper travelled to Cardiff and began a detailed investigation. They quickly learned that not only did Cover have a violent history, often involving razors and sharp objects, going back to at least 1949, but that he had received £100 of the reward money offered by Lily's family for the evidence he had provided at trial. The journalists also learned that Cover's decision to alter his statement to name Mattan came only after the offer of a reward had been made.

Laura informed them she had always believed her husband to be innocent and that she had been speaking to him at her parents' home between 7 p.m. and 8 p.m. on the night of the murder. If this conversation had taken place at the latter time, it meant it would have been impossible for him to have got to Volpert's at the right time, but with no way to prove the actual time, it was never strong enough to provide Mattan with an alibi.

They also spoke to Margaret Bush, the woman who, along with Mary Tolley, had been the last to be served in the shop before the murder. She too provided new evidence that was dramatic; the journalists insisted that she swear an affidavit. The new document recounted how, after leaving the shop, she and Mary had seen Mattan in Bridge Street, several minutes away from the shop. She said she had not mentioned this sooner as the police had only ever asked her whether she had seen Mattan in the shop itself, not whether she had seen him later that day.

The journalists also made contact, through a third party, with the local MP for the area including Tiger Bay. That man was Jim Callaghan, and he also happened to be the Home Secretary at the time. In years to come, he would become Prime Minister.

The result was a front-page story on the 1 June edition of the paper under the headline: WAS THE WRONG MAN HANGED?

After questions were asked in Parliament the Home Secretary revealed he had asked the chief constable of South Wales Police (which had formed on 1 June 1969 following the amalgamation of four forces including Cardiff City Police, the force that had investigated the Volpert murder) to take a fresh look.

Around a week later, a reply came back dismissing virtually all the evidence raised by the investigation. The chief constable suggested that Margaret Bush may have changed her story because the paper had offered to pay her to do so. While Cover's record of violence was substantial, he noted that none of his previous crimes had been motivated by theft which had clearly been the case with the death of Lily Volpert.

Margaret Bush would eventually withdraw her statement, saying she had only made it in order to get rid of the reporter from the *People* who had begun to harass her.

The paper ran a few more stories in the weeks that followed, each one prompting a further investigation from officers both inside and outside the force, but ultimately no evidence pointing to a miscarriage of justice was found. As a result, the Home Secretary declined to reopen the case. The family would have to wait a further twenty-seven years for justice.

In 1993 Neil Sinclair, a local historian who had grown up in Tiger Bay, published his debut book, *The Tiger Bay Story*. It was part social snapshot, part love letter to the people and the place he had known for the past fifty years. One chapter in particular dealt with three historic murder cases, including that of Lily Volpert. Sinclair learned that many locals felt the case had been a miscarriage of justice and that the family had unsuccessfully campaigned for years to have Mattan's name exonerated.

The book soon came to the attention of Philip Mattan, Laura's son and half-brother to Omar, David and Mervyn. The case had barely been discussed by the family, but Philip was eager to know more and began to investigate. On a visit to Cardiff docks he met an old Somali seaman who told him it was about time Mahmood's name was cleared.

'I started digging around in old files and what came out was a very sad story of great injustice. I started a leaflet campaign and the feedback we got was that very few people had ever believed he did do the murder,' Philip later told the *Independent*.

Philip began writing letters, hundreds of them, to local councillors, community leaders and MPs. He also wrote to the *South Wales Echo* which began running a series of articles.

It was through the efforts of the paper that, in August 1994, Laura Mattan was given permission to enter Cardiff prison and lay flowers on the unmarked grave where her husband's body had been buried.

Coverage of this event came to the attention of renowned Cardiff solicitor Bernard de Maid. He had made his name defending people of different backgrounds during a time when racism was rife throughout the courts and South Wales Police. Two years earlier he had been instrumental in quashing the conviction of one of three men wrongly accused of murder in one of the worst miscarriages of justice in British legal history – the case of the Cardiff Three.

It was not until 2 September 2022, seventy years to the day after Mahmood Mattan had been hanged, that South Wales Police finally issued a formal apology to his surviving descendants.

'There is no doubt that Mahmood Mattan was the victim of a miscarriage of justice as a result of a flawed prosecution, of which policing was clearly a part,' said then chief constable Jeremy Vaughan.

> This is a case very much of its time – racism, bias and prejudice would have been prevalent throughout society, including the criminal justice system . . . It is right and proper that an apology is made on behalf of policing for what went so badly wrong in this case seventy years ago and for the terrible suffering of Mr Mattan's family and all those affected by this tragedy for many years.
>
> Even to this day we are still working hard to ensure that racism and prejudice are eradicated from society and policing. Police investigations would have been totally different then and a long way off today's excellent investigative standards.
>
> Even when reflecting on a case from seventy years ago, we do not forget those who have been affected by miscarriages of justice and we do not underestimate the impact this has on individuals.

But for the family itself, the apology was too little, too late. 'It's far too late for the people directly affected as they are no longer with us and still, we are yet to hear the words I am/we are sorry,' said Laura's granddaughter Tanya Mattan.

Despite facing decades of abuse, Laura Mattan always believed her husband was innocent. Because of this, she refused to change her surname or that of her children, believing that doing so would have amounted to a betrayal. Her loyalty came at a heavy price.

The family had been awarded a payout of £1.4 million in 2001, but the money did nothing to ease their suffering. Mahmood's execution had blighted the lives of his three sons. Omar, who had long struggled with his mental health and other difficulties, was found dead on Murkle Beach in northern Scotland in April 2003. He had been drinking and was three times over the limit at the time of his death. The inquest recorded an open verdict.

Not long before he died, Omar spoke of the racism and injustice that he had experienced: 'Until I was eight I was told my father had died at sea. Then one day the Salvation Army band was playing near our house and I went out to sing with them. One of the leaders said: "We don't need the sons of hanged men." That knowledge felt like a cancerous growth in my head.'

His younger brother, Mervyn, had also led a troubled life, serving time in prison. In 2011, he was found dead at home, with several empty sherry bottles nearby. An inquest found his death had occurred due to his dependence on alcohol. In both cases, it seems as though the weight of the wrongful conviction of their father had made it impossible for them to live normal lives.

As I know only too well, no amount of money and no number of apologies, however sincere, can ever undo the damage caused by this kind of institutional racism or bring back what has been lost.

It took me thirty-one years to get justice for my mother. The family of Mahmood Mattan had to wait for seventy. And let's not forget that the family of Lily Volpert will likely never know who was responsible for her death and therefore will never receive closure.

The bitter truth about Mattan's death can be summed up in the headstone his family erected in 1996 when they were granted permission to exhume and move his body to the Muslim section of the Western Cemetery in Cardiff.

Spelled out in gold lettering against a black background, the legend is a simple one. Mahmood Hussein Mattan. Husband of Laura. Father of David, Omar and Mervyn. KILLED BY INJUSTICE.

The story of Mahmood Mattan is the ultimate example of a miscarriage of justice. It's one thing incarcerating someone for something they did not do, but it's quite another killing someone who is innocent.

In some cases there is a difference of opinion about whether someone was truly innocent or not, but here there was a full police admission that the wrong person was hanged. It's a matter of public record that this person lost their life because of the way the criminal justice system views Black people.

I was also deeply touched by the impact Mattan's death had on his family – an element that is not always fully taken into consideration.

I remember talking to a friend about another man, around my own age, whose mother had died at the hands of the police while he was present. He had been left so damaged by the experience that, years later, he was still unable to function in any meaningful way. In my experience, it's more the norm for someone to be affected like that. I consider myself fortunate to have emerged through it all in the way I have.

It's also important to keep in mind that you can end up just as traumatised from seemingly minor incidents, especially if they are repeated often enough. The first time you are stopped and searched, it's really scary, but then if it keeps on happening, it becomes truly damaging.

In February 2024 an investigation was launched after a sixteen-year-old boy from south London lodged a complaint after being stopped and searched on six occasions over the course of five months. One of the reasons given was that the child was said to resemble individuals linked to robberies and knife-related offences in the vicinity. Nothing illegal was ever found and none of the stops resulted in any action.

If someone keeps telling you that you fit the description of someone wanted for a crime, after a while you start to think, Do I just look like a criminal? You start to internalise and surrender to those thoughts which can be incredibly detrimental, especially if you're just a child. It cuts really deep.

But there's no consideration given to the harm caused by all of this and no process for helping people to heal. These kind of encounters with the police just leave a lot of damaged people in their wake. In the case of Mattan, it was the accumulation of damage caused by the racism he experienced that led to his combative relationship with the police and ultimately contributed to his own demise.

5

Kelso Cochrane

It was a murder that would become a defining moment in the history of race relations in Britain. The victim was a young Black man, full of drive and ambition, who was stabbed to death in cold blood on the streets of London, having been accosted by a gang of white youths.

The police investigation that followed was an utter shambles, featuring a mixture of apathy, incompetence and corruption. The names of those thought to be responsible were an open secret in the local community but though some of the suspects were arrested in the days that followed the murder, they were released without ever being charged.

Despite overwhelming evidence to the contrary, the police insisted the crime was not racially motivated and refused to pursue this line of enquiry. They also colluded with the press to suggest that, rather than being an innocent victim, the dead man had himself been a violent criminal and that the knife used to kill him may well have been his own.

As the police investigation floundered, activists rallied to demand justice for the family of the victim as well as a wider reckoning on the issue of racism within British society. Yet despite their best efforts, the guilty men walked free for decades.

But if you think this chapter is about the 1993 murder of London teenager Stephen Lawrence, you're sadly mistaken. This eerily similar crime took place more than thirty years earlier and remains unsolved to this day.

Yet, like the Lawrence case, this murder became a defining moment in the battle against racial discrimination and in its aftermath, campaigners used it as an example of how the criminal justice system was failing to protect Black people and other minorities. Six years after it happened, in 1965, the UK's first Race Relations Act was passed into law.

Kelso Benjamin Cochrane was born in September 1926 to a working-class family living in Antigua, one of a group of small islands known as the Lesser Antilles that forms the border between the Caribbean Sea and the Atlantic Ocean.

Kelso, one of eleven siblings, grew up assisting his carpenter father in the family business before deciding to take up the trade for himself. At the age of nineteen, believing he would find better opportunities further afield, he headed off to nearby Dominica and made it his home for the next three years.

In 1949, still eager to expand his horizons, he made his way to America where he worked as a farm labourer in Florida and spent a short spell in the US Army. It was around this time that he met a woman from South Carolina who, following a whirlwind romance, became his wife and soon after that, the mother of his daughter Josephine. Kelso moved his family to New York and, in a bid to make the switch from a trade to a profession, began studying to become a lawyer in his spare time.

But just as his career goals began to come together, so his

domestic situation began to fall apart. Despite their best efforts, the relationship between husband and wife became increasingly acrimonious and the pair agreed to split.

This decision had unexpected consequences. In February 1954, Kelso was deported back to Antigua on the grounds that his visa had expired, and, following the end of his marriage, he could no longer remain in the country.

Although Kelso could reapply for entry to America there was no guarantee he would be successful. In the meantime, he decided to head to a destination that would guarantee him a permanent home with none of the red tape or bureaucracy the Americans insisted upon. Antigua was part of the British Empire and that meant that Kelso was automatically a citizen of the United Kingdom. He had the exact same rights to live and work in the country as someone who had been born and bred there.

Within weeks he was aboard the SS *Colombie* which travelled around various West Indian ports to pick up passengers before heading across the Atlantic, arriving at Plymouth on 4 September 1954, along with some five hundred other, mostly male West Indians.

Kelso had arrived in London at an increasingly dangerous and challenging time for Black people. As the number of migrants grew and they began to be a dominant presence in the few parts of the capital where they could find work, so resentment grew, especially among the close-knit, working-class white population that had been there since before the war.

In October 1954, just a month after his arrival, the *Belfast Telegraph* reported: 'Recently there was a riot in Camden Town, London, when a car belonging to a negro G.I. was smashed up, a petrol bomb exploded in a house where coloured people lived and many coloured persons were attacked.'

Like others, Kelso would have quickly learned to avoid the streets at night when travelling alone and to keep himself to himself whenever possible to avoid being physically attacked by racists.

A key problem faced by all new migrants was finding somewhere to live.

When the *Windrush* landed in England, many of those aboard had not organised any accommodation so arrangements were made for around two hundred to be temporarily housed in deep air-raid shelters on Clapham Common. The nearest Labour Exchange was based at Brixton which is why that part of London quickly became home to many of them, sowing the seeds of the thriving community that persists today. It also helped that the area had been bombed heavily during the war and was still in a state of disrepair, meaning only the most desperate would choose to live there. After Brixton, the most popular destination was Notting Hill which, back then, was a far cry from the glamorous and highly desirable district it has become today. Extensive development had taken place there during the late nineteenth century, with a view to turning the area into a fashionable suburb of the capital, filling it with formidable townhouses with plenty of space for large families as well as the servants they employed to look after them.

But the area never really took off as wealthy families preferred to be in more central areas such as Mayfair or Belgravia. By the early 1950s Notting Hill was very run down. Rubbish, rats and ruin were everywhere, and around half of all houses were unoccupied.

Unable to rent out individual homes in their entirety, landlords had chosen to split the properties into individual rooms which could then be let out to poor families. While this initially kept the landlords happy, controls on rent introduced during the First World War and extended during the Second made it almost impossible for them to charge enough to keep up with the cost of repairs and maintenance, so many simply stopped trying and allowed their properties to fall into disrepair.

Conditions were often harsh. There was no electricity and multiple households usually shared a single toilet, which was unusual at the time, even in the lowest quality private rented accommodation. In addition, many flats lacked running water and tenants had access to only a single communal stove on a landing. The only source of heating available throughout these damp and draughty properties were paraffin stoves, meaning that fires were commonplace.

However, the same rent controls protected sitting tenants from having their rents raised to the market value for as long as they remained in situ. Only if a tenant left of their own accord could a new one replace them at a more realistic cost. Despite the problems, the poorest families knew they had no choice but to stay put.

One man who exploited this situation was Perec 'Peter' Rachman, a Polish-born landlord whose surname would go on to become forever associated with slum properties and the exploitation of tenants. During the 1950s, when the first members of the *Windrush* generation were still struggling to find places to live, Rachman promoted himself as one of the few landlords willing to allow Blacks to rent his properties, most of which were in Notting Hill.

In a rare newspaper interview he said: 'The government does nothing to house these West Indians when they come here. That's why they come to me.' But this was no act of kindness. Knowing they were desperate, Rachman packed these new arrivals into tiny rooms which he rented at many times the going rate. The only way the West Indians could afford it was to install as many people as they could into each property and share the cost, often taking it in turns to sleep on the limited number of mattresses available.

In addition, Rachman also placed them in properties where large numbers of sitting tenants remained paying the same low rents they had a decade earlier. By favouring West Indian musicians and encouraging them to have all-night parties, Rachman quickly drove out these other tenants and replaced them with even more West Indians, earning him huge profits.

As the number of migrants grew rapidly throughout the 1950s, so did concerns among the white population that they were 'taking over' areas of London as the high rents they were being forced to pay hiked up prices for everyone else.

These concerns were exploited by right-wing extremists such as Oswald Mosley's Union Movement, members of which began daubing the local streets with their slogan, KEEP BRITAIN WHITE.

Attacks on migrants remained commonplace. Suspicions about the culture and lifestyles of the migrants were not helped by the fact that there was very little mixing between the races, thanks to what amounted to an unofficial apartheid.

As the 1950s progressed, one particular subculture would be seen as dominant when it came to street violence. At first their attacks were aimed at one another, but they soon united and turned their attention to a common enemy.

Their origins can be traced back to the crisis facing the men's tailoring industry following the end of the Second World War. Many of their would-be customers were either still posted abroad, waiting to be demobilised, or had been killed. And with wartime rationing still in place, there was far less choice when it came to materials.

In order to stimulate sales, high-end tailors from Savile Row and Jermyn Street devised a new style, based on a revival of the Edwardian look from the turn of the century. The hope was that it would appeal to members of the officer class whose soldiering career had come to an end. It turned out to be a huge error of judgement on the part of the tailors as the look completely failed to take off and shops found themselves with huge piles of unsold clothing. In order to get some return on their investment, they sold the items in job lots to menswear shops in the south and east of London at extremely low prices.

When these shops put the items up in their windows, they quickly found a new market – local working-class teenagers from the council estates, post-war prefabs and the likes of the Peabody and Guinness Trust estates. They were eager to distinguish themselves from the way their parents, and in particular their fathers, dressed. Through increasing exposure to American youth culture, these teenagers had seen pictures of young men wearing what were known as 'zoot suits' and were eager to find a way to create a style of their own.

Growing up largely without the benefit of strong male role models during a time when unemployment was extremely low and decently paid manual work was easy to find, this generation of young people had more disposable income than their parents had done, with plenty of money to spend on clothes and entertainment. They grafted by day and danced and drank in the music halls by night.

As children of the Blitz, they had grown up against a backdrop of violence and destruction but, unlike their fathers, they lacked an easily identifiable enemy they could take on in the quest for adventure and excitement. Instead of taking up arms for Queen and country, they formed themselves into tight-knit and fiercely loyal gangs based in the dilapidated streets in which they lived and then went into battle against gangs from rival areas while also indulging in acts of petty crime on their own turf.

Initially known as Spivs, Cosh Boys or Creepers, they also developed a taste for violent street robbery. Their targets were frequently old ladies who would be coshed and have their purses stolen.

Fights between gangs became increasingly vicious. Newspapers soon became dominated by stories of razor-wielding working-class teenagers in unusual clothing roaming the streets ready to strike at anyone considered vulnerable. The *Daily Express* coined the name 'Teddy Boys' to describe the eccentric Edwardian-style dress of the young defendants in a murder trial.

The fact that the Teddy Boys of west London saw the district as their own territory and therefore felt threatened by the arrival in increasing numbers of 'outsiders' was thoroughly exploited by groups such as the White Defence League and the National Labour Party.

The Black & White News, a paper produced by an anti-immigration group known as the Britons' Publishing Society, carried headlines such as BLACKS MILK ASSISTANCE BOARD and

BLACKS SEEK WHITE WOMEN which proved incredibly effective at stirring up hatred and convincing many locals that all the disturbing myths they heard about the newcomers were actually true.

When a reporter from *The Times* visited the area to gauge the mood of inhabitants, what he found shocked him.

> There are three main causes of resentment against coloured inhabitants of the district. They are alleged to do no work and to collect a rich sum from the Assistance Board. They are said to be able to find housing when white residents cannot. And they are charged with all kinds of misbehaviour, especially sexual. Talking to housewives at their garden gates, menfolk in saloon bars and teenagers in corner cafés, your Correspondent had no doubt that these charges are universally believed to have some substance in them.

Immersed as they were in all things American, the Teddy Boys also embraced the use of the n-word as an insult, picking it up as a result of the influx of three million American G.I.s who were stationed in Britain towards the end of the Second World War. It became an additional weapon in their arsenal.

The number of attacks on members of Black communities increased steadily throughout 1958 and intensified with the heat of the summer, and not just in London.

Tensions in Nottingham had been building up, especially around competition in the job market, as the number of migrants in the city rose and the number of available jobs fell due to the end of the post-war economic boom. Some companies, such as the renowned bicycle manufacturer Raleigh, attempted to appease the white majority by refusing to employ Black workers at all, despite the fact that one of the company's largest export markets was Jamaica.

However, Oswald George Powe, a Jamaican-born trade union-
ist and activist living in Nottingham, orchestrated a campaign to
change this policy. Direct negotiation with the company failed, so
Powe appealed to Norman Manley, Jamaica's inaugural premier.
Manley's ban on bicycle imports from England was instrumental in
altering the company's stance – and Raleigh would in time become
a major employer of Caribbean workers in Nottingham. However,
Black workers were paid lower rates than their white counterparts
and many complained of the 'racist atmosphere' in the factory.

Tensions continued to build. On 23 August, violence flared
up after a blonde British woman was seen enjoying a drink in a
pub in the St Ann's district while in the company of a Black man.
Once again this was seen by many as a sign that integration of
the races was simply going too far. The man was attacked and, as
word spread, a crowd of more than one thousand gathered in the
area and began to seek out others to attack. The violence lasted for
many hours and saw eight people taken to hospital, one requiring
thirty-seven stitches after his throat was slashed.

The then Chief Constable of Nottinghamshire, Captain
Athelstan Popkess, strived to play down the notion that the outbreaks of violence were racially motivated and the force would
later produce a report claiming it was nothing more than an incident of 'generic hooliganism'.

The incident made the papers and led some Conservative MPs
to issue warnings that further trouble could be expected. They
renewed their demands for controls to be placed on immigration
from the Commonwealth as soon as Parliament resumed after the
summer break.

Back in Notting Hill, late the following evening, perhaps inspired by news of events in Nottingham, nine Teddy Boys, aged
between seventeen and twenty, armed themselves with a variety
of weapons, somehow packed themselves into a small family car
and went out on what they would later describe to the police as a
'nigger-hunting' expedition.

Their first target was MacDonald Waldron, a kitchen porter, who was heading towards Ladbroke Grove station during the early hours of Sunday morning when he was knocked down and struck over the head with a cosh, suffering a concussion and requiring six stitches.

Less than an hour later, Mattthew Lucien and his friend John Primal were walking home from a night out in the West End, having missed the last train, when a black car pulled up alongside them and a group of white youths piled out and attacked them.

The brutality lasted only seconds before the youths dived back into the car and drove off, leaving both their victims sprawled on the pavement. Primal had been stabbed while Lucien had been struck about the head.

Another hour passed before the next attack. Joseph Welsh, a labourer for a gas board, was making his way home along Shepherd's Bush Green when a black car appeared on the other side of the road. A white man exited the vehicle and came running directly towards Welsh, punching him in the face. Welsh began to fight back but others left the car and joined in the melee, beating Welsh unconscious and leaving him with a series of cuts requiring nine stitches.

As 5 a.m. approached, James Ettiene was walking along Wood Lane, heading home after finishing his night shift with London Transport, when he felt a blow to the back of his head. He quickly realised he was being attacked by a gang and began to run. He came across a crate of milk bottles and began throwing them at his pursuers in a bid to slow them down, then jumped onto the rear platform of a passing trolley bus. Two of the Teddy Boys managed to get on the bus, too, one of them holding a lump of wood. They implored the conductor to 'throw the nigger off' but instead the bus stopped by a public police phone box and the attackers melted away into the night.

By this time overnight reports about the beatings and stabbings were reaching the authorities. The police in Notting Hill had earned a reputation for generally ignoring attacks where the victims were Black, but such an alarming situation could not be allowed to develop any further.

Details of the vehicle suspected of involvement were radioed to all patrols and at 5.40 a.m., PC Eric Wilding and his colleague PC White spotted the car driving along the Uxbridge Road. Commandeering a taxi, they gave chase and eventually confronted the youths, who then escaped into the White City housing estate.

PC Wilding inspected the abandoned car and found it filled with an array of potential weapons, including iron bars, several pieces of wood and an air pistol. It was clear that, had the police not confronted them, they had intended to carry out further assaults.

With the car in the police's possession, it would only be a matter of time before the youths were tracked down. The first was arrested the following day when he went into Shepherd's Bush police station and reported that his car had been stolen. The remaining eight were quickly traced and taken into custody.

The investigating team worked for twenty hours without a break, interviewing each of the youths separately under caution. Most freely admitted their involvement, though usually attempted to downplay the number of blows they had personally struck against the victims.

'These niggers keep on taking liberties with us,' said one. 'I swear on the Bible that although I joined in giving the niggers a whacking, I had nothing to do with any stabbing.'

Another finished signing his statement and added: 'I don't like niggers.'

Within a few days all nine appeared at West London Magistrates' Court where they were denied bail and remanded at Wormwood Scrubs Boys' Prison to await trial at the Old Bailey three weeks later.

It meant none of them were around to participate in the events that took place the following weekend, but their actions would serve as a catalyst for even more violence.

A few days after the attacks, just ahead of the August bank holiday weekend, groups of Teddy Boys began to congregate on the streets of Notting Hill, looking for trouble. When they saw Majbritt Morrison, a young blonde Swedish woman, walking along the street close to Latimer Road Tube station while having a heated argument with a Black man, they believed they had found the opportunity they had been seeking.

Rushing to defend her, they were shocked to learn the man was actually her husband. Close up, they could also see that she was pregnant. Majbritt told the youths to mind their own business. Humiliated, they decided to attack Mr Morrison anyway, but hadn't counted on the fact that several of his Black friends were nearby and quickly came to his rescue. The scuffle between the two groups lasted only a short time but news of what had happened soon spread with the story becoming more distorted and outrageous with each retelling.

By that same evening, rumours were going around that a white woman had been raped by a Black man. This sparked a wave of anger that would build up over the course of the next day.

Just before midnight, Majbritt was heading to her home in Bramley Road after attending a blues party when she realised the property had been set alight. She broke into a sprint, eager to rescue her two cats, but one of the Teddy Boys in the crowd recognised her from the night before. 'There's another black man's trollop,' he shouted. 'Get her. Kill her.'

A crowd surged forward and she was struck with an iron bar but managed to make it into the house and rescue her cats. She then returned to face the crowd but found herself arrested for obstruction, most likely for her own safety.

In the meantime, the crowd had grown and at least four hundred angry white youths were in the vicinity of Bramley Road. The small group of police officers attempted to head them off and restore calm, but without any success.

PC Richard Bedford reported hearing the mob shouting: 'We

will kill all black bastards. Why don't you send them home?' Elsewhere another officer, PC Ian McQueen, was told: 'Mind your own business, coppers. Keep out of it. We will settle these niggers our way. We'll murder the bastards.'

Once the mob realised the police were attempting to prevent them reaching their destination, the officers themselves became the target with milk bottles and bricks being hurled at them. 'Why are you helping the black bastards?' the crowd demanded to know. 'You are a lot of nigger lovers.'

Though a few further scuffles took place that night – including an attack on the house hosting the blues party that Majbritt had attended earlier – it wasn't until the following evening that the situation fully deteriorated.

As word of a potential riot spread throughout the capital, more and more youths converged on the area. They poured out of nearby Tube stations or arrived in cars or vans, all of them armed with a variety of weapons and intent on violence. The sheer number of Teddy Boys and other youths meant the police were unable to exert any form of control.

A petrol bomb was thrown into a house that was home to several Jamaicans, forcing them out into the street where they could be viciously attacked. Other homes were targeted with windows smashed. The police also came under repeated attack as they attempted to prevent the Teddy Boys carrying out any further assaults.

One local journalist reported seeing 'a mob of over seven hundred men, women and children stretching two hundred yards along the road. Young children of ten were treating the whole affair as a great joke and shouting "come on, let's get the blacks".'

But by this time, members of the Black community were fed up with hiding inside their homes and simply accepting their fate. Upon learning that further attacks were being planned, preparations were made. Men got ready to take the fight to the enemy while women were told to keep pots of boiling water and packs of caustic soda on hand so that if anyone tried to break into their homes, they would be able to repel them. In the meantime, the men arranged an ambush, climbing onto the rooftops of their homes, armed with milk bottles and petrol bombs. Others took to the streets carrying iron bars and machetes, ready to launch a second attack wave.

Jamaican Baker Baron was there, watching the crowd from behind the curtains of a second-floor room when he heard them begin to chant: 'Let's burn the niggers, let's lynch the niggers.' The ex-serviceman then gave the order for the others to begin throwing Molotov cocktails.

The tactics worked, driving the Teddy Boys back. The next morning Baron and his friends were able to walk the streets with their heads held high, having shown their enemies they would not simply 'go down like dying dogs'.

Emboldened by their success, the Black community became more proactive in the hours that followed. Detective Sergeant Walters of Notting Hill Police reported seeing a 'large group of coloured men' walking along Ladbroke Grove: 'What can only be described as a mob were shouting threats and abuse, and openly displaying various most offensive weapons, ranging from iron bars to choppers and open razors. One Black man, Denton Boyd, had a chopper in his hand and was shouting: "Come and fight" and "What about it now?"'

Although Notting Hill was the centre of the disturbances, trouble spread to other parts of London including Paddington, Shepherd's Bush, Kilburn and Marylebone. It would later emerge that some of the white rioters had come from as far away as Tottenham.

The violence continued night after night, filling both the hospitals and the police cells, but eventually petered away at the end of the bank holiday, most likely because many of the white youths involved in the fight had to return to work.

In all, 108 people were charged with offences ranging from

grievous bodily harm to affray and riot and possessing offensive weapons; seventy-two were white (and most aged twenty or under) and thirty-six were 'coloured'. The latter almost certainly felt they were acting in self-defence but this was not taken into account. Denton Boyd, for example, received twelve months' imprisonment.

Considering the level of violence, the use of indiscriminate weapons such as petrol bombs and the sheer number of people involved, it was remarkable that no one was killed.

The official police report, written by DS Walters, refuted the press's suggestion that there had been a 'racial' dimension. Instead, he wrote, 'Whereas there certainly was some ill feeling between white and coloured residents, it is abundantly clear much of the trouble was caused by ruffians, both coloured and white, who seized on this opportunity to indulge in hooliganism.' Despite this official denial, it was crystal clear from the events in Notting Hill and Nottingham that many parts of the country were a powder keg just waiting for the spark to ignite further violence. This no doubt played a significant part in the treatment of the nine youths who had preceded the violence with their 'nigger-hunting' expedition when they came to court on 18 September 1959.

Presiding over his very first Old Bailey case, Mr Justice Salmon delivered a seven-minute-long speech that left both the boys and the members of the public crowded into the courtroom in no doubt that what had taken place was utterly unacceptable.

'Your object was to instil stark terror and inflict as much pain and grievous injury as you could,' he said.

During that night you savagely attacked five peaceful, law-abiding citizens without any shadow of an excuse. None of them had done you any harm. None of them had given you the slightest provocation. Indeed, you knew nothing about them, except that their skin happened to be of a colour of which you apparently did not approve. [. . .]

You are a minute and insignificant section of the population who have brought shame upon the district in which you lived, and have filled the whole nation with horror, indignation and disgust.

Everyone, irrespective of the colour of their skin, is entitled to walk through our streets in peace, with their heads erect, and free from fear. That is a right which these courts will always unfailingly uphold.

As far as the law is concerned, you are entitled to think what you like, however vile your thoughts; to feel what you like, however brutal and debased your emotions; to say what you like, providing you do not infringe the rights of others and imperil the Queen's peace.

But once you translate your dark thoughts and brutal feelings into savage acts such as these, the law will be swift to punish you, and to protect your victims.

It was a stern reprimand but what happened next would make headlines across the country. Mr Justice Salmon sentenced each of the boys to four years' imprisonment – an unprecedentedly harsh sentence at the time, even considering the level of violence that had been involved.

The case was immediately seized upon by the far right with a campaign launched to have the sentences reviewed. In the ongoing battle over issues of race and immigration, Notting Hill soon became the front line.

The Union Movement, a political party founded by the notorious fascist Oswald Mosley, began distributing leaflets in the area and the man himself paid a visit, further stirring up racial hatred.

One of the many people deeply shocked and upset by the events and the deteriorating relationships between the Black and white communities was London-based journalist and human rights activist Claudia Jones.

Born in Trinidad in 1915, her family had emigrated to New York when she was eight years old and growing up, she considered herself to be more American than Caribbean. A bright student who won prizes for her academic achievements, as she entered her teens she became increasingly aware of the racial injustices she saw all around her, especially the case of the Scottsboro Boys.

In March 1931, nine Black boys, aged between thirteen and twenty, were falsely accused of rape by two white women on a train in Alabama. They were quickly tried in the city of Scottsboro, and despite flimsy evidence and unreliable witnesses, all but the youngest were convicted and sentenced to death.

The case was taken up by a number of political and civil rights organisations including the Communist Party USA, which provided legal assistance and argued that the boys had been denied fair trials due to racial prejudice. (It would take many years and two appearances at the US Supreme Court before all the boys were exonerated or pardoned.)

Jones found herself inspired and signed up for the party's youth wing, the Young Communist League. In 1941 she was appointed national director of the League and seven years after that was elected to the national committee of the main party.

A powerful orator whose speeches drew large crowds during her travels across the country, Jones was also appointed the 'negro affairs' editor of the party's newspaper, raising her profile even higher.

But in the aftermath of the Second World War, rising concerns about the spread of communist ideology in countries such as Korea, along with mounting Cold War tensions, meant that such views were often treated with extreme suspicion and became the subject of both police and government action.

Jailed on no fewer than four occasions, Jones – who had never applied for US citizenship – was set to be deported for un-American activities and sent back to her home country, but Trinidad refused to allow her to return on the grounds that she might cause trouble there. As Trinidad was still part of the British Empire at this time, she was able to claim asylum. And that was how Jones came to find herself living in Notting Hill.

She arrived in 1955. Alarmed by the growing influence of local racist groups, in particular the White Defence League led by Colin Jordan, Jones immediately picked up where she left off, joining the Communist Party of Great Britain and working with various activist organisations to campaign against housing injustices, discrimination in the workplace and racist immigration policies.

Although many of those Commonwealth citizens who emigrated to Britain during the 1950s had great political and administrative acumen – especially those who had studied here – a large number had simply returned to the Caribbean or Africa to fight for local causes such as independence.

This placed Jones in an almost unique position. Building on her previous journalism experience, she decided to give a voice to the growing Caribbean community by launching the country's first 'Black' newspaper, the *West Indian Gazette*, because 'people without a voice were as lambs to the slaughter'. Creating the newspaper was a way of providing a platform where that voice could be fully heard.

The first edition was published in March 1958 and one of its key aims was to present West Indian talent to the public at a time when many saw them as only capable of working as manual labourers. The paper was well received by the community but struggled financially. Mainstream businesses did not pay for advertisements as they felt the audience was too niche for their products while Black-owned businesses simply didn't see the point in spending money to reach an audience already committed to supporting them.

Despite this, the *Gazette* quickly became an important and influential publication, drawing attention to key issues of the day. It campaigned against the colour bar and regularly exposed companies, pub chains and retailers who refused to employ or serve Black customers. Its offices, above a barber shop in Brixton, received a string of visits from influential political figures and Black civil rights leaders from around the world including Martin Luther King and the presidents of Trinidad and Tobago and Jamaica.

The unrest had come along just a few months later, dramatically highlighting the racial tensions that existed between the newly arrived Commonwealth emigrants and the white community but crucially bringing the issue to a far wider audience. Jones quickly realised much more needed to be done in order to 'wash the taste of the riots out of the mouths of Black people', to bring the community together and prevent further outbreaks of violence.

Making extensive use of her friends and contacts, she organised an indoor festival to celebrate Caribbean culture. It took place on 30 January 1959 at London's St Pancras Town Hall and was even televised by the BBC.

But just when it seemed the situation for Black communities in London might be improving and that people could go about their ordinary business without fear of being attacked, tragedy struck.

Kelso Cochrane had been one of the lucky ones, finding work as a carpenter and earning enough to settle into relatively comfortable lodgings in Notting Hill.

Although he was free to remain in England for as long as he wanted, Kelso still hoped to return to America. In May 1957 he learned that his application for US citizenship had been successful, thanks largely to the support of his estranged wife who wanted the best for their daughter. But before he could act on this, his former wife became involved with someone else and changed her mind, leading to his citizenship request being rescinded. Having initially intended to stay in London only for a year or two, he now resigned himself to making it his permanent home. It turned out to be a great decision – within a few months he found himself in a relationship with Olivia Ellington, a Jamaican trainee nurse eleven years his junior.

By April 1959 Olivia had moved into Kelso's bedsit on the first floor of a house at 11 Bevington Road and the pair began planning a summer wedding.

Around three weeks before their big day, Kelso fell while working on a carpentry job and landed on his left thumb, fracturing the bone. He attended Paddington General Hospital where an X-ray confirmed the fracture. An operation to reset the thumb was performed but proved unsuccessful as, in the days that followed, Kelso was still in a significant amount of pain.

On the morning of Saturday, 16 May, he returned to the hospital where his thumb was repositioned, and a new plaster cast fitted. He and Olivia spent the rest of the day shopping and listening to talks at Speaker's Corner in Hyde Park before heading home.

It had been an enjoyable day but as bedtime approached, Kelso's thumb became increasingly painful and he realised it would be impossible for him to sleep, so he decided to return to hospital once again to see if they could do anything more. Arriving at around 10.30 p.m., he was eventually seen by the same doctor who had treated him that morning and prescribed even stronger painkillers.

Kelso then set about walking the mile or so back to the bedsit. Around midnight, he was heading along Southam Street (now the Edenham estate), and close to the Earl of Warwick pub on the corner of Golborne Road.

As Kelso headed down the road, a group of five or six Teddy Boys spotted him from the other side of the street. 'Hey, Jim Crow,' they shouted, crossing the road and quickly forming a circle around him.

Joy Okine, a twenty-one-year-old clerk, lived in a first-floor flat on the corner of Golborne Road. She was at home with her mother when she heard a commotion outside the window and the two women looked out.

They saw a group of white boys jostling with a Black man. Punches and kicks were being thrown. The Black man was trying to defend himself as best as he could, but with one arm in plaster and overwhelming odds, he had no chance. One of the youths jumped on Kelso's back and he fell to the ground.

Just then, two Jamaican friends, Horatio Lewis and Ken Steele, arrived on the scene. They had been out at a nearby dance hall and were walking home, just in time to see Kelso fall.

Steele yelled out and both men started running towards the melee, causing the attackers to run off. By the time they reached Kelso, the Teddy Boys were nowhere to be seen.

Kelso didn't seem to be badly hurt. Steele and Lewis helped him to his feet and asked what had happened. 'These chaps asked me for money,' he replied, 'I told them I didn't have any. They started to fight me.'

The last moments of the attack had also been witnessed by taxi driver George Issacs as he was dropping off a group of passengers across the road. He pulled up alongside the kerb and Steele told him about the attack. He too didn't think the victim was badly hurt and offered him a lift home, but within a few moments Kelso deteriorated and started to show signs of real distress, moaning in pain and falling to his knees.

Issacs suggested they take Kelso to the Charles Hospital, some half a mile away. It was only as the men were lifting him into the back of the taxi that they noticed for the first time a tiny spot of blood had begun seeping through his shirt, directly in line with his heart.

At the hospital, Issacs, Steele and Lewis all waited while Kelso was examined. By now he was in a state of shock, slipping in and out of consciousness and only barely able to give his name and respond to the doctor's questions. There was hardly any blood on his clothing, but a post-mortem would later reveal he had been stabbed on the left side of his chest with a very sharp, stiletto-type knife.

The blade had been driven in with considerable force, entering through his fifth rib and penetrating to a depth of two inches, piercing the main chamber of his heart where it caused massive internal bleeding.

As doctors fought to save Kelso's life, a message was sent to Harrow Road police station, informing them of the incident. Detective Sergeant Sidney Coomber and another officer arrived a few minutes later.

'I entered a cubicle where I saw a coloured man I now know as Kelso Cochrane, lying on the floor being attended by a doctor, a sister and a nurse,' Coomber would later say in a statement. 'I assisted giving this man artificial respiration.' But it was too late and within moments, Kelso had been pronounced dead.

Coomber stepped out of the cubicle to where Steele and Lewis were still waiting. 'I told them that the man had died and on hearing this they burst into tears.'

Around this same time, a junior reporter working the night shift on the *Sunday Express* answered the phone. 'Are you interested in a murder?' the caller asked before adding: 'Three white youths have stabbed a darkie named Cochrane on Golborne Road.'

Much to the young reporter's relief, the call had come early enough to make it into the 4 a.m. edition of the paper. It made the front page, under the banner headline MURDER IN NOT-TING HILL.

The police officer assigned to the task of finding Kelso's killers was Detective Superintendent Ian Forbes-Leith, a former soldier who had studied at Sandhurst and taken part in the D-Day landings.

At the time of the murder he was already quite familiar to the public thanks to his starring role in a number of cases, some of which had resulted in flattering newspaper profiles and led to him ultimately being appointed the youngest ever detective superintendent in the force at the age of thirty-eight. Now forty-two, he had only recently taken up a new post running the X Division of CID which included the area where the murder had taken place. This would be his first major case with the unit.

Woken from his sleep with news of the murder at 1.15 a.m., he arrived at Harrow Road police station around an hour later to find officers taking witness statements from the likes of Lewis and Steele, the men who had attempted to assist Kelso immediately after the stabbing.

After assigning various roles to what would become a twenty-strong team of detectives, Forbes-Leith was alarmed to see coverage of the killing on the front of the *Sunday Express*. It seemed clear that the leak had come direct from the police and that didn't bode well for the integrity of the rest of the investigation.

Just before dawn, officers knocked on the door of Olivia Ellington and told her that her fiancé was dead. In the statement she gave to officers later that day she said the couple had been to-gether for eight months. 'My heart broke,' she said later.

It was Kelso's cousin James – who learned about the death around the same time – who attended the morgue to identify the body, sparing Olivia the task. The pair had been as close as brothers. The only reason James was in the UK at all was because Kelso had encouraged him to make the journey. As soon as James caught sight of the body of his cousin, he fainted.

Olivia spoke to the newspapers the same day: 'Kelso was a nice quiet man and so very kind.' She insisted he was not the type to seek out trouble or get involved in fighting. She was convinced the only reason he had been targeted was due to the colour of his skin.

Considering the violence that had broken out in Notting Hill the previous summer, an immediate concern was a backlash on both sides of the racial divide. Taking no chances, Detective Superintendent Forbes-Leith drafted fifty anti-riot officers into the area, along with extra police dogs. Black Marias were stationed in strategic locations. Uniformed officers went on patrol in pairs while radio cars cruised the streets, all in the hope that any signs of public disorder could be suppressed before they had a chance to spread.

Extensive searches were made of the area around the murder scene in an attempt to find the knife, to no avail. But the investigation would be less than forty-eight hours old when Forbes-Leith made an important announcement that he hoped would go some way to alleviating concerns about racial hatred. 'The stabbing has absolutely nothing to do with racial conflict,' he told the press. 'The motive could have been robbery.'

The next day's edition of the *Daily Mirror* confirmed that this was the line of enquiry the police were pursuing, quoting an unnamed senior Scotland Yard officer as saying: 'You will be doing the community a service by refraining from any suggestion that this is a racial murder.'

He continued: 'We are satisfied that it was the work of a group of about six anti-law white teenagers who had only one motive in view – robbery or attempted robbery of a man who was walking the streets in the Notting Hill district alone in the early hours of the morning. The fact that he happened to be coloured does not, in our view, come into the question.'

Further evidence of the robbery motive came from Kelso's dying words – about being asked for money – and the fact that his wallet was empty, despite him earning £15 per week (a good wage for the time) and having been paid the day before.

(In reality, Kelso, far more concerned about the prospect of being robbed than being attacked because of the colour of his skin, had emptied his wallet at home, shortly before heading to the hospital.)

Sir Oswald Mosley, having been widely condemned for stirring up racial hatred in the area, jumped on the police announcement to defend himself. In a statement to the press he thanked the police for 'bringing to an end this particular nonsense' and reiterated calls for repatriation.

'The only cure for these troubles is to send the Jamaicans back to a fair deal in their own country by restoring the prosperity of their sugar industry.'

In the meantime, the investigation began to focus its attention on a house party on Southam Street, which had been attended by a number of Teddy Boys, some of whom had a reputation for being involved in acts of violence in the past.

Six of them were kept overnight but two in particular were detained for almost an entire extra day. They were twenty-year-old Patrick Digby and his close friend John 'Shoggy' Breagan, who was twenty-four. They were questioned but subsequently released without charge.

Shoggy later told a newspaper of his fears as he waited in the police cell. 'I am completely innocent of all connection with this crime but two weeks ago I came out of prison after serving a three-year sentence for attacking a negro. What would happen if they thought I was easy meat and tried to bring a murder charge against me?'

He acknowledged that he had seen Kelso, but only after he had been stabbed. 'I was at the party in Southam Street with my friend Pat Digby. We left the party together after midnight and walked the streets looking for a couple of girls. Then I saw a coloured man lying on the ground. Digby saw him too. "It's got nothing to do with us," I told Digby. "Leave him alone."'

Digby was also interviewed and described it as 'the worst experience I have ever gone through': 'We saw this black man lying on the pavement, clutching his chest. Two spades – that's what we call coloured men here – were standing beside him. We decided to get out of it fast. It was not our business.'

Although it seemed to the outside world that Forbes-Leith and his team were making huge efforts to find the killers, the reality was somewhat different.

It was only later that the reason why Digby and Breagan had been held longer than the others would emerge. During their initial interviews, aspects of their stories had not matched, leading to them falling under greater suspicion. During their second interviews, all the questionable small details lined up perfectly and both were allowed to go free.

No one seemed to have realised that during the period in between, the two men were housed in adjoining cells, giving them the perfect opportunity to get their stories straight.

It was one of a number of failings that emerged from the early days of the investigation. Simple steps that should have been taken were overlooked. Eyewitnesses had reported seeing one of the men attacking Kelso trying to rip an iron railing out of the ground to use as a weapon, but no fingerprints were ever taken. In the case of Pat Digby, while his clothes had been taken away for examination, his home was never searched for clues.

This was especially astonishing considering that rumours abounded that the murder weapon had been hidden under his floorboards.

Claudia Jones, the activist who had been working hard to improve relations between the races in Notting Hill and beyond, was especially shocked by Kelso's death. It seemed that all her efforts to bring peace to the area following the 1958 uprising had been in vain and that the country had returned to square one.

In the immediate aftermath she joined forces with the Coloured People's Progress Association to march on Whitehall to express their anger about the rising levels of racial violence and racism in Britain. She also led the formation of a brand-new organisation – the Inter-Racial Friendship Co-ordinating Council. They organised a memorial meeting for Kelso and a public funeral (raising £257 to cover the costs) which turned into a huge public event.

Newspapers reported how scores of people packed themselves into Kensal Green cemetery to watch the proceedings. 'They clung to stones and crosses and stood on tiptoe on raised graves.

Some tried to use a hearse as a "grandstand". More than a thousand, most of them coloured, were at the graveside and when the ceremony was over, many stayed on to sing hymns. Men wept and one woman fainted.'

The reports also noted that a young West African man in white robes and a fez was seen handing out leaflets urging people to join a march from Hyde Park to Trafalgar Square the following day.

The leaflets said: 'It could be you. Kelso's murder is Britain's shame. All Africans and Afro-Asians must make this Sunday a day of remembrance for a dear brother who was murdered because of the colour of his skin.'

In the weeks after the funeral, the council sent a letter to the Prime Minister calling for the introduction of new laws against incitement to racial hatred (which was not illegal at the time) in order to prevent the likes of Colin Jordan from spreading his message of hate.

What's particularly striking in terms of the concerns they outlined is that an identical letter could have been written at any time in the decades that have followed. 'Lack of police on beats and police bias have been developing and have led to a situation of lawlessness and a growing lack of confidence by all citizens in the law enforcement agencies.'

The following Sunday, 24 May, saw a rally held in Trafalgar Square jointly organised by the White Defence League and the National Labour Party to protest against what both groups referred to as 'the coloured invasion'.

The event saw a large banner reading KEEP BRITAIN WHITE stretched between the lions at the foot of Nelson's Column. (They were seemingly unaware of the presence of a Black man on the column itself.) During a series of speeches, Colin Jordan claimed that 'coloured immigrants' were 'riddled with infectious diseases' such as leprosy and referred to Cochrane as a 'manufactured martyr'.

The following week, Jones and her supporters met up with

officials from the Home Office and once more asked for racial hatred to be outlawed. They made requests for a substantial increase in the number of police to be stationed around Notting Hill, but crucially for the removal of those with 'racial bias'. On 1 June the group staged a vigil just outside 10 Downing Street, to 'express a lack of confidence in arrangements for the security of coloured people'.

In the meantime, the police investigation into the murder began to flounder. The identities of the men responsible for Kelso's death quickly became 'the worst kept secret' in Notting Hill but the authorities seemed either unwilling or unable to press forward.

Decades later it would emerge that corruption, incompetence and a lack of empathy for the victim had all played their part in the failure but some of the reasons were the result of decisions being made well above the pay grade of Detective Superintendent Forbes-Leith.

A key consideration within government circles at the time was the potential impact Kelso's murder would have on the wider community. The 1958 Notting Hill Riots were very much top of mind and there was a fear that the incident might trigger a new round of violence.

These fears went all the way to the top with Prime Minister Harold Macmillan hosting a series of ministerial meetings to discuss the matter. This may have been a factor in why police were so keen to rule out a racial motive in the early stages of the case.

A wider issue, beyond that of race, was growing opposition to the death penalty during the post-war period. In particular, the public began to question the use of capital punishment following the 1950 execution of Timothy Evans for the murder of his wife and child. It later emerged that Evans was entirely innocent, and the deaths were the work of serial killer John Christie.

Then there was the hanging of nineteen-year-old Derek Bentley in 1953 for being party to, but not directly responsible for, the murder of a police officer. It was his friend, Christopher

Craig, who fired the fatal shot that killed the officer while he attempted to arrest him for burglary. Another officer was holding Bentley. Craig, at sixteen, was too young to receive the death penalty, but Bentley was not. Bentley was granted a posthumous pardon in 1998.

In 1955 Ruth Ellis was sentenced to hang for the murder of her boyfriend, David Blakely, despite evidence that he had been physically abusive to her. Ellis attracted huge public sympathy, with many seeing her crime as one of passion rather than malice, meaning the judge could have commuted her sentence to life imprisonment. This was the case with 90 per cent of women sentenced to death at the time. Hundreds wrote letters or signed petitions begging for clemency and there was an eleventh-hour attempt at an appeal for a reprieve, but it was all in vain. She was the last woman to be executed in Britain.

Growing concerns about the use of the death penalty led to the 1957 Homicide Act which introduced a number of reforms so that there were only six categories of murder for which capital punishment would apply:

- In the course or furtherance of theft.
- By shooting or causing an explosion.
- For resisting arrest or during an escape.
- Killing of a police officer.
- Killing of a prison officer by a prisoner.
- The second of two murders committed on different occasions.

Eight days before Kelso was killed, a twenty-five-year-old scaffolder and Teddy Boy named Ron Marwood had been hanged for fatally stabbing police officer Ray Summers in the back as he attempted to break up a fight outside a dance hall in north London.

More than 150 MPs appealed for the sentence to be commuted and one thousand protestors gathered outside Pentonville Prison on the morning of his execution. Later that same day, a gang of Teddy Boys rioted outside Tower Hill police station, chanting 'all coppers are bastards' and 'revenge for Marwood'.

Kelso's death plunged the authorities into a vicious circle from which there was no escape and which served only to highlight the racial injustice of the state.

If Kelso had been the victim of a racist attack and killed simply because of the colour of his skin, then his killers would not face the death penalty because this did not fall among the six categories for which capital punishment could apply.

If, however, the motive for his death was indeed robbery, as the police were insisting it was, then it would fall into the category of being murdered 'in the furtherance of theft' and his killers would face the gallows.

If the victim had been white and the perpetrator Black, the outcry over the imposition of a death sentence would have been far less, but it was all too easy to see how the reverse could easily prompt more violent outbreaks in areas with large migrant communities across the country.

A tactic the police deployed in order to water down the level of public sympathy for the victim was one they would also make use of in the aftermath of the murder of Stephen Lawrence: they would do their best to discredit the dead.

On 24 May 1959, the *People* newspaper carried a front-page item about the case under the headline GANG VICTIM LED DOUBLE LIFE.

A new theory about the death of 32-year-old Kelso Cochrane, the coloured carpenter stabbed in Notting Hill a week ago, emerged last night from a detailed investigation of Cochrane's background. The facts are that Cochrane had been drinking on the night of his death and was known to be truculent after a few drinks.

He had a conviction for causing grievous bodily harm to a

workmate who he attacked with a spanner. The knife that killed him was probably his own. He liked to carry one. And police think he may have lied to his friends about his wrist injury, which he said was caused at work.

Even allowing for poetic licence by the paper's journalists, the story was riddled with inaccuracies. A post-mortem had found no trace of alcohol in Kelso's body and Olivia Ellington had already told police that he only ever drank in moderation.

Rather than allowing the public to consider the implications of an entirely innocent Black man being killed by members of a white gang while making his way home and minding his own business, the story implied he was at least partly to blame for his own demise.

On the back of such stories, racists had hoped that the death of a Black carpenter would finally push the capital into the 'race war' they had tried to spark the previous summer. In fact the effect was the total opposite. The case brought the people of the west London district together, ensuring they were more determined than ever to stamp out racism once and for all.

In October 1959 Sir Oswald Mosley briefly returned to Britain to stand as a candidate in the general election for the seat of Kensington North. Anti-immigration policies, including the forced repatriation of immigrants from the Caribbean, was the foundation of his platform. He also called for a ban on mixed marriages. But a paltry 8.1 per cent share of the vote disillusioned him into leaving England.

On 3 June 1960, a year after Kelso's death, the *Kensington News and West London Times* ran a story headlined COCHRANE KILLER IS STILL FREE on its front page, which noted that the 'savage and brutal crime with its disturbing possibilities of race hatred remains unsolved'. A local police officer was quoted as having said, six months earlier: 'We know who killed Kelso Cochrane – but we can't prove it.' The killer is believed to have been Pat Digby. Years later, Digby's stepdaughter would claim that he admitted responsibility for the murder.

Although the case was never officially solved and the killer or killers ultimately escaped justice, the murder of Kelso Cochrane was a significant milestone for race relations in Britain. As would be the case with the murder of Stephen Lawrence more than thirty years later, the Cochrane case cast light on just how deeply embedded casual racism and violence had become all across the country.

The small Caribbean fayre organised by Claudia Jones in the wake of the Notting Hill Riots became an annual fixture and, after her death in 1964, was taken up by others who helped it to grow and evolve in line with her wishes.

In 1966 it moved outdoors for the first time, taking place as a multi-day event in the same area of west London where it occurs today under its new name: the Notting Hill Carnival.

It's amazing to think how many people attend the event each year, enjoying the music and the costumes, with no idea of its origins or true appreciation of the trauma, adversity and injustice that led to its creation.

In 2003 Kelso's brother Stanley asked for the case to be reopened so that the very latest forensic techniques could be used to pinpoint the killer. It then emerged that Kelso's clothes had been destroyed in 1968 so the case could not proceed any further in that direction.

Once almost forgotten, the death of Kelso Cochrane is increasingly being recognised as a pivotal moment in race relations. On 17 May 2009, a blue plaque, paid for by the Nubian Jak Community Trust, a charity with a mission to shine a light on the historic achievements of Britain's Black and ethnic minority people, was unveiled at the spot opposite where Kelso was attacked, to mark the fiftieth anniversary of his death. A new social housing development named after Kelso was opened in 2024, with members of his family taking part in the official opening; the street that runs alongside the building was also renamed Kelso Cochrane Lane.

Pat Digby died of a heart attack in 2007, but the fight continues.

The police files into the murder of Kelso Cochrane now reside at the National Archives in Kew. They are closed from public view and will not be released until 2054, the year Kelso's youngest daughter, Josephine, will turn one hundred years old.

While it's not especially unusual for the files of unsolved murder cases to remain restricted for this length of time so that all those directly involved will have died, there are plenty of precedents from cases that occurred years after the death of Kelso where such restrictions have been fully lifted. This has not yet happened in this instance.

The most recent attempt was made by BBC investigative journalist Mark Olden who submitted a Freedom of Information request in 2020 asking for permission to access the restricted files. This too was turned down.

Police protocol states that, even though there may have been no activity in decades, no unsolved case is ever closed. This means that, should new evidence turn up, it will be taken into account and investigated accordingly.

According to Scotland Yard, officers from the Special Casework Team have reached out to the family of Kelso Cochrane in an attempt to discuss details of the investigation. The force says these efforts have not been successful.

Daniel Machover, a lawyer working on behalf of the Cochrane family, says they are planning to challenge the ruling that the files should remain closed. These efforts are also supported by a number of journalists who wish to access the files.

Unexpectedly, some of these files were released in July 2024. They showed that Breagan had been freed from prison ten days before Kelso was killed, for carrying out unprovoked knife attacks on three Black men in 1957. When he was arrested for these offences, the files reveal that he swore to two police officers that if he went to jail, he would kill the first Black person he saw when he got out.

While it is too late for anyone to face the force of criminal justice in connection with the death, Kelso's family live in hope that gaining access to the file will make it easier to satisfy themselves that the police truly did all they could to bring his killers to justice.

That need to continue fighting for justice, even years or decades after an event, is something I understand only too well.

People often use the word 'closure', but I never feel that's quite right. It can come across as something that signifies that you've reached the end, that everything is fine and all will be OK because you have all the answers, that your life can be reset to normal.

The truth is there will always be a void. In my case, I always felt that my mum could never rest in peace until the truth was known. There had to be some kind of recognition of what had happened, acknowledgement of who was responsible and why.

Getting justice for my mum felt like the greatest gift I could give her, in her absence. I would imagine that Kelso Cochrane's family feel the same and I wish them well.

6

David Oluwale

Thirty years after the death of Charles Wotten, history seemed to be repeating itself as violence broke out between Black and white workers, this time on the streets of the capital.

According to one newspaper report, published on 23 July 1949:

London's most violent race riot for years broke out this week when 1,000 yelling white men, armed with bottles, sticks and knives, invaded the East End coloured quarter.

Bands of whites detached themselves from the main throng to search East End cafés and hotels for coloured men. A big mob gathered outside the Coloured Workers' Hostel in Deptford shouting: 'Throw the dirty blacks into the river!'

The report goes on to describe a series of pitched battles between Blacks and whites and how it took more than one hundred police officers several hours to restore order. Three officers and thirty Black men were reported injured, two of them seriously.

As had been the case during the unrest of 1919, the targets of the mob were mostly Black seamen, but the hostel was also home to a significant number of West Africans, many of whom had arrived in the UK as stowaways.

For those unwilling or unable to pay the fare to travel to England, stowing away had always been a popular option. When the *Windrush* had arrived in Portsmouth a year earlier, there had officially been two stowaways onboard, but as many as fifteen more who apparently slipped off unseen.

For those who were caught, the punishment was a fine of £1 or a sentence of between seven and twenty-eight days in prison. Many opted to pay the fine – a bargain compared to the minimum £28 the *Windrush* charged for paying passengers.

In the case of stowaways from countries such as Nigeria, they usually carried British Travel Certificates. Such documents were intended to facilitate travel between the British and French colonies of West Africa, but as they included a statement that the holders were British citizens, many stowaways used them to prove they had a right to both enter and remain in Britain.

Following the disturbances in Deptford, the Home Secretary faced calls to repatriate all those who had come to the UK as stowaways but admitted he did not have the power to do so as they remained British subjects.

The chosen solution was to render the British Travel Certificate invalid for the purpose of entering the country. The legislation was enacted in late September 1949 meaning that in the future, stowaways faced being returned to their home countries on the next available boat.

For that reason, David Oluwale appeared to be one of the lucky ones. He arrived in Hull earlier that same month, having stowed away on board the cargo ship *Temple Bar* which had left Lagos, Nigeria, two weeks earlier.

As David set foot on British soil, the mass migration that began with the *Windrush* was just getting underway. As we have already seen with the hanging of Mahmood Mattan and murder of Kelso Cochrane, the idea that the residents of their 'mother country' would welcome them with open arms into a brave new world of racial tolerance was not at all realistic.

Many suffered as, during the 1960s, the climate became increasingly hostile towards Blacks. Like Mahmood and Kelso before him, David Oluwale would pay the ultimate price for seeking a better life for himself.

Twenty years after his arrival, his dead body was discovered lodged between two rocks on the banks of the River Aire in the city of Leeds. And two years after that, in the first ever case of its kind, two police officers would go on trial to face charges that they were the ones that had killed him.

Relatively little is known about the early life of David Oluwale. He was born in Lagos, most likely in 1930, and had one younger sister. His father appears to have died when he was young leaving his mother as the sole breadwinner in the family.

Through the support of relatives, David was able to attend a Christian grammar school which took its blueprint from England and taught a curriculum heavily biased towards British history and values, as well as Nigeria's place in the wider Empire. The intention was to turn out well-qualified, proper little English gentlemen who could enter high-profile professions, such as law or medicine, and support their families for years to come.

But David never got the chance to earn any such qualifications as he left school in 1944, most likely because his family could no longer afford the fees. He worked a few manual jobs and was eventually taken on as an apprentice tailor, but, along with many others, struggled with constant food shortages and soaring prices.

In those post-war years, many set their sights further afield and hoped the place they knew as the 'mother country' would provide the opportunities they sought. From 1945 to the end of the decade, some sixteen hundred stowaways are estimated to have arrived in Britain, two-thirds of them from West Africa.

One day in mid-August 1949, at the age of nineteen, David made his way to Apapa Wharf, the oldest and largest port in Nigeria, and slipped aboard the *Temple Bar* which was about to set sail for the city of Hull with a cargo of groundnuts – an important cash crop and one of the country's main exports.

Eight further stowaways had boarded at the same time. Six were discovered and thrown off before the *Temple Bar* set sail but David and two others evaded detection. Their luck did not last for long. After only a day at sea the captain suspected more stowaways were on board and called for smoke to be pumped into the hold in order to drive them out.

The three men were put to work for the rest of the voyage and handed over to the police as soon as they arrived in Hull on 3 September 1949.

Appearing before a magistrate at the local police court, the men were told they would have been better off staying at home to dig groundnuts. He sentenced each of them to twenty-eight days in prison. The sentence would be served at Armley prison in Leeds, some sixty miles to the west. Despite his first night there being in such unfavourable conditions, this was the city David would soon come to regard as home.

With his sentence complete, David joined other West Africans, many of them fellow stowaways, in this new phase of their lives. So long as you didn't mind hard and dirty manual labour, work was easy to find.

In those first few years David took on a variety of jobs including hod carrying on building sites, labouring in a slaughterhouse and working in a foundry. Racism in the form of discrimination at work or when it came to housing was never far away but this was generally a happy time for him.

David and his friends would regularly attend dances at the Mecca Ballroom where they had the opportunity to mix with local women and show off their moves. He spent a significant proportion of his wages on clothes to make sure he always looked sharp and soon acquired the nickname Yankee because of his love of American culture. Always cheerful, smiling and cracking jokes, friends described him as the life and soul of the party.

Discrimination, however, was constant and at around 5ft 5in, David was often picked on. Powerfully built, he wasn't afraid to fight back when confronted and would use any means possible to make up for his lack of height. His speciality was biting the fingers of his opponents.

In March 1951, David had been working in Sheffield and was eating in a snack bar one evening when the proprietor asked him to leave, claiming he was drunk. When David refused, the police were called and took him away in the back of a Black Maria. During the journey, things turned violent, and a police officer received a bite wound that was serious enough for him to require hospital treatment.

In what would be his first conviction, David was fined £2 for assault and ordered to pay a further ten shillings for being drunk and disorderly.

Two years later, in April 1953, there was another restaurant dispute, this time over an allegedly unpaid bill. Police were called and a scuffle broke out, during which David was either struck with a truncheon or banged his head somewhere else. At least one police officer was badly enough injured to require medical treatment.

The details of what actually happened are questionable but what cannot be disputed is that from that day onwards, David Oluwale was never the same.

He was charged with disorderly conduct, assault of a police officer and damage to a police uniform. He was jailed for two months but towards the end of his sentence, he began to act strangely. Doctors described him as loud and excitable but also frightened without cause.

On 6 June, he was admitted to the psychiatric unit of a local hospital on a fourteen-day court order but after just a few days, it seemed clear his condition was not going to improve. He was committed to the nearby Menston Asylum. He was soon diagnosed with schizophrenia and treated with a combination of brutal electroshock therapy and a powerful cocktail of antipsychotic drugs. The latter, sometimes referred to as a 'chemical cosh', effectively turned him into a zombie.

David would remain at Menston for the next eight years. During his whole time there, he did not have a single visitor.

In April 1961 David was released from Menston Asylum but the therapy and the drugs had changed him. Gone was the happy, smiling man who had once been the life of the party and in his place was a nervous, twitchy figure who shuffled around slowly and would often break out into peals of laughter, seemingly for no reason.

He found work at a local foundry but got sacked just a few months later after getting into a fight with a Jamaican worker. Without employment he soon found himself living on the streets, his welfare benefit payments not enough for him to secure a roof over his head. Although some hostels and homeless shelters were available, the majority refused to take in Black men – which at the time they were legally able to do – leaving him no choice but to sleep in shop doorways.

In September that same year, he was jailed for six months for malicious wounding after almost biting off the finger of a park warden who was trying to prevent him from entering a derelict house he had been using for shelter.

It was around this time that David first began to express what were assumed to be paranoid delusions about the police. He told psychiatrists that they were treating him badly, stealing his money and persecuting him.

In November 1965 his odd behaviour escalated, and he complained of hearing voices. He was detained under the Mental Health Act and returned to Menston, then known as High Royds Hospital. He would spend a further two years there.

One consultant psychiatrist, Dr Richard Carty, would report that he was 'restless, noisy and restive'. He noted that he 'spoke English fairly well but he was so confused he could give no clear account of himself' and did not know where he was. He was also hallucinating, seeing imaginary creatures which he described as 'lions with fishes'. He was convinced these creatures were trying to kill him.

After a couple of months David settled down and became quiet and lucid, though there were also periods when he was completely withdrawn and would not speak to anyone.

He was occasionally violent and aggressive, prone to biting the fingers of those around him.

In April 1967 he was released from the hospital and once more returned to the streets of Leeds.

As a result, David was regularly arrested, charged and sentenced for the crime of 'wandering abroad'. The term refers not to leaving the UK but rather to sleeping rough and is defined as 'lodging in any barn or outhouse, or in any deserted or unoccupied building, or in the open air, or under a tent, or in any cart or wagon'. Anyone arrested for wandering abroad is required to give 'a good account of himself or herself'.

The archaic language is because the criminal offence comes under Section 4 of the Vagrancy Act 1824. A separate section of this same law will crop up later in this book time and again, especially in the direct run-up to the events that led to my mother being shot.

David's troubles continued. In December 1967, he was jailed again, this time for three months, after admitting that he had exposed himself to two women. Released at the end of March 1968 he found himself back on the streets of Leeds just as traders and shopkeepers were putting the police under increased pressure to keep the streets clear of vagrants.

As the only Black man sleeping rough in the city at the time, David stood out. In particular two officers from Leeds City Police, both based in Millgarth station, took exception to his presence. Inspector Geoffrey Ellerker and Sergeant Kenneth Kitching made it their personal mission to get him to leave, arresting him on multiple occasions in the months that followed.

During his brief spells in prison that resulted from these arrests, it seemed that David's mental health was getting ever worse with medical and welfare officers convinced he could no longer tell the difference between reality and his own delusions. 'Strong persecutory feelings of anti-authoritarian,' wrote one. 'Insists police frequently take him outside Leeds and leave him in the forest,' recorded another. All his allegations and protestations were dismissed as they were seen as nothing more than symptoms of his illness.

Officers from Millgarth continued to make his life a misery. A charge sheet from March 1969 makes it abundantly clear that racial prejudice was a factor in his treatment. In the space for the prisoner's nationality, the word 'British' had been typed in, but then crossed out with 'Wog' scrawled in its place.

On 10 April 1969, David was released from prison for the last time. On 4 May, his body was discovered face down in the River Aire, lodged between two rocks at Knostrop Weir, close to the city's main sewage works.

The officer dealing with David's body made note of the various injuries he had found but other than that, there was little interest in finding out more about the events leading up to his death. More senior officers decided that it would be best to wait for the results of a post-mortem before deciding whether the death had been the result of foul play or misadventure.

The post-mortem was conducted the day after the body had been found and confirmed the presence of a large bruise on David's forehead, though the pathologist was unable to say whether this was the result of something which had occurred before or after his death as the tests to determine this were inconclusive. It was inevitable, therefore, that the pathologist ruled that David's death was the result of drowning.

An inquest took place on 14 May. By this time his identity had been confirmed through matching the fingerprints the police held on file.

A month after his body had been recovered, David was buried at Killingbeck Cemetery. The only persons present were the cemetery superintendent and his undertakers. The few items found on his person when he was pulled out of the river were used to decide the kind of service he received.

A string of blue rosary beads had been found in his pocket, so he was buried in the Catholic section of the graveyard. The small amount of money he carried – eleven shillings and ten pence – was put towards the costs of his flimsy coffin and pauper's grave.

There were plenty of questions that needed to be asked but no one around to ask them. With everyone willing to accept that this was simply a case of a troubled, mentally ill man who had somehow fallen into the river and drowned, there was no need to look any further.

Indeed, the story might have ended there had it not been undone by a poorly conceived attempt at a cover-up in the aftermath of a road accident a few months later.

On Christmas Eve 1969, a seventy-two-year-old woman named Minnie Wein had been fatally injured after being struck by an unmarked police car driven by Superintendent Derek Holmes, known throughout the force as 'Big Red'.

A number of officers, among them Inspector Geoffrey Ellerker, tried to cover up for their boss. They insisted the dead woman, who was returning home after a bingo session, had smelled of alcohol when they found her, that she had crossed the road away from the pedestrian crossing and that Big Red himself had not been drinking. In reality, Minnie Wein had been teetotal for her entire life.

Employing what would later be described as a threatening manner, Ellerker prevented two junior officers from the traffic division from giving Big Red a breath test and told them to alter their statements to ensure the superintendent would not be held responsible for the accident. Initially compliant, the men quickly had a change of heart and took their concerns to their superiors.

Soon Ellerker and three other officers found themselves suspended on suspicion of misconduct. The subsequent court case saw them facing a total of eleven charges, including conspiracy to pervert the course of justice, preparing false evidence for an inquest, failing to administer a breath test and altering statements.

Some of the officers called to give evidence and make statements in relation to the trial were quite new in service, with several still going through probation, meaning they had been with the police for two years or less. Because they had been so junior and had been concerned about starting their careers off on the wrong foot, many had said nothing about the shocking behaviour they had regularly seen from Ellerker and Kitching. The latter was known to regularly drink on the job and often used excessive force against people he arrested, who would inevitably be charged with being the aggressors.

Ellerker would back Kitching up when necessary, but it was when they acted together that they were at their worst. In particular, the pair were known to have waged a year-long war of harassment and physical violence directly against David Oluwale.

The most troubling allegation was that Ellerker, Kitching and another officer were known to have delivered an especially savage beating to David while he was sleeping in a shop doorway in mid-April 1969. Ellerker had even borrowed a truncheon from a junior officer – inspectors did not carry them at the time – moments before getting involved. Two weeks later, David's body had been pulled out of the river and judged by the coroner to have been in the water for around that long. The implication was clear and highly disturbing.

When Ellerker was found guilty, sentenced to nine months and kicked out of the force, many officers who had worked with him finally felt able to unburden themselves about some of the incidents they had experienced.

One, Gary Briggs, told his roommate, an eighteen-year-old police cadet named Gary Galvin, how he had been on duty one night when Kitching and Ellerker had beaten up a Black man who had been sleeping in a shop doorway. Briggs had not seen the actual attack itself, but shortly before Ellerker had asked to borrow his truncheon and it was clear what he intended to do with it. Briggs added that the assault had not been an isolated incident. Whether it was simply the strength of his own moral compass or the fact that he was so very young, the moment Galvin heard about the assault, he knew he had no choice but to take action and relate what he had been told to an inspector.

Before the end of the day, following a two-hour interview, Sergeant Kitching had been suspended from duty and an official inquiry was underway with officers sent from Scotland Yard to Leeds to investigate.

What emerged was a horrifying catalogue of abuse and torment against David, especially in the last few months of his life. Kitching, in particular, was revealed to have an intense hatred of vagrants, believing they were a drain on society and that the best way to deal with them was to make their lives so miserable that they would leave the city and never come back.

Eager to lead by example, he would often go out on patrol in the division van rather than remaining behind at the station, in order to hunt down the homeless. He would inevitably wake them up with the tip of his boot, delivering a good kicking until they ran away.

For some reason – race being by far the most likely as David was the only Black man sleeping rough at the time – he became especially obsessed with the Nigerian who he had given the nickname 'Uggy'. He made it very clear to his fellow officers that if any of them came across Uggy during their patrols, they should not attempt to move him themselves but instead call Kitching or Ellerker so they could deal with him personally.

Kitching regularly abused his position to drink on the job,

visiting pubs after last orders had been called for a beer or two. Ellerker soon joined him on these trips. One Christmas Eve, Kitching got carried away and was found asleep on a market stall. Ellerker was himself so drunk he had to be driven home.

Although David took plenty of beatings from the pair, they also tortured him in other ways. On 7 August 1968, he was spotted in Cookridge Street at 3 a.m. They chased and caught him, bringing him roughly down to the ground before loading him into the back of their car. They then drove him to the Fox and Hounds pub in Bramhope, some seven miles outside the city centre.

Pulling up into the car park, Kitching told a terrified David that they would be leaving him there for a short time as they had to return to the station briefly. He pointed to the door of the pub, which was in total darkness. 'If you knock on the door, they will give you a cup of tea,' he said. 'And we'll be back in a few minutes to pick you up.'

David got out of the car and thanked the pair, and as he made his way towards the pub door, Kitching and Ellerker drove off, laughing. They had deliberately abandoned him knowing he would have to walk miles in order to return to the city and might think twice about returning.

Later that same week, they pulled the same stunt again. Kitching woke David with a kick as he slept in the doorway of a bridal store. Ignoring his protests, the pair led him to their car explaining that they were not going to hurt him, only take him for another drive.

This time they took him to Middleton Woods in the south of the city, about five miles away from the centre. On the way, Kitching relentlessly teased David about his family back in Africa and what they would think about the fact he was constantly getting into trouble with the law. David broke down and began to cry.

When they arrived in the heart of the woods, David refused to get out of the car, so Kitching and Ellerker simply dragged him out. He began swearing at them: 'You never leave me alone. I've got to sleep somewhere.'

Kitching told him to shut up and then shoved him so hard that he ended up falling backwards into the trees. Back at the station Kitching proudly told another officer what he had done. 'He should feel at home in the jungle,' he added.

The torment amounted to sport for the pair. One time, they placed him inside a dustbin and rolled him down one of the shopping arcades. Another time, Kitching urinated on David as he slept, with Ellerker holding a torch so Kitching could be sure every drop hit its target. They had once also set fire to the newspapers he was using as a mattress.

Another encounter saw David kicked so hard in the groin that his body lifted off the ground slightly. 'He was holding his private parts with both his hands and he was crying,' a witness recalled. Many of these abuses were witnessed by other more junior officers who were driving the cars or vans that the pair used to hunt down their quarry, but it's likely there were many more such attacks where the only witnesses were Kitching and Ellerker themselves. When they ran out of more creative ideas, the pair would simply resort to delivering a vicious beating, raining down blows with fists and boots until David was bloody and bruised all over.

Police Constable Keith Seager, who was based in the same station as Kitching and Ellerker, told investigators that, three hours before he is thought to have died, he and Kitching had found David sleeping in a doorway and called in Ellerker.

Seager said: 'I heard blows being struck. I saw Oluwale run out of the doorway covering his head with his arm. I saw Kitching and Ellerker come out. They were smiling. They seemed quite contented with themselves.'

The last time David was seen alive was a few hours later when a bus conductor saw two police officers in hot pursuit of a man along Call Lane, close to the banks of the River Aire. All the officers in the Leeds police force were asked to account for their whereabouts at that time. Only Kitching and Ellerker were unable to do so.

Questioned by investigators, Kitching admitted roughing up

Oluwale on a number of occasions but claimed he only did so to clear the area of the homeless. He said his course of action was justified because Oluwale was a 'wild animal, not a human being'. Kitching said occasionally he had 'kicked his behind' and 'tickled him with my boot' to get him to move on when simply telling Oluwale to leave the area had been unsuccessful. As for the allegation about driving him to Middleton Woods and abandoning him there, Kitching claimed it was a 'fine August night' and that the woods were a delightful spot to sit out.

Ellerker was far less forthcoming, seemingly bitter about being grassed up by his colleagues. He told the man leading the investigation, Detective Chief Superintendent John Perkins, that, somewhat conveniently for him, his notebook covering the period under investigation had been lost. Pressed further on his actions, he claimed the degree of force used on Oluwale was never more than was required.

Although there was no direct evidence to support the assertion, Perkins felt certain that David Oluwale died as a direct result of being chased by Ellerker and Kitching. In his final report he said: 'By their horrible actions they have brought shame and discredit on an honourable and hardworking force.'

Despite the lack of direct proof, Perkins urged his superiors to consider charging both officers with murder. But the officers heading up the prosecution team (prior to the establishment of the Crown Prosecution Service the police conducted prosecutions themselves) did not agree. They found the level of evidence provided by the detective to be 'extremely poor' and concluded that an acquittal would be 'almost inevitable' should the case be taken to court.

Even if the evidence had been stronger, the chances of a successful prosecution would still have been low. Back then a police officer's word was considered to be law and the idea that two men entrusted with such power would choose to abuse it would be hard for any jury to swallow. And in any case, the jury would not be taken from a cross section of classes and races across the city. In those days only those who owned property were eligible to be called for jury service, meaning, inevitably, virtually every case was heard by twelve white, middle-class men.

After conferring for a short time, the prosecution team decided to take the safer option. Both officers were charged with manslaughter.

The trial of Geoffrey Ellerker and Kenneth Kitching began in November 1971. They both denied the charges against them.

Despite the good work done in gathering evidence against the pair, it was clear early on that the chances of a successful conviction were slim. The witness who had seen the two officers running was unable to say for sure who they were chasing. This meant there was no direct evidence available to prove they had contributed to David's death.

The prosecution, believing that no jury was ever going to be sympathetic to the death of a homeless Black man, opted to portray him in a negative way, as a dirty, mentally defective dosser. The defence case went even further, praising Kitching's actions as those of an 'old-fashioned British bobby' and painting David as an out-of-control savage.

Giving evidence, Eric Dent, a staff nurse at Menston Hospital, said Oluwale had been involved in a number of attacks on patients and that he was a fearsome opponent. 'He was all muscle. He went in at the waist and out at the shoulders.'

Mr Dent added that when Oluwale became violent he would kick, bite, punch and spit. 'He usually snarled. He resembled an animal. He came in with everything.'

He later said: 'He could take more punishment than Cassius Clay and give back far more.'

Ellerker's barrister went further still, questioning whether Oluwale should have been in the country at all. 'What right have we to call him a citizen? His only claim to being a citizen was that now and again he was lodged in the local prison.' The fact that David was a fully-fledged British citizen with all the same rights as someone born in the UK did not appear to have occurred to them at all.

Despite his supposed independence, even the judge made comments that made it clear he had prejudices of his own. He said: 'It is accepted on all hands that he was a dirty, filthy, violent vagrant,' adding that David was a 'menace to society' and 'a frightening apparition to come across at night'.

During the trial, the judge ordered that the charge of manslaughter be dropped as there was not enough concrete evidence to support it. When the jury delivered their verdicts, they found Ellerker guilty of three assaults and Kitching guilty of two. Ellerker was handed a sentence of three years while Kitching was jailed for twenty-seven months.

Justice Hinchcliffe told the men: 'By your wicked misbehaviour to this coloured vagrant, you bring disgrace and shame not only on your wives and family, but on the whole of the police force of this country.'

Although it was never raised during the court case, it was clear that Kitching and Ellerker would never have been able to maintain their brutal campaign of harassment for as long as they did, had it not been for the support of other officers. There was evidence of notebooks and station records being altered. In addition, there was a suspicion that many of those officers that ultimately gave evidence against the pair had likely taken a more active role in the abuse than they had admitted.

Gary Galvin, the police cadet who first brought the whole scandal to light, paid his own price. His son, Carl, himself a senior officer with West Yorkshire Police, later said:

The events of 1969 had a profound effect on my father, a man who up until that point had been a team player with a

wide circle of friends and involved in a lot of team sporting
activities.

As a result of some of the reaction he got from colleagues
and other people within society at that time, he became quite
a solitary individual, but with that came a lot of strength because he would never ever let his morals and ethics waver and
that is something he instilled in me and my brother as we were
youngsters growing older.

Despite dozens of incidents of Black men dying in custody or
following police contact in the years that followed, no other police
officers would be successfully prosecuted for their involvement
in the death of a Black person until Benjamin Monk was found
guilty of the manslaughter of former Aston Villa footballer Dalian
Atkinson in 2021.

Although the prosecutors in the case felt there would be little
sympathy for someone of David's status, the people of Leeds were
moved by his story and his death became a catalyst for change,
elevating him to the status of folk hero. There was shock and
embarrassment that such a vulnerable man could have suffered so
much right under their noses.

Fans of Leeds United, once known for being one of the most
racist clubs around – visiting Black players were regularly pelted
with bananas – began using David's name in one of their chants,
aimed at taunting the local police: 'The River Aire is chilly and
deep, Ol-u-wale; Never trust the Leeds police, Ol-u-wale,' sung
to the tune of 'Michael, Row the Boat Ashore'.

During the 1980s graffiti urging people to REMEMBER OLU-
WALE regularly appeared in huge white letters across the city
centre. Anyone growing up in Leeds since that time has long
known all about the case, though the same hasn't always been true
for other parts of the country.

But many were determined to keep his name alive: 2012
saw the founding of the David Oluwale Memorial Association

(DOMA) with its aim to 'educate the city of Leeds in coming to terms with its past, improving its care for those who remain marginalised, and to promote equality, diversity and racial harmony for our people'.

It was through the work of DOMA that David Oluwale was appointed king of the Leeds West Indian Carnival in 2017 with a large papier-mâché head in his likeness used to lead some of the parades.

Then, in April 2022, a blue plaque commemorating David Oluwale was installed on Leeds Bridge, close to the spot where he was last seen alive. The plaque was unveiled during a ceremony led by the leader of the city council and attended by upwards of two hundred guests.

It reads: 'David Oluwale. A British citizen, he came to Leeds from Nigeria in 1949 in search of a better life. Hounded to his death near Leeds Bridge, two policemen were imprisoned for their crimes.' The plaque also has a quote from the novelist Caryl Phillips, a co-founder of the David Oluwale Memorial Association. 'The river tried to carry you away, but you remain with us in Leeds.'

Less than five hours after it was unveiled, the plaque was stolen, an act West Yorkshire Police logged as a hate crime.

The plaque was replaced but has been damaged or stolen on at least two further occasions. It is now monitored by CCTV.

Another theme that emerges from the sad case of David Oluwale is the way that police treat people – especially Black men – who are suffering with mental health issues. It's an early example of a pattern that continues to this day.

Take, for example, the case of Sean Rigg. On 21 August 2008, the forty-year-old musician was having a medical emergency and mental health crisis. The police were called and were expected to take him to hospital. Instead, he was pursued by officers along the streets of Balham, south London, and eventually restrained in a dangerous prone position for up to eight minutes.

Arrested for allegedly stealing his own passport, Sean was then once again placed in a dangerous position inside the caged area of a police van, wearing only Speedos and handcuffs. When officers eventually removed him from the van, he was unconscious but those present claimed they thought he was faking it.

Less than an hour later, Sean was dead. In 2012 an inquest found that Sean's death was the result of a cardiac arrest which occurred due to the 'unnecessary' and 'unsuitable' prone position he had been restrained in. (It is because of this incident that all police vans and custody units are now fitted with CCTV cameras.)

Time and time again we see the police being unable or unwilling to see these people as vulnerable and instead treating them as stereotypical 'angry Black men' who need to be suppressed.

As with injustice overall, this is an issue that has a disproportionate impact on the Black community. Government statistics show that Black people are 3.5 times as likely as white people to be detained under the Mental Health Act.

In recent years we're increasingly seeing the police pushing back against dealing with people with such issues, claiming they are not the best organisation to do so. While it's true that specialists are often better equipped, the nature of police work means they are always going to be interacting with people who have special needs, mental health issues or have neurodiverse backgrounds. Often, you have no idea what issues there are until after the interaction begins.

Better training is required, partly because of this but also because the presence of the police can sometimes make such situations worse. We talked earlier about the accumulation of trauma from being stopped and searched or the negative impact of living in a society that sees you as a stereotype, not an individual.

Walking around Brixton in south London, I see a lot of people with mental health issues but that doesn't always mean they are scary or dangerous. If you can put yourself in their position, it can help to take away the fear. Sometimes the way a person presents themselves is a direct consequence of the way the police attempt to deal with them, nothing more.

Mental health issues aside, the casual police brutality experienced by David Oluwale was far from an isolated case. In those days, for Black people across the country, it was simply part of everyday life. For the most part, it took place behind closed doors or in the heart of communities where the only witnesses would be other Black people. But every now and then, such activities would receive more mainstream attention.

During the late 1960s, London's Metropolitan Police had flagged a number of popular community venues as the kind of places frequented by criminals and bohemians who in their eyes were equally likely to be troublemakers. One such venue was the Mangrove Restaurant in Notting Hill, about which we shall hear more later. Another was Desmond's Hip City, the first Black-owned record store in Brixton, situated on Atlantic Road. Both would be subjected to close scrutiny and frequently raided.

On 15 November 1969, a Nigerian named Clement Gomwalk had just parked his white Mercedes directly outside the record shop so he could join his wife and children who were already inside. His car was in a 'no waiting' zone and when officers on patrol went to examine more closely, they noticed that the number plate did not match the details of the tax disc.

Under the 'sus' laws, this gave the police more than enough reason to take action. The officers roughly pulled Gomwalk from the vehicle and accused him of stealing it. He not only denied any offence but also informed the officers that he was a diplomat, attached to the Nigerian High Commission.

By now a crowd of onlookers, many of them from inside Desmond's, had formed around the officers, objecting to

Gomwalk's arrest. As the diplomat was roughly thrown into the back of a police van, some of the crowd surged forward and tried to intervene.

As a series of scuffles broke out, the police called in reinforcements. Among the crowd was seventeen-year-old Olive Morris, a member of the Black Panther movement (which we shall encounter in the next chapter) with a reputation for being fearless when it came to confronting misjustice.

Seeing a friend of hers have his arm broken as police officers sought to detain him, she went to his aid and soon got caught up in the melee. With her very short hair and androgynous clothing, the arresting officers assumed she was a young Black man and therefore did what they always did while travelling in a van towards a police station: they delivered a flurry of kicks, punches and blows from truncheons until their victims – unable to fight back or defend themselves because they had been handcuffed – were bloody and on the verge of unconsciousness.

She was kicked in the chest and punched in the face. Soon blood was pouring down her face and throat, making it difficult for her to breathe. One other woman was in the same van and yelled out 'She's just a girl, you know,' but the assault continued.

When they reached the station, Morris was separated from the others. She would later recall: 'The policemen who stood around me teased me about my sex. Some of them said I was a girl but looked like a man. Others said, "No, that ain't no girl, that's a bloody wog" and they all laughed. They made me take off my jumper and my bra in front of them to show I was a girl.'

One officer held up his truncheon and pointed it towards her. 'Now prove you're a real woman. Look, it's the right colour and size for you. Black cunt.'

Morris and five others were later charged with threatening behaviour, assaulting a police officer and the possession of offensive weapons. She was released from the police station that evening and immediately went to King's College Hospital in order to have her wounds treated. Her brother Basil later recalled he 'could hardly recognise her face, they beat her so badly'.

Morris was subsequently found guilty of the assault and handed a fine of ten pounds. She was given a suspended sentence, allowing her to avoid prison.

Her strident beliefs had led her to join the British Black Panthers in 1968 and her direct experience at the hands of the police would drive her deeper into the movement. She struck up friendships with the likes of beat poet Linton Kwesi Johnson and was one of the leading voices in the movement that supported the idea that real change could only ever come about as the result of direct action.

Sadly, Olive never got to see the fruits of her labour, dying from blood cancer at the age of twenty-seven. But others would be inspired by her actions and take up the fight on her behalf.

7

The Mangrove Nine

The *Windrush* generation was barely five years old when Frank Gilbert Crichlow left his hometown of Port of Spain, Trinidad, to embark on a new life in England, travelling aboard the SS *Colombie*.

He started out living in Paddington and, like many new arrivals at the time, found work with British Railways.

Frank's day job involved maintaining gas lamps at railway stations, but he had always had a far greater interest in being directly in the spotlight himself. In 1956, at the age of twenty-four, he quit to form an act called the Starlight Four, which was successful enough to provide him with a solid income thanks to regular bookings in clubs and on television and radio. At one point the band even provided the music for a cinema advert.

By 1959 the project was running out of steam and bookings dried up. Frank decided to dissolve the band and move on, investing his savings in a café in Westbourne Park Road which he called the El Rio.

Opening in the wake of the 1958 Notting Hill Riots and in the run-up to the murder of Kelso Cochrane, and being one of the first Black-focused coffee houses in the country, El Rio quickly became a lively focal point for the whole Caribbean community but also attracted interest from a rapidly growing and highly fashionable bohemian set who were eager to embrace multicultural London life.

It was a place where people could come and share the many difficulties faced by the community at a time when white supremacists such as Oswald Mosley and Colin Jordan were pushing their repatriation policies and police were harassing the local Black population. Speaking about those times, Frank Crichlow said:

> A lot of West Indians came to the Rio and it got very popular . . . Local whites used it and a lot of musicians used to be there as well . . . It was a West Indian scene but it had a lot of mixture. It created a tremendous atmosphere . . .
>
> What started to give the black community strength was places like the Rio. The Rio was a meeting place. People would work all week and at the weekend they would go to the cafés and meet and talk. It gave us the strength to keep going.

The Rio became a key first port of call for those arriving in the capital from the West Indies with Frank and others happy to provide advice about housing and employment options. Well aware that many of the newcomers were short of money, out of work and living in constant fear of the racist Teddy Boys prowling the streets, Crichlow longed to offer them a way to replace the sense of neighbourhood cohesion that they had left behind.

El Rio frequently faced police scrutiny and became especially embroiled in controversy in the early 1960s when government minister John Profumo and his showgirl lover, Christine Keeler, were among the regular guests. Both would later become infamous for their part in a security scandal known as the Profumo Affair and this would draw even more attention to El Rio. The police went on to prosecute Crichlow seven times in quick succession for not having gambling and dancing licences.

Frank was convinced he knew exactly why: 'The basic reason was racism. A lot of officers in west London were fired up by people like Oswald [Mosley]. White people who were in the race riots in 1958 and in their teens would then go and join the force and end up as police officers. There is no doubt in my mind about that. That is why I think Notting Hill has a heavy history between the black community and the police in the early days.'

In 1968 Frank decided to take things upmarket and opened the Mangrove Restaurant at 8 All Saints Road, Notting Hill. Serving authentic Caribbean food using recipes Frank had been taught by his mother, the restaurant continued the success of his other ventures and quickly became the heart and soul of the local Black community, as well as being popular with celebrities such as Jimi Hendrix, Sammy Davis Jr, Diana Ross and Vanessa Redgrave.

As an extension of the restaurant, Frank established the Mangrove Community Association, which offered practical assistance to the local community, from legal advice to youth projects, as well as support for the elderly and those struggling with substance abuse.

Increasing numbers of Black radicals also headed to the Mangrove to discuss the political fortunes of the Caribbean where an increasing number of countries were moving towards independence. The burgeoning British Black Power movement also found a home there with many of its ideas being spread through the pages of *The Hustler*, a small community newspaper printed on the premises, and there were regular visits from many Black intellectuals including C. L. R. James and Lionel Morrison.

Frank was strongly anti-drugs – a popular joke among the community was that he was the only man from Trinidad who had never smoked ganja – but had previously been more relaxed about other vices. (In December 1960 the Rio had been fined for allowing gambling to take place on the premises.) He wanted the Mangrove to be wholly legitimate but found himself fighting a constant battle to keep out undesirables and potential trouble-makers. Despite his success in doing so, the local police saw things very differently.

At 11 p.m. on 24 January 1969, police raided the Mangrove for the very first time.

Frank was not working at the time, and the officers would not let the manager call him or even see the search warrant they said they had obtained to authorise them to enter the premises. Nothing illegal was found.

The next day, Frank contacted the Notting Hill police to complain, but the officers there said they had no knowledge of any such raid and told him to contact nearby Notting Dale police station. They too denied any involvement. Frank eventually went to Scotland Yard itself and finally got acknowledgement that officers from Notting Hill had been responsible all along.

Another police raid took place during the summer and again yielded nothing. Soon afterwards Frank was told that all the charges lined up against him had been dropped, which was something of a concern as he had no idea he had been facing any charges in the first place.

From this point the police changed tactics, giving their support to a local petition that had been started by some of Frank's competitors to prevent the Mangrove from having a late-night licence. In court, the magistrate dismissed the evidence given by the police, which mainly consisted of the fact that they had raided the premises on two previous occasions.

Two days before Christmas, the local council revoked the 'all-night café' licence, restricting service to takeaway only after 11 p.m. on the grounds that individuals with criminal backgrounds, along with prostitutes and other undesirables, frequented the Mangrove. However, police never uncovered any evidence of drugs or illegal activities. Crichlow lodged a complaint with the Race Relations Board, arguing that the police actions were unjust, and stating his belief that the raids were purely because he was Black.

A third raid took place in May 1970 and on this occasion, Frank was arrested for assaulting a police officer as well as 'using premises at night without a licence', but this would be just the beginning of a campaign of harassment.

Over the course of the next six weeks, the Mangrove would be raided nine more times. On each occasion the police again said they were searching for drugs, but no contraband of any kind was ever found. Many of the raids were brutal with officers striking both staff and customers with truncheons if they failed to comply quickly enough.

Regular customers began to desert the venue, worried about being caught up in one of the raids. When it started out, the Mangrove regularly took £100 each night and people would sit in their cars in the streets outside, waiting for a free table. But by the early 1970s, this had fallen to around £10, making the business unsustainable. For Frank and a key member of his staff, Darcus Howe, enough was enough.

A fellow Trinidadian and a decade younger than Frank, Darcus had first arrived in the UK at the age of seventeen and intended to study law. He had gone directly to the Rio on arrival in London and met Frank along with other radical thinkers. He soon discovered he had a flair for journalism and became a firm believer in the power of the printed word as a catalyst for political change.

Darcus went back to Trinidad where, under the tutelage of his uncle C. L. R. James, he began writing for the *Vanguard*, a trade union newspaper. He then returned to Britain to play his part in the growing politicisation of the Black community.

To support himself while back in London he worked regular shifts at the Mangrove and saw first hand how the local police were treating the place. Incensed at the brutality he witnessed during

the raids, Darcus convinced Frank to turn to the local community
for support and take a more radical approach, drawing inspiration
from the growing civil rights movement which had started in
America and was beginning to spread around the world.

The British Black Power movement originated during the
summer of 1967. This emergence followed a public speech delivered in north London by Stokely Carmichael, an American
political radical, who spoke out against 'white power' in Britain.
Other radical activists and thinkers followed in his footsteps
and visited London, including Martin Luther King Jr and
Malcolm X.

In America such movements had often resulted in violent con-
frontations with the police, so Scotland Yard set up a Black Power
Desk in 1967 to monitor the group's activities, working with the
intelligence services and reporting to the Home Secretary.

Of all the groups that emerged at that time, one was considered
to pose the greatest risk. Founded by Nigerian playwright Obi B.
Egbuna in the summer of 1968, it would go on to be the largest
and most influential Black Power movement and went by the name
of the British Black Panthers.

Although linked ideologically to the American group of the
same name, the British chapter of the Panthers operated separately.
The American Panthers had been involved in a number of fatal
gunfights with the police which was a key reason there was so
much concern about them coming to the UK. In 1969, J. Edgar
Hoover, the director of the FBI, described the Panthers as 'the
greatest threat to the internal security of the country'. In the UK
their leader was a PhD student, recently arrived in London from
her native Trinidad, named Altheia Jones-LeCointe. The group
regularly met up at the Mangrove.

With letters of complaint about the police raids going unanswered, Frank and Darcus agreed to pursue a more direct strategy
and air their grievances by taking to the streets. A new organisation, the Action Committee for the Defence of the Mangrove,

was formed and issued a public statement to explain exactly why the protest was taking place.

> We, the Black People of London have called this demonstration in protest against constant police harassment which is being carried out against us, and which is condoned by the legal system.
>
> In particular, we are calling for an end to the persecution of the Mangrove Restaurant of 8 All Saints Road, W.11, a Restaurant that serves the Black Community.
>
> These deliberate raids, harassments and provocations have been reported to the Home Office on many occasions. So too has the mounting list of grievances such as raids on West Indian parties, wedding receptions, and other places where Black People lawfully gather.
>
> We feel this protest is necessary as all other methods have failed to bring about any change in the manner the police have chosen to deal with Black People.
>
> We shall continue to protest until Black People are treated with justice by the police and the law courts.

But tensions were running high. Two weeks earlier the police had arrested four young Black men at a summer fair at Finsbury Park, taking them back to a police station on Caledonian Road. Within a short time, twenty friends of the arrested men had arrived at the police station to protest their innocence and demand their release. Officers at the station believed they were under attack and called in reinforcements. All twenty of those involved in the protest were arrested.

Guardian journalist Vince Hines later reported: 'The police seemed to have been panicked by the presence of a large number of black youths making demands and more youths were arriving. Urgent police reinforcements were called in. A fight broke out between the police and the youths inside and outside the station.'

On 9 August 1970, 150 protestors took to the streets close to the Mangrove, carrying placards bearing slogans like FREAK OUT OR GET OUT, CALLING ALL PIGS and POWER TO THE PEOPLE. Despite this, the mood was one of celebration, with all those involved believing they were simply making a stand and pleading for change by taking their concerns to the streets, where they would be seen by a wider audience.

The event kicked off with an opening speech by Howe himself:

It has been for some time now that black people have been caught up in complaining to police about police; complaining to magistrates about magistrates; complaining to judges about judges; and complaining to politicians about politicians. We have become the own shapers of our destiny as from today.

But the police had other ideas. They hoped that by dramatically over-policing the event, they could spark conflict which in turn would allow officers to arrest, charge and prosecute those running the Mangrove and by doing so, shut it down.

More than two hundred police officers accompanied the protestors and a further five hundred officers were held back in reserve. At one point in the march a brief struggle broke out and the police were accused of attempting to snatch some of the placards out of the hands of the marchers who then resisted.

'The demonstration literally exploded,' Darcus would later recall, going on to describe the police as taking part in a fifteen-minute 'orgy of violence' involving 'pure, unadulterated, unlicensed brutality': 'We gave as good as we got. Bricks, stones and bottles, any ammunition at hand we threw at the police. Whole building skips were emptied at them.'

By the time it was over, Frank, Darcus and seven others were under arrest.

The others were Rhodan Gordon, Altheia Jones-LeCointe, Barbara Beese, Godfrey Millett, Rupert Glasgow Boyce, Anthony

Carlisle Innis and Rothwell Kentish. Collectively, they would come to be known as the Mangrove Nine.

Recently released documents from the Home Office and Special Branch, obtained through the Freedom of Information Act, show that the police's actions were part of an intentional plan to undermine the growing Black Power movement. Reginald Maudling, the Home Secretary, ordered the Metropolitan Police to compile a thorough report on the activists within two days of the protest. The report's proposals involved applying the Immigration Act in order to deport Crichlow, or prosecuting the leaders of the march for inciting racial hatred. Ultimately, both were rejected on the grounds that they might arouse sympathy for the protestors. Instead, the Home Secretary ordered the Director of Public Prosecutions to charge them all with affray and incitement to riot.

Police and government plans hit a roadblock when the case made its first appearance in the magistrates' court. Unwilling to accept the police suggestion that the presence of Black radicalism within the Mangrove was equivalent to criminal intent, the magistrate dismissed the case out of hand.

That would normally have been the end of the matter but any celebrations among the Nine were short-lived. Unwilling to let the case go, the DPP made the unusual decision to reinstate the charges, meaning the Mangrove Nine would have to go to trial at the Old Bailey.

Darcus and Altheia chose to represent themselves, with a young Scottish barrister with a reputation for activism, Ian Macdonald, acting as liaison. It was to be a powerful statement. Few people facing serious charges represented themselves in court at the time and the idea that Black people would choose to do so was considered extraordinary.

One of the first acts of the defence was to apply for a jury composed only of Black men and women. Citing Magna Carta, they claimed this would be the only way to ensure their case was truly being heard by their 'peers'. When the application failed – as they all expected it would – they focused their attention on the way the members of the jury were being selected, using up all the challenges available to them (seven per defendant) to strike out sixty-three candidates.

This action ultimately led to the inclusion of two Black jurors on the panel and highlighted that the Mangrove Nine, along with Macdonald, had no intention of passively adhering to the court's strict and limiting procedures. The main prosecution witnesses were police officers and during their cross examination, the defendants managed to erase what little legal legitimacy appeared to exist. They exposed the prejudice on which the prosecution had built its case. It soon became clear that the main aim was to suppress the most radical elements of the Black political types who were regular visitors to the restaurant.

Darcus, in particular, proved to be a master orator, tying up the witnesses in knots. His co-defendant Barbara Beese later recalled that the witnesses for the prosecution were 'going down like nine-pins, faced with their contradictions'.

A major turning point in the trial came when Darcus began to cross examine the four police officers who claimed to have observed the specific acts upon which some of the charges were based.

The four officers claimed to have simultaneously seen the defendants taunting the crowd while inside the van. Darcus initially insisted the van be driven into the middle of the courtroom so this claim could be tested. Though this request proved impractical, members of the jury were taken out to see the van. It was then that Darcus spotted that the 'observation window' through which the officers had supposedly watched the events was nothing more than a slit in the side of the van.

'They had all said they were looking through this hole the size of a letterbox from the side of their van and had seen everything,' Darcus later recalled. In court he produced a piece of paper, cut to the same size as the slit in the van, and asked PC Pulley to demonstrate exactly how this worked. The officer explained that each of the four men in the van had one eye looking out of the slit. 'I said, "Yeah, the four of you? And where was your face?" I looked at the jury and repeated "Where was your face?" I will never forget that day, after that I knew we couldn't lose.'

After a trial that had lasted fifty-five days, the jury needed only eight hours to reach their verdict. All defendants were acquitted of incitement to riot, and Darcus and Altheia were acquitted of all the charges they had been facing.

What is more, twenty-eight years before the publication of the Macpherson Report, the judge would find evidence of institutional racism within the Met. He publicly acknowledged that there was clear 'evidence of racial hatred' within the capital's police force.

The Assistant Commissioner, appalled by the judge's remarks, requested that the Director of Public Prosecutions speak to the judge and ask him to retract his comments. Reginald Maudling organised a meeting between the judge and top civil servants, urging him to take back his statement, but the judge stood firm.

The case did not eliminate systemic racism, but, as Crichlow stated, it was a pivotal moment. It challenged the police, the Home Office and society's views towards the Black community. 'We took a stand, and I am proud of what we achieved – we forced them to sit down and rethink harassment.'

The trial played a significant role in changing public perception. The jury's verdict demonstrated that not all white individuals held prejudiced views, and it gave impetus to the Black Power movement by showing that resistance against the state could lead to real success, rather than being seen only as a noble yet futile effort.

Interviewed by the *New Internationalist* in 2013, Darcus Howe commented: 'It was a time of vulgar racism. The everyday abuse Black people would get from strangers on the street and the police alike would shock you today. But I never once believed what they wanted us to believe – that we as Black people are inferior to whites – and fighting my corner at the Mangrove Trial was part of that.'

Frank Crichlow would go on to be one of the co-founders of the Notting Hill Carnival with the event using the Mangrove as its headquarters for many years. However, the harassment continued.

Although Crichlow was recognised in the community for his strong opposition to drugs, he himself faced charges related to drug offences in 1979. He was eventually acquitted. In 1988, the police forcefully entered the Mangrove, using sledgehammers to smash through the doors, under the suspicion that there were drugs hidden inside. Crichlow was detained for five weeks before receiving bail, with restrictions that prohibited him from visiting his business premises for more than a year, leading directly to the Mangrove's eventual decline.

By the time the case came to court what little evidence there was failed to pass muster and the jury dismissed all the charges. As a result, Crichlow initiated a lawsuit against the Met, accusing them of false imprisonment, malicious prosecution and battery. He won his case and was awarded damages of £50,000 – a record for the time.

The case of the Mangrove Nine represents one of the first times that the Black community began to question and fight back against the injustices they were increasingly facing. In following the example of high-profile civil rights leaders in America, they must be commended.

The irony was, this was a group of campaigners who had been advocating for the rights of others who suddenly found themselves in the Central Criminal Court. Thankfully their intelligence and ability to represent themselves allowed them to succeed where others had failed. It could so easily have gone the other way.

It was a watershed moment for the courts and the community alike. Whereas once the word of a police officer was felt to be above question, a new reality was dawning and with it came an official acknowledgement that many of those wearing uniforms were every bit as prejudiced and biased as those without.

8

The Oval Four

During the last few months of his short life, languishing in prison after having been convicted of robbery, disgraced former Detective Sergeant Derek Ridgewell would answer the question of how he ended up turning to crime with a simple reply: 'I just went bent.'

The reality, as it turns out, was somewhat different. For the man who today is best remembered as the single most corrupt officer in the history of British policing, the rot had been there right from the start.

Born in Glasgow in May 1945, Ridgewell moved to London at the age of seven and left the South-East London College of Technology a decade later with four O levels. He went through a handful of jobs before being sworn in as a probationary constable with the British Transport Police (BTP) in May 1964 and posted to Paddington.

He had been in the job only a few weeks before one of his fellow officers caught him attempting to steal parcels from the depot. Rather than being reported, Ridgewell was treated to a good hiding from his colleagues and told in no uncertain terms that such behaviour was not acceptable.

Little is known about what he got up to in the months that followed but in October 1965, Ridgewell resigned in order to take up a three-year post with the British South Africa Police of Southern Rhodesia, now Zimbabwe.

The difference between life there and back in mid-1960s Britain – where the flow of migrants who were part of the *Windrush* generation was just reaching its peak – could not have been more stark. In Rhodesia, the races were so strictly segregated that mixed-race individuals were not allowed to join the force out of fear they would cause confusion.

There were no Black recruits – the only non-whites inside the barracks were the young Black men lining up to work as servants for their white masters.

The police force was far closer to being a military unit than anything back in Britain. Ridgewell would have been woken up with a bugle call at 5 a.m. every morning and on the parade ground in full dress uniform by six. He would have spent his time learning to ride a horse and deploy a wide range of weapons, from shotguns and revolvers to CS gas launchers and sub-machine guns.

But just a few weeks into his training the newly formed state of Rhodesia declared independence from Britain. This led to immediate political turmoil and ignited fears that a military intervention might be required to bring the rogue country under control.

Concerned for their safety, Ridgewell and two other new recruits decided to leave the country immediately, crossing over to Mozambique by train and seeking sanctuary at the British consulate. But desertion was a crime and the trio soon had arrest warrants issued in their names. Once safely back in England, Ridgewell gave interviews to the newspapers and TV cameras explaining a key reason he wanted to leave was that he had been appalled by the terrible way Black people were treated in the country.

The coverage made him come across as a heroic type who had left his job on principle because of his opposition to racism, but it was all a lie. Ridgewell was deeply racist and his attitudes towards Black people would be at the heart of his corrupt practices.

A few weeks later, the warrant against him was dropped and he rejoined the BTP, initially working as a dog handler before moving to a specialist unit bringing down crooked detectives. By 1971 he was considered something of a rising star in the force and asked to take charge of the 'dip' squad – the name given to the undercover team assigned to catch pickpockets operating on the London Underground.

Not only was this crime on the increase but those behind it were becoming ever bolder. Rather than relying on stealth and skill, they would simply use force – backed up by weapons if necessary – in order to get their hands on people's handbags and wallets.

Shortly before 11 p.m. on 18 February 1972, Ridgewell and two members of his team were undercover on the platform at Stockwell Underground station when they spotted six young Black men acting in a suspicious manner.

When the next train arrived, the six men boarded an empty carriage and Ridgewell followed them while his colleagues moved into adjacent carriages. The plan was for Ridgewell to be a decoy, a tempting target that would prove irresistible to any group of criminals hell-bent on robbery and violence.

It worked, almost too well. According to Ridgewell, within seconds the six youths had surrounded him. One, nineteen-year-old Courtney Harriot, pulled out a knife and waved it in Ridgewell's face and hissed: 'Give us bread, man. Your wallet or it's this!'

The scene quickly turned chaotic. Ridgewell pulled out his truncheon and knocked the knife from Courtney's hand while shouting 'Police!' Courtney responded with a shout of 'Fuzz!'

and the other youths began tightening their semi-circle around Ridgewell, lashing out with punches and kicks.

After a brief melee with more blows exchanged on both sides, the officers – despite being outnumbered two to one – managed to get the upper hand and when the train reached the next station, Oval, all six youths, aged between seventeen and nineteen, were dragged off and arrested for attempted robbery.

For Ridgewell, it was exactly the kind of operation he excelled in and the reason he had been appointed the head of the squad in the first place.

Two weeks earlier he had achieved a similar success. On 2 February 1972, four young Black men travelling on the Underground between Oval and Waterloo had been arrested on suspicion of attempting to steal handbags. They were subsequently charged under the 'sus' law for loitering with intent to commit an arrestable offence on the Tube.

All four had signed confessions admitting their guilt and, as was the case with the six men who had been arrested after the attack in Stockwell, the case would soon be heard in court.

So far as the BTP was concerned, the timing could not have been better. These kinds of attacks were becoming all too common, spreading not just across the transport network but also onto the streets themselves and the public needed to be reassured that action was being taken.

On Saturday, 29 July 1972, fifty-two-year-old freelance photographer Leonard Bestwick was stabbed to death in the centre of Chester during an attempted robbery. A few days later the *Cheshire Observer* published an interview with Chief Superintendent Arthur Benfield, the officer in charge of the case. He explained that Mr Bestwick appeared to be the victim of a type of attack usually associated with inner-city areas of the United States of America.

'From what we have learned in this investigation,' the officer continued, 'it appears this was a mugging gone wrong.'

That same phrase turned up once more on 15 August when sixty-eight-year-old Graham Arthur Hills, a retired railway worker, was stabbed to death a short distance from Waterloo station in London as he made his way home after a night at the opera. Alone, smartly dressed and carrying a briefcase, Hills was no match for the three-strong gang that attacked him. He was murdered trying to fight them off.

The London detective chosen to speak to the press about the case had recently returned from a study trip in the US and said that the murder of Hills also appeared to be 'a mugging gone wrong'.

It might surprise you to learn that up until the summer of 1972, the term 'mugging' was virtually unknown on this side of the Atlantic. This was why, when the *Daily Mirror* covered the death of Graham Hills on 17 August, it provided its readers with a handy explanation of what it actually meant.

'It has its origins in America. The word itself is derived from attacking a mug – an easy victim. American police describe it as an assault by crushing the victim's head or throat in an armlock or to rob with any degree of force, with or without weapons. In America this crime has grown by more than 229 per cent in ten years.'

The article went on to explain that there had been 150 incidents in each of the past three years on the London Underground alone. It concluded: 'slowly, mugging is coming to Britain'.

Of course, people had been being attacked and robbed on the streets of London ever since the days of highwaymen, but somehow the papers of the day decided that mugging wasn't just a new name for an old crime but a whole new crime in itself. In the weeks and months that followed, muggings began to dominate the headlines of local and national newspapers alike.

The problem with this was that there was no actual crime of 'mugging' on the statute books. Those accused of such offences, like the ones caught up in the operations being run by Detective Sergeant Ridgewell, would find themselves charged with either robbery or assault with intent to rob.

But as public concern grew, police chiefs were tasked with going back over their recent records to calculate the scale of the problem. What they did was to collate a range of crimes involving various kinds of bag snatches, assaults with intent to rob and other similar offences and report back.

This meant that mugging went from a crime that simply didn't exist on the record books prior to 1971 to suddenly having dozens of offences committed each week, creating a moral panic that also had a strong racial element.

Multiple studies by academics have shown that when it comes to violent crime, the vast majority of it is carried out by only a small proportion of offenders. The numbers vary but in general, 5 per cent of the criminal offenders (not 5 per cent of the general population) in any given town or city will commit at least 50 per cent of the local violent crime. Some studies have suggested the figure might be even more shocking with just 1 per cent of offenders committing up to 60 per cent of violent crime.

There are, of course, criminals from all classes, races and corners of society and there is no doubt that some muggings in the early 1970s were carried out by Black youths. In fact, there is some suggestion that unofficial segregation among criminals at the time meant that young Blacks who were desperate for cash were more likely to turn to mugging (where they could access cash directly) rather than burglary (where items would have to be sold on to realise cash) as they were unable to access the long-standing, white-dominated networks used to fence stolen goods.

Once you bear this in mind and sprinkle in a few high-profile court cases involving Black muggers, it's easy to see how you get to the point where the police – and therefore also the public – begin to see every Black person as a potential mugger, despite this being very far from the actual case.

By way of example, leave aside the issue of race and consider two fictional council estates which we'll call A and B. Based on local intelligence, the police decide that A is a den of criminality while B is not. As a result, they pour additional resources into patrolling and conducting stop and search operations on estate A.

The natural consequence of this is a rise in the number of arrests and convictions from estate A. In police eyes, getting results reinforces the idea that their tactics are successful, so they continue and potentially even increase the pressure on estate A whose residents – the vast majority of whom will be entirely innocent – then become increasingly hostile towards the police.

It remains a fact that Black individuals are more likely to be stopped and searched by the police compared to white individuals. This can lead to higher rates of recorded crime among Black individuals, not necessarily because they commit more crimes, but because they are more frequently targeted by police.

While in reality, young Blacks in south London were no more likely to be involved in low-level criminality than those from other ethnic groups, the fact that they were being disproportionately targeted by the police meant there was a greater likelihood that those who committed offences were being caught. This created a vicious cycle where any small amount of success that resulted from this tactic would simply encourage other officers to do the same.

At the same time, the constant harassment led to growing hostility among the community and, in turn, increased resistance to police action. This then resulted in people being taken into custody for offences such as obstruction, resisting arrest or assaulting a police officer that simply would not have occurred if the police had not been so heavy-handed in the first place.

The implications of this mindset would continue to be felt all through the next two decades, leading directly to the situation that resulted in my mother being shot.

But in the case of Ridgewell, there was an additional factor at play – virtually all the people he had targeted had been entirely innocent.

When the case of the four young men arrested at Waterloo station opened at Southwark Juvenile Court, the judge had immediate concerns. Although all four had signed confessions soon after being arrested, they had retracted them ahead of the court case, claiming they were coerced into signing through threats of violence from Ridgewell and members of his team.

Their own account of the events leading up to their arrests was markedly different. They explained that they had been on the Tube minding their own business when they suddenly came under a vicious and unprovoked attack by a group of white passengers.

As the train reached Waterloo and the doors opened, the four men found themselves being manhandled onto the platform. It was only then that the group of white men who had launched the attack revealed that they were not passengers but rather plain-clothes police officers.

When the police came to give their own evidence, they couldn't seem to get their stories straight and much of what they said was outright rejected by the white girlfriend of one of the accused, who had witnessed the entire incident.

The judge was unimpressed and not only threw out the case but also referred the entire matter back to the British Transport Police, calling on them to launch an investigation into the way their officers had behaved. This was quite an extraordinary turn of events, taking place in a time when the word of a police officer alone was usually considered enough to warrant a prosecution. But any wider concerns about Ridgewell were brushed under the carpet and he carried on as usual.

(Back then, the police lacked any kind of independent oversight agency to carry out such an investigation, so the police essentially marked their own homework. No surprise then that it found no evidence 'to support any allegation against any person'.)

While others may have considered the case to have been a failure, it didn't seem to bother Ridgewell at all.

When the case of the six men arrested two weeks later – who would come to be known as the Stockwell Six – was heard at the Old Bailey, similar concerns about the strength of the evidence against them were aired.

Once again, the defendants claimed they had only signed confessions because they had been threatened with being beaten. Once more, contrary to Ridgewell's account of how he had been attacked by the gang, the defendants said no such attack had taken place and that the police – who had failed to identify themselves at the start of the confrontation – had been the aggressors.

Certainly, much of the police evidence seemed extremely far-fetched. The idea that a streetwise Black nineteen-year-old from London would use the white, hippie word for money – 'bread' – seemed almost laughable. Similarly, Courtney would have been highly unlikely to shout 'fuzz' on seeing police officers. Within the Black community at the time, they were almost exclusively known as 'pigs'.

Despite these huge shortcomings in the evidence and the fact that all six pleaded their innocence, all but one was found guilty. Courtney Harriot was sent to prison for six years, Paul Green was sent to borstal while three others, Cleveland Davidson, Texo Johnson and Ronald De'Souza, were convicted of related offences. The sixth member of the group, Everet Mullins, was the only one to be acquitted. His defence team was able to prove that he was illiterate so he would clearly have been unable to read the confession that he signed.

Passing sentence, Judge Alexander Karmel, QC summed up the mood of the times and demonstrated he had wholeheartedly believed Ridgewell's version of events:

Mugging is becoming more and more prevalent, certainly in London. We are told that in America people are even afraid to walk in the streets late at night for fear of mugging. This is an offence for which deterrent sentences should be passed.

Little did you know that the man you attacked, struck and kicked was a detective-sergeant of the British Transport police in plain clothes and that in the adjoining carriages were two other officers who were part of a patrol formed because of what had been taking place on the Northern Line.

Ridgewell had not slowed down in the run-up to these court cases. On 16 March 1972, he was back on the Underground network and targeted another group of four young Black men. One of them was Winston Trew, a twenty-one-year-old married father of two.

Born in Jamaica, Winston had been given his name as a tribute to Britain's much admired wartime leader. His father, who worked as a police sergeant, decided to bring the family to England when Winston was a young boy in the hope he would get a better education here than he could have done back in the Caribbean.

His life in England had been defined by racism from the very first day in infant school when a fellow pupil punched him square in the face, simply because he was Black. The white drivers of passing cars would shout abuse at him and in the streets he was regularly stopped, harassed and searched by police officers whenever he left his home. The constant feeling of fear and oppression drove him towards community politics and the youth division of the fast-growing Black Power movement.

He had actually been making his way home from an activist meeting – they always travelled in small groups for their own protection – when he and his friends found their way blocked by several white men as they made towards the exit of Oval station. As the men initially failed to identify themselves, Winston and the others thought they were simply facing a bunch of white guys looking to make trouble.

Then Ridgewell appeared. 'We're police. Some of you blokes have been nicking handbags and we're going to search you lot.'

Winston and the others objected. The accusation was so ridiculous it only reinforced the idea that these men could not be police officers. A small scuffle broke out as the Black youths tried to get away, flooring at least one of the white men with a well-aimed kick to the stomach.

Uniformed officers ran to the aid of Ridgewell's team and Winston found himself in a headlock so tight that he was only barely able to breathe. Weakened, he was then placed in the back of a police van.

It was then that Winston became increasingly afraid. An officer he had knocked to the ground punched him twice then hissed into his ear, 'Just you fucking wait until we get to the station.'

On arrival, Winston immediately demanded his mandatory phone call – something he knew he was entitled to thanks to his community activism and life-long experience of police harassment. 'You blacks got no bloody rights,' Ridgewell told him.

Once inside a cell, Winston was attacked again. An officer tried to knee him in the groin then smashed his head against a wall, leaving him dazed.

A short time later he was taken into a room where Ridgewell and two other officers were waiting. Ridgewell produced a pre-written statement which said Winston admitted trying to pick a man's pocket on the station platform and another on the escalator. It also said that when the officers had identified themselves as policemen (which they never had) he had immediately attacked them.

Winston refused to sign. As Ridgewell looked on, the other men in the room began slapping and punching him around the face and body, shouting out: 'Just bloody sign it.'

When he still refused, he was taken back to his cell. A short time later, Ridgewell entered with a grin on his face. He explained that one of the others had signed his confession and named Winston as the leader of the pickpocketing gang.

A second interrogation followed with more threats and more violence. Winston knew that the more he continued to deny the offences, the greater the chance that Ridgewell and others would simply plant some stolen purses or wallets in the carrier bag he'd had with him, strengthening their case even further.

Seeing no way out of the situation and terrified at the prospect of further beatings, Winston reluctantly agreed to comply.

'In the end I signed a false confession that I had committed a number of these offences. I did it because I was frightened and also because I knew I had a cast-iron alibi for the times I gave and therefore thought that the case would fall apart later as a result. I was honestly afraid I would not come out of the station alive.'

When the case – by then known as the Oval Four – came to the Old Bailey, inconsistencies in police evidence once again surfaced, as did the blatant racism behind the targeting of certain individuals. There were, after all, no witnesses apart from the arresting officers and no named victims. The four faced seventeen charges of 'robbing persons undetermined'.

Ridgewell was asked by a defending counsel if he was 'particularly on the lookout for coloured young men'. He replied: 'On the Northern line, I would agree with that.'

At the end of the five-week trial, Winston and his three companions were found guilty of assaulting the officers, as well as of two pickpocketing offences the police claimed to have witnessed, although they were acquitted of the other charges to which they had confessed in their statements. They were sentenced to two years in prison, reduced to eight months on appeal.

Ridgewell was clearly getting bolder and seemed to think himself untouchable. But he was about to take his scheme of fitting up innocent young Black men just one step too far.

On the night of 4 August 1972, two Black students were 'set upon' by five heavily built white men at Tottenham Court Road Underground station. In keeping with other incidents, it was only after a scuffle had taken place that the students were shocked to learn that their 'attackers' had been undercover police officers led by Ridgewell. Both men were charged with having assaulted the officers, as well as handbag theft.

But Ridgewell had chosen his targets poorly. Rather than being streetwise members of the south London Black community who had grown up against a backdrop of casual police violence and harassment, the two men were devout Jesuit priests from Rhodesia who were studying at Oxford University with a view to becoming social workers.

At the Old Bailey, Judge Gwyn Morris felt no need to hear all of the prosecution case or any of the defence case before throwing it out. The whole thing was implausible, there were no independent witnesses and the accounts given by the various police officers involved varied so widely that it made no sense at all.

'It is wholly unsafe to allow this matter to go any further,' he said. 'One is dealing with highly reputable . . . students. One is not dealing with people of bad character. How can any possible reliance be placed on these officers?' He added: 'I find it terrible that here in London people using public transport should be pounced upon by police officers without a word by anyone that they are police officers.'

With increasing concern that Ridgewell's exploits were about to bring the force into disrepute, his BTP bosses decided to quietly move him from the 'dip' squad in early 1973, giving him a de facto promotion by moving him to Force Headquarters.

Later that same year, an investigation was conducted by the BBC's *Nationwide* programme. It demonstrated that Ridgewell's version of events was almost certainly a tissue of lies. The situation just could not have unfolded as he had said during a mere two-minute Underground stop. An article in an anarchist publication looking at similar claims made reference to a calypso song heard in pubs around Brixton: 'If the muggers don't get you, Ridgewell will.'

Although there was a flurry of public interest at the time, it soon faded away and Ridgewell was all but forgotten by everyone. Except his victims, the nine young Black men who had been convicted and sent to prison for crimes they did not commit.

For Winston Trew and the others like him, Ridgewell's actions had a devastating effect. Few of his family or friends believed he was entirely innocent. Not only did they have doubts that the police could lie so blatantly, there was also the fact that Winston and the others had all signed confessions admitting their guilt.

By the time he emerged from prison, his wife had left and taken his son to live in Jamaica. 'Ridgewell threw a hand grenade into my life,' he said later.

After being released from prison, Winston made a complaint of violence and perjury against Ridgewell and other officers to the Director of Public Prosecutions. The following year he received a reply informing him that: 'Having carefully considered all the evidence, I have reached the conclusion that it is not such as to justify the institution of criminal proceedings against the officers concerned.'

There can be little doubt that Ridgewell's corrupt actions did much to fan the flames of the fire that saw mugging become a crime associated with Black inner-city youth. As public alarm continued to grow in response, so all aspects of the criminal justice system responded. Police conducted more raids and arrests, especially in areas such as Notting Hill and Brixton where there were large numbers of Black residents. Judges began imposing heavier sentences on those involved.

This trend came to a head in March 1973 when three teenagers – Paul Storey, sixteen, Mustafa Fuat and James Duignan, both fifteen – appeared at Birmingham Crown Court, accused of a vicious mugging.

Prosecuting counsel Patrick Bennett, QC told the jury that thirty-one-year-old Robert Keegan, a maintenance worker, had been heading home one evening the previous November when 'he had the misfortune to encounter these three young persons.

'They knocked him to the ground and dragged him to some waste ground where he was robbed. They used more violence on Mr Keegan and Storey used a brick in the attack while the other two used their feet.'

The trio went off and examined their haul which amounted to just five cigarettes, thirty pence and a bunch of keys. Seemingly infuriated, they returned and attacked Mr Keegan again, leaving him with such severe head injuries that he was unable to work and was expected to suffer permanent changes to his behaviour and some loss of mental capacity.

Storey, who was mixed race and said to be the ringleader, was found guilty of attempted murder and jailed for twenty years, bursting into tears upon hearing his sentence. His two younger accomplices were given ten years each.

Ridgewell did not limit himself to 'fitting up' young Black men. In 1975 he turned his attention to a twenty-one-year-old white man named Stephen Simmons who, out of the blue, found himself under arrest and accused of stealing mail bags. Simmons and another man were both convicted and sent to borstal, losing their jobs and their homes.

Later that same year Ridgewell led an operation that saw the arrest of twelve workers from the Bricklayers Arms goods depot off the Old Kent Road in south-east London, all of them accused of being part of a criminal enterprise. In what is known as a 're-labelling operation' they were said to have been stealing parcels by redirecting them to an address under their control where they could access the goods inside and sell them on. During the court hearing that followed, complaints that confessions had been forced surfaced once again, but eight of the accused were found guilty regardless, each receiving a sentence of around nine months.

In 2013, having tried but failed to clear his name for decades,

Simmons made a call to an LBC radio show offering legal advice to ask for help with his case and was told to try running an online search for the name of the officer that had arrested him. What he discovered was shocking and would have dramatic implications for all those whose paths had crossed with that of Ridgewell during the early 1970s.

Not only had Ridgewell been fitting up innocent people by claiming they had been implicated in mail theft, he had been deeply involved in the crime himself. Using the same relabelling method he had accused others of, Ridgewell had been making hundreds of thousands of pounds selling stolen goods. However, he fell out with one of his fellow criminals and in May 1978 he found himself under arrest after police received a tip-off.

Though still only a detective sergeant, Ridgewell had been living well above his means, owning several properties, and had opened multiple bank accounts including one in the Swiss city of Zurich. No one seemed to have paid too much attention to any of this.

In January 1980, Ridgewell and two other officers, all of whom had been involved in the operation to prosecute the depot workers, appeared at the Old Bailey, only this time in the dock rather than the witness box. The three were found guilty of conspiracy to steal goods worth £364,000 – more than a million pounds' worth in today's money – in the form of sixty van loads of parcels. Ridgewell was sentenced to seven years while his colleagues got six years and two years.

In 1982, Ridgewell died from a heart attack while still in prison. But there are rumours that he was killed because he knew too much about corruption at the highest levels in the police.

Simmons took this new proof that Ridgewell had been corrupt and instructed an appeal lawyer. The Criminal Cases Review Commission – the body which had previously overturned the conviction of Mahmood Mattan – sent his case back to the Court of Appeal, which in 2018 overturned his conviction.

His success saw others following in his footsteps. In December 2019, Winston Trew was one of three members of the Oval Four to have their convictions quashed by the Court of Appeal. The fourth could not be tracked down. Delivering his ruling, the Lord Chief Justice, Lord Burnett, told them: 'Our regret is that it has taken so long for this injustice to be remedied.'

In 2021, Courtney Harriot and two other members of the Stockwell Six were also cleared, though once again the remaining two convicted members could not be traced.

In a statement released shortly after the quashing of the Stockwell Six convictions, the BTP's deputy chief constable, Adrian Hanstock, said:

> It is wholly regrettable that the criminal actions of a discredited former officer of this force over four decades ago led to these unsound prosecutions.
>
> I apologise unreservedly for the distress, anxiety and impact this will have undoubtedly caused those who were wrongly convicted. We understand that nothing can ever make up for the period of time that they spent in custody or the longer-term effect it may have had on them.
>
> We have examined all available records which suggest that Ridgewell was the principal officer in other investigations and have not identified any additional matters that we feel should be referred for external review.

Despite the apology, the BTP has never been able to explain why it failed to sack Ridgewell in 1973 when questions first began to be asked about his behaviour. There are also question marks over why, when Ridgewell was jailed for seven years in 1980, the police failed to immediately conduct a review of all the cases he had been involved in.

*

As with the Mangrove Nine before it, the case of the Oval Four was a turning point in the way the public, and particularly the Black community, began to view the police but also a shift in the way the public began to view Black people.

Many of the earliest arrivals of the *Windrush* generation grew up believing that all the authority figures they encountered – be they police officers, teachers or even the managers at their place of work – were equally fair and just in their dealings with everyone. For many, it was a given that these people could be trusted. If you got punished because your teacher said you did something wrong in class, then your parents would generally side with the teacher.

It's how so many Black children from around that time ended up being classed as educationally subnormal and sent to special schools. The parents just accepted there must be something wrong with their offspring because teachers were telling them so.

It was the same story with law and order. If a police officer stopped you in the street, it must be because you did something wrong. In their mind, there could be no other explanation. That further empowered the police. Before his corrupt conduct was exposed, officers like Ridgewell took full advantage of the fact that they could walk into court and tell a pack of lies safe in the knowledge that they would still be fully believed.

The consequence was that once Black people became poster boys for muggings and other street robberies, the wider public found it hard to see them in any other way. I remember being at school among a group of Black boys and chatting to a white boy called Dean. We said to him, 'We know you lot tell jokes about Black people, tell us one of them.'

He said, 'Nah, I don't want to say anything because you lot will beat me up,' but we assured him we would not – we just wanted to know the kind of things that were being said about us behind our backs.

Eventually we convinced him he was safe and then it was like a switch had been pulled – he just let off, one after another, after another. The one that stuck most in my mind was this: 'Why don't people like the black jelly babies?' The answer: 'Because they steal your rings when you put your fingers in the pack.'

I remember thinking, *Wow, you lot just have us down as criminals right from the start!* It was a real revelation. We were doomed. Once he was finished with the jokes we did rough Dean up, but only a little bit.

Those attitudes are still there today. I recently talked to a Black woman about my life. She was one of those consciously aware types, a proper 'conscious sista'. I told her my mum had been shot by the police and she was naturally shocked. 'Wow,' she said. 'Was your mum a gangster?'

It wasn't the most sensitive response but unfortunately a lot of people still think that way, automatically assuming that the person must have done something to deserve it. And that was from a fellow Black person.

Today Winston Trew works as a university lecturer but continues to actively campaign against police corruption and racial injustice.

In July 2021 he told the *Daily Mail*: 'There is still police corruption, there is still antagonism between young black men and police. I am old now and so invisible on the streets. But I wouldn't like to be a young guy today. The sus law has gone but others which have similar negative impact are in its place. There still needs to be a fundamental change in the way police approach young black men.'

As the 1970s continued, so the nature of racism began to change. On the surface it seemed that Black people had finally become fully integrated into the fabric of UK society. Trevor McDonald became the first Black newsreader in 1973, Lenny Henry became a hugely popular comedian having won a TV talent show, *New*

Faces, aged seventeen in 1975 and Daley Thompson was a rising star in athletics who would go on to win a gold medal at the 1980 Olympic Games.

In reality, changes introduced under the 1971 Immigration Act effectively ended the free movement of members of the Commonwealth by making it much more difficult for anyone to claim the right to live in Britain. Only those who were British citizens because they were born in the country or those who had an ancestral connection to the country, such as having a British parent or grandparent, or who had resided in the country for the past five years, were able to claim the right to abode. Whereas prior to the Act anyone living in the Commonwealth had been awarded a special status, there was now no difference between them and the citizens of any other country in the world.

The new laws were brought in by a Conservative government led by Edward Heath which came to power in 1970. Their manifesto had pledged to tackle the 'social problem' of migration which many believed was getting out of control.

The impact of the new law was not only to dramatically reduce the number of West Indian and African immigrants heading to the UK but also to change how Black people living in Britain perceived themselves and the nature of the opposition to their presence.

The tap had been turned off which meant that in some circles, there was an acceptance that those who continued to live here would be sticking around and should therefore be more integrated into society. The other side of the coin was that, having successfully stemmed the tide, those on the far right now looked at ways to reverse it and return those who were here to their 'homeland' as quickly as possible.

Casual racism became commonplace, with 'traditional' comedians such as Jim Davidson and Bernard Manning filling their sets with jokes that played to racist stereotypes. Little wonder when you look at the way Black people were depicted in the popular media with shows such as *Love Thy Neighbour* which portrayed Black people as savages and cannibals, as well as insisting that insults such as 'nig-nog' and 'sambo' were hilariously funny.

It all supported the notion that there was nothing wrong with being racist, that it was a form of political opinion and nothing more. But the rise of far-right parties such as the National Front meant more extreme views were finding their way into the mainstream, and it was suddenly OK to express such thoughts out loud, no matter who you were.

In August 1976, they found their way onto the stage of the Birmingham Odeon.

Do we have any foreigners in the audience tonight? If so, please put up your hands. So where are you? Well wherever you all are, I think you should all just leave. Not just leave the hall, leave our country. I don't want you here, in the room or in my country.

Listen to me, man! I think we should vote for Enoch Powell. Enoch's our man. I think Enoch's right, I think we should send them all back. Stop Britain from becoming a black colony. Get the foreigners out. Get the wogs out. Get the coons out. Keep Britain white. I used to be into dope, now I'm into racism. It's much heavier, man.

Fucking wogs, man. Fucking Saudis taking over London. Bastard wogs. Britain is becoming overcrowded and Enoch will stop it and send them all back. The black wogs and coons and Arabs and fucking Jamaicans don't belong here, we don't want them here. This is England, this is a white country, we don't want any black wogs and coons living here.

We need to make clear to them they are not welcome. England is for white people, man. This is Great Britain, a white country, what is happening to us, for fuck's sake? Throw the wogs out! Keep Britain white.

Among the audience was a teenage Caryl Phillips, who had been born in St Kitts and immigrated to England when he was just four months old, settling in Leeds. He would later win a place at Oxford University, go on to become a successful novelist and is currently Professor of English at Yale. But on that night, he struggled to believe his ears.

He later said of the evening: 'When he started talking about Enoch Powell, and how "Enoch was right", I felt embarrassed, and I could that tell my best friend felt embarrassed, and we couldn't really talk about it.

'It was a betrayal, in a way that is kind of primal, in a way that only an adolescent, a late adolescent could feel it . . . I never wanted to listen to Eric Clapton again.'

Clapton wasn't the only one. In April 1976 David Bowie was detained on the Russian–Polish border while travelling to Moscow by train. He was found to have a cache of Nazi memorabilia in his possession, along with books about Joseph Goebbels and other Nazi leaders. Bowie claimed the materials were required to help him research a film about Hitler's propaganda tactics, but they were seized anyway. It didn't help that, returning to Victoria station soon afterwards, he was pictured waving to fans in a way that suggested he was delivering a Nazi salute.

Then, shortly after Clapton's concert rant, the September 1976 edition of *Playboy* appeared on the shelves, featuring an interview with Bowie. He was asked to explain how he had previously stated that he strongly believed in fascism but also expressed an interest in running to be Prime Minister.

Bowie responded: 'I'd love to enter politics. I will one day. I'd adore to be Prime Minister. And, yes, I believe very strongly in fascism. The only way we can speed up the sort of liberalism that's hanging foul in the air at the moment is to speed up the progress of a right-wing, totally dictatorial tyranny and get it over as fast as possible [. . .] Rockstars are fascists, too. Adolf Hitler was one of the first rock stars.'

When the interview was over, the reporter asked Bowie if he was prepared to stand by the comments he had made. 'Everything but the inflammatory remarks,' came the reply, leaving a huge level of ambiguity about just how seriously he meant what he had said.

There had been a major heatwave across the UK during that summer of 1976 and perhaps that stopped people thinking straight. It was around this time that the likes of Sid Vicious from the Sex Pistols and Siouxsie Sioux from Siouxsie and the Banshees began adorning their punk outfits with swastikas and claiming they were using them as 'fashion statements'.

Eric Clapton would later claim he was extremely intoxicated at the time he made his comments. Later that same year, in an interview with *Sounds* magazine, he offered: 'I thought it was quite funny actually. I don't know much about politics. I don't even know if it would be good or bad for him [Enoch Powell] to get in. I don't even know who the Prime Minister is now. I just don't know what came over me that night. It must have been something that happened in the day but it came out in this garbled thing.'

It wasn't until the mid-2000s that he began to express true regret for his remarks, but he always stopped short of making a full apology.

Tensions were rising. During the local elections in Blackburn during the spring of 1976, 40 per cent of the vote had gone to the National Front. A few weeks earlier an Asian teenager named Gurdip Singh Chaggar had been stabbed to death by a gang of white racists in Southall.

The response of National Front leader John Kingsley Read was potentially incendiary: 'One down, a million to go.'

For Red Saunders, a rock photographer and political activist, something needed to be done to redress the balance. He penned a protest letter which went on to be published in the major music press of the day – the *NME*, *Melody Maker*, *Sounds* – along with the *Socialist Worker*.

When I read about Eric Clapton's Birmingham concert when he urged support for Enoch Powell, I nearly puked. What's going on, Eric? You've got a touch of brain damage. So you're going to stand for MP and you think we're being colonised by black people.

Come on ... you've been taking too much of that *Daily Express* stuff, you know you can't handle it. Own up. Half your music is black. You're rock music's biggest colonist. You're a good musician but where would you be without the blues and R&B?

You've got to fight the racist poison, otherwise you degenerate into the sewer with the rats and all the money men who ripped off rock culture with their chequebooks and plastic crap. Rock was and still can be a real progressive culture, not a package mail-order stick-on nightmare of mediocre garbage.

Keep the faith, black and white unite and fight. We want to organise a rank-and-file movement against the racist poison in rock music.

The letter ended with a call for anyone who was interested in joining to write in. Within two weeks, more than six hundred replies had been received. In the months that followed, a new movement, Rock Against Racism, came into being and in November 1976 staged its first ever show.

In the years that followed the movement would go on to stage dozens of concerts, carnivals and other events, bringing together the biggest punk, ska and reggae bands of the day, as well as music and fans of all races.

I was only a couple of years old when all this was starting and still living in blissful ignorance about such issues. But the fact that such high-profile characters felt able to say and do such things in public at the time – and that their careers did not come to a crashing halt as a result – says a great deal about the attitudes towards race within society as a whole.

Things could not be more different today. During the 2024 general election – which was dominated by issues around immigration and racial tension – three candidates for Reform UK were dropped by the party prior to polling day for making racist or offensive comments.

One shared remarks online that suggested those hailing from sub-Saharan Africa had a low level of intelligence. Another commented that Blacks should 'get off [their] lazy arses' and stop behaving 'like savages'. The third reportedly used the word 'scum' in a social media post talking about those arriving in the UK on small boats. Modern-day responses to this kind of racism are a useful barometer of how far we have come. But back in the first new decade of Thatcher's Britain, things were about to get a lot worse.

9

New Cross Fire and Beyond

As we have repeatedly seen in the pages of this book, racist attacks had been part and parcel of the Black experience in Britain even before the arrival of the *Windrush*. But the 1970s saw a particular upsurge in the level of violence, especially in south-east London, where regular attacks were taking place in the streets, community centres and youth clubs.

Support for the National Front began to wane with the rise of Margaret Thatcher, and many believe she deliberately aimed her anti-immigration policies at bringing their supporter network over to the Conservatives.

In 1978 she had said during an interview for the documentary strand *World in Action*:

> There was a committee which looked at it and said that if we went on as we are then by the end of the century there would be four million people of the new Commonwealth or Pakistan here. Now, that is an awful lot and I think it means that

people are really rather afraid that this country might be rather swamped by people with a different culture and, you know, the British character has done so much for democracy, for law and done so much throughout the world that if there is any fear that it might be swamped people are going to react and be rather hostile to those coming in.

The following year the Conservatives swept to power and it was clear that the politics of race had played a significant part in their victory.

One of Thatcher's first acts as Prime Minister was to implement a 45 per cent pay rise for all police officers. This figure had come from an independent review of police pay initiated by James Callaghan in 1977 and reported the following year. Thatcher knew only too well that many of the plans and policies she was determined to introduce, in particular those concerning immigration, union representation and the reform of some industries, would prove deeply unpopular. The only way to minimise the civil unrest that was likely to follow would be to have the police fully on her side.

During the early hours of Sunday, 18 January 1981, an eyewitness reported seeing a white man approach the door of 439 New Cross Road in Deptford, south-east London. The man was seen raising his arm, as if throwing a cricket ball, then ran back out of the garden gate and climbed into a white Austin Princess car which quickly drove away.

Inside the three-storey Victorian house, up to two hundred young Black Britons were enjoying themselves having come together to celebrate the sixteenth birthday of Yvonne Ruddock as well as the eighteenth birthday of her good friend Angela Jackson. The festivities had started on the Saturday evening – at some point the police had attended following a complaint about the noise — and the revelry was still in full swing many hours later.

People were dancing on all the floors or spilling out to chat to one another on the narrow staircases. The sound of lovers' rock mingled with people laughing and singing along. The vibe was good.

Just minutes after the white car was seen driving away, party-goers on the upper floors began to smell smoke. Some of those on the ground floor came up to report that a small fire had broken out in the kitchen at the front of the house and that the party would have to come to an end.

But the moment they reopened the door, they found the stair-wells had already filled with choking black smoke and saw flames racing up to meet them. People started to panic, scrambling over one another in an attempt to reach the safety of the upper floors.

The flames came up after them and the staircase collapsed. 'In seconds, there was no electricity and everything was dark,' sixteen-year-old DJ Wayne Haynes later recalled in the BBC documentary *Uprising* by Oscar-winning director Steve McQueen.

All hell broke loose. People were screaming and shouting, trying to climb out a window and other people pulling them back.

Heat was coming up from underneath and it was getting hotter. I remember sweating and wiping my forehead, but the sweat was actually my skin peeling off my face. It felt like I had sand all over my face and the more I wiped, the more skin came off.

He took the only possible route out and crawled through the second-floor window. But as he climbed down the drainpipe, it tore away from the side of the house and he fell through the roof of the outside toilet. In total he broke 163 bones.

Others were not so lucky. Thirteen people lost their lives that night including Yvonne and her twenty-two-year-old brother

Paul, the oldest to die. The youngest victim, Andrew Gooding, was just fourteen. The others were Rosaline Henry, sixteen; Patrick Cummings, sixteen; Patricia Johnson, fifteen; Owen Thompson, sixteen; Lloyd Hall, twenty; Humphrey Brown, eighteen; Steve Collins, seventeen; Gerry Francis, seventeen; Peter Campbell, eighteen and Glenton Powell, sixteen.

Many suffered horrific burns while others who followed Haynes out of the windows were also left severely injured. (Two and a half years later, Anthony Berbeck became the fourteenth victim; traumatised by the experience, he died by suicide.)

Each and every one of those who lost their lives in the fire had been Black or mixed race. This, combined with the eyewitness reports of someone possibly throwing a Molotov cocktail at the building, meant the first line of enquiry revolved around the idea that this had been a racially motivated attack.

New Cross lies within the London Borough of Lewisham, an area known for high levels of support for the far right, and fire was known to be their chief weapon of protest. The group had a reputation for shoving burning envelopes filled with excrement through the letterboxes of Black and Asian families in a bid to drive them out of the area.

In January 1971, a decade before the fire at New Cross Road, another Afro-Caribbean house party, this time in Sunderland Road in nearby Ladywell, had burst into flames after three firebombs were thrown at it. No one died on that occasion but twenty-two people were left injured, some of them seriously.

As is so often the case when Black victims of crime are concerned, the early days of the police investigation were lacklustre at best and quickly made matters worse by targeting the wrong people. When eight members of the Black Unity and Freedom Party, an offshoot of the Black Power movement, were on their way home after visiting some of the injured in Lewisham Hospital, they were stopped and harassed by a group of police officers. A scuffle followed leading to several arrests and worsening police/ community relations.

Two white racists were later arrested and jailed for their part in what became known as the Sunderland Road Firebombing, but as the decade continued meaningful progress in restoring good relations between the police and the Black community remained elusive.

In August 1977, the National Front organised a protest march from New Cross to Catford, passing through the centre of multicultural Lewisham, using rising levels of street crime as justification for the action. Members of the far-right party from all over the country were encouraged to attend – it was to be the ultimate show of strength.

Although it had been established more than a decade earlier, in February 1967, the National Front (NF) had initially failed to be accepted as a serious political party. It had been born out of an amalgamation of three fascist groups – the Greater Britain Movement, the League of Empire Loyalists and the Racial Preservation Society – and as a result lacked coherence.

This all changed in April 1968, following the infamous 'Rivers of Blood' speech by extreme right-wing Conservative MP Enoch Powell which brought a powerful anti-immigration rhetoric into the mainstream. Seeing that the speech had gained traction among the white working class, the National Front took the opportunity to capitalise on this and raise its profile.

By 1970, the NF had lined up eighty-four candidates to stand in the general election and achieved 5.2 per cent of the vote, a figure that was modest but also significant. As the 1970s continued the party saw dramatic growth as it further widened its appeal. In May 1973, in the West Bromwich by-election, the NF achieved 10 per cent of the vote in what had previously been considered a safe Labour seat.

By 1976, the National Front claimed to have upwards of

fourteen thousand members paying monthly dues. In the May 1977 Greater London Council local elections, the party received 119,000 votes.

The party sought to build on growing concerns about unemployment, housing availability and the dubious increase in the crime of 'mugging' that continued to be associated with Black youths. Party associates also proved willing to carry out physical attacks on anyone who opposed their ideology or showed sympathy for migrants. Their targets included Laurence Spicer, a journalist handing out leaflets for the Liberal Party, who was called 'a Liberal bastard, wog lover, traitor' before being knocked to the ground.

In response, the local labour party set up an extensive initiative called the All-Lewisham Campaign Against Racism and Fascism (ALCARAF). This aimed to keep track of far-right activities and try to improve community relations.

Despite these efforts, the National Front continued to gain influence, capitalising on false stories about Black crime.

In May 1977, the Metropolitan Police carried out early-morning raids on properties housing dozens of young Black people supposedly associated with mugging. Police records listed the raids as 'Operation PNH' – widely believed to be a reference to 'police nigger hunting'. They resulted in twenty-one residents being charged with 'conspiracy to steal' and led to a community campaign in their defence. Known as the Lewisham Twenty-One, large-scale public meetings were held in central Lewisham to work out how best to defend them.

The NF reacted by sending in groups of thugs to attack the meetings and break them up. One incident saw more than two hundred skinheads burst into a meeting and begin attacking those present. More than eighty arrests were made.

The racists began to attack people selling socialist papers and Black shopkeepers on a daily basis. Lewisham was rapidly becoming a no-go area for the Black community.

It was against this backdrop that the National Front announced its plan to parade through Lewisham on 13 August. Their chosen campaign slogan, 'Muggers Out', aimed to provoke the Black community and inflame local racial tensions. ALCARAF had attempted to have the march banned by appealing to the High Court, but this had been rejected. They planned to hold a peaceful demonstration against this decision.

The Anti Racist/Anti-Fascist Co-ordinating Committee and Socialist Workers Party decided on more direct action. Although the racists would be under heavy police protection (a move that only widened the gap between the community and the police) they would set up a blockade to prevent the march from reaching its final destination.

As the march got underway, clashes began almost immediately with protestors throwing smoke bombs and screaming obscenities at one another. The police attempted to force them back onto New Cross Road so they could clear a path for the National Front while protecting them on three sides.

But the police were unaware the protestors had laid a clever trap, allowing the police and the honour guard of the NF to pass before turning their attention to the main body of the crowd. Several of the houses along the route were derelict and dozens of the anti-fascists had concealed themselves on the upper floors or behind garden walls, just waiting for the right moment to attack.

When it came the assault was brutal with bricks and bottles and firebombs raining down on the marchers. Dozens were injured and attempted to hide in doorways to get away from the storm of missiles.

Another group of protestors had gone ahead, amassing in central Lewisham to prevent the NF from reaching their finish line. Unable to proceed in any direction, the racists were forced to hold a brief rally in a car park before their police escort returned them to Lewisham train station.

Having thought they were protesting in an area with strong

local support, the NF quickly found themselves hugely outnumbered by at least four thousand counter-protestors. Within a few months, the unity shown by the protestors on that day would lead to the formation of what would become the primary group leading the fight against the far right – the Anti-Nazi League.

Suzy Harding, one of those present, recalls: 'There was a bit of fighting but most of the [fascists] were so terrified that they just ran away. I have to confess I didn't have a clue what to do in the middle of all this. I caught the eye of this one particular [fascist], a big, scary-looking, middle-aged bloke. He just turned and ran off down the road. Most of his mates did the same.'

It was the first time ever that a National Front march had been prevented from completing its intended route and a significant victory for the protestors. But before they could celebrate, the police returned in force in order to take their revenge. Armed with riot shields and batons, they descended upon the crowd. Now the whole community became involved with dozens more locals joining the fight. One witness even recalled elderly Black women standing at their upstairs windows and throwing cauliflowers at the police lines.

In total, 250 police officers took part in the day's events, leading to 214 arrests and at least 111 people being injured, fifty-six of them police officers. Seven police vehicles were also damaged, and it turned out to be the very first time that the police had deployed riot shields on the UK mainland.

The clash would become known as the Battle of Lewisham. Although the National Front had suffered a severe blow in an area where it believed it had widespread support, it would continue to pose a threat to the Black community for some time to come.

In November 1977 a journalist who had attended a National Front meeting reported that he had overheard conversations about burning down the Moonshot, a popular youth club in New Cross that had been the target of regular police raids. The next month saw a major firebomb attack that left it so badly damaged it had to be completely rebuilt.

In July 1978 the Albany Empire community theatre in Deptford, a popular venue that had hosted a number of Rock Against Racism gigs, suffered an arson attack. The following day a handwritten note was pushed through the letterbox. It read: 'Got you.'

No surprise, then, that in 1981 the whole community believed the New Cross Fire had also been started deliberately and targeted the property because it was occupied by Black people. It was with some relief that people saw the police immediately pursuing this exact line of enquiry, with the *South-East London Mercury* reporting that the police were trying to trace the driver of the Austin Princess that had been seen outside the house shortly before the attack.

It did not last long. Within days the police had switched their theories. Despite the wealth of precedent and high levels of racial tension in the area, the police decided the fire was not the result of an attack by a third party but instead had been started by some of those attending the party, possibly as the result of a fight taking place between guests on the ground floor.

Rather than treating the survivors as victims, the police began treating them as criminals, all but ignoring the trauma and shock they undoubtedly felt at the time, and putting them through lengthy interrogations to find out who had been involved in the alleged fight and where the fight had occurred.

On the Sunday following the deadly blaze a mass public meeting was held at the Moonshot Club. While the organisers – who included Darcus Howe of Mangrove Nine fame – expected only a few hundred, it was attended by over a thousand people. The group then relocated to the scene of the fire itself, leading to New Cross Road being blocked for several hours as they protested about the way the police were dealing with the case.

As the press promoted the theory that the partygoers had been responsible for their own demise, so public sympathy began to fade. Some of the families of the victims even began receiving abusive letters.

For the members of the local community supporting the

families of the victims, the switch of police focus was difficult enough, but they also struggled to deal with a wider lack of official support. Such a tragedy would normally lead to some kind of acknowledgement or the release of messages of condolence from the Queen or the Prime Minister, but in this instance, there was nothing at all.

The lack of wider support became all the more evident when, three weeks after the New Cross Fire, another fatal blaze occurred, this time at the Stardust nightclub in Dublin. More than eight hundred young people were attending a disco there at the time. Of these, forty-eight died and 214 were left injured. Both Margaret Thatcher and the Queen offered immediate condolences to the families of those who had been lost. All the victims of the Dublin fire had been white.

In addition, the families of those who died at New Cross were only offered the lowest possible levels of compensation. It amounted to barely half of what they had spent on the funerals. Meanwhile, those who survived, regardless of whether they had been physically injured or left mentally scarred, were refused compensation for the trauma they had suffered.

Angered by all this, activists from across London established the New Cross Massacre Action Committee (NCMAC). The group sought to raise awareness of the tragedy, raise money for the bereaved and establish the true cause of the fire, through their own investigation if necessary.

The key development to come out of the committee was the setting up of the Black People's Day of Action which was set to take place on Monday, 2 March 1981. Despite being a wet workday, somewhere between fifteen thousand and twenty thousand people turned up for the twelve-mile march through central London, from New Cross Road to Hyde Park. It was the single largest political mobilisation of Black people the UK had ever seen.

Many of those who attended carried placards with the pictures of the thirteen victims, along with their names and dates of birth. The crowd chanted a range of slogans including: 'No Police Cover-Up', 'Thirteen Dead and Nothing Said' and 'Blood Ah Go Run If Justice No Come'.

As it passed through various communities, so the crowd grew as passers-by and onlookers sought to join in. Some reported school children clambering over fences while others spoke of people simply walking out of their offices or workplaces, eager to be part of such a memorable and important event.

Although the march was mainly peaceful, a small, brief scuffle with the police took place close to Blackfriars over confusion about which route the march was planning to take. This minor incident was enough for the *Sun* to report on the event with the headline THE DAY THE BLACKS RAN RIOT IN LONDON, while other papers went with equally biased headlines including BLACK DAY AT BLACKFRIARS and WHEN THE BLACK TIDE MET THE THIN BLUE LINE.

The first inquest into the New Cross Fire began in April 1981. The coroner was Arthur Gordon Davies, and the families of the victims were represented by Michael Mansfield, Ian Macdonald and Rock Tansey.

Initially, the police said they were looking into four theories of how the fire started. The first was that there had been a planned firebomb attack from outside the building; the second was that a passing opportunist had launched an arson attack from outside the building. The final two theories were that the fire had started inside the building, either deliberately or accidentally. However, as the inquest proceeded, it became clear that any notion of a racial motive had been ruled out by the police, in favour of the theory based on a fire starting inside the building involving chemicals.

NCMAC closely monitored the inquest proceedings and were disturbed to find some aspects of the forensic examination of the scene in the immediate aftermath of the fire appeared to be flawed.

Certain objects had not been fully checked, mistakes seemed to have been made in testing substances found, and a metal tube discovered on the ground floor containing traces of a chemical, perhaps the remains of a possible incendiary device, had not been considered significant.

Many witnesses were cross examined during the proceedings but the coroner did not make notes during this evidence, preferring instead to take information directly from police statements. At the end of the inquest, the jury returned an open verdict. The coroner's refusal to take notes was later ruled to have been a breach of Section 6 of the Coroners Act 1887, and the Attorney General agreed that an appeal could be lodged on behalf of the relatives of the dead.

A second inquest, conducted in 2002, also concluded with an open verdict. But, importantly, it completely exonerated the party attendees.

Over the years, various events have been organised to honour the tragedy and pay tribute to those who perished. There are also several public memorials to commemorate the fourteen young victims, including plaques at 439 New Cross Road and Lewisham Town Hall, as well as a stained-glass memorial window in St Andrew's Church, Brockley.

The cause of the New Cross Fire is still the subject of debate. The police both failed to prove whether it was or was not the result of an arson attack and failed to reassure the community that the incident was properly investigated.

The case also highlights just how openly racist many officers were at the time. A white teenager who had attended the party but managed to escape from the fire was repeatedly asked why he had attended, the officers seemingly unable to understand that he had simply been among friends.

The way both the police and the media reported on the tragedy seemed to make it easier for people to emotionally distance themselves from it. Instead of thinking how tragic and sad it was that so many young people had died, they questioned why so many of them were in the house and why they were there so late. But this was a time when racist attitudes all too often meant that Black people were being denied entry to pubs and clubs, leading to house parties becoming the norm. Just like the Black-only parties of London in the eighteenth century, it was the only way they could get together and enjoy themselves.

Finally, those same racist attitudes meant both police and public failed to connect with the fact that those who died were not immigrants but British citizens.

Years later I would meet Wayne Haynes through my work as a DJ. We talked about the thirteen dead who then became fourteen. As with all such tragedies, it's sometimes easy to forget what it's like to experience that kind of trauma at an early age. It had taken a heavy toll.

Surviving a fatal fire is at the extreme end of the spectrum, but for many members of the Black community, exposure to a low level of trauma was part and parcel of daily life.

The 1979 election of Margaret Thatcher had widened the gulf between the rich and poor in the country, and inner-city areas like St Paul's in Bristol (where an uprising would take place in 1980) and Brixton were at the sharp end of the suffering.

By the spring of 1981 the housing waiting list in Brixton had climbed to eighteen thousand, meaning there was no chance of getting a home for several years. Even if you did, a third of the housing stock had been declared sub-standard. Meanwhile, unemployment was reaching record highs and having a disproportionate impact on minority groups with two out of three of all unemployed in the area being Black.

The effect of higher levels of poverty was a rise in street crime, and the media once again whipped up concern about the rise of street 'muggings', implying that such crimes were almost exclusively carried out by young, working-class Black men.

In a bid to restore order to the streets, the Metropolitan Police decided to focus attention on the area for a while. Their name for this operation? Swamp 1981. It was a direct reference to Thatcher's earlier comments about people having concerns about being 'swamped' by those from a different culture.

It should have been obvious that this kind of racist rhetoric would only serve to further embolden groups preaching race hate, such as the National Front, and also provide additional justification for the increased use of racist policing strategies such as stop and search.

It was a poor choice at the time and an even poorer one in retrospect, but you have to remember that, fresh from their 45 per cent pay rise, officers were eager to show their support for the government. The choice of name was not just a reference but also a tribute to their new paymaster.

It began on a smaller scale. At 11 p.m. on Friday, 3 April, the front-line area around Dexter and Leeson Roads, in Brixton, was sealed off by police with no one being allowed in or out for over an hour. More than twenty arrests were made. Then, in the following week, Operation Swamp 81 launched properly. It saw over one thousand people (mainly young Blacks) stopped and searched, all adding to more frustration among the community. To make matters worse, the searches were often violent, degrading and arbitrary. Many locals reported being stopped as many as three times in a single day. Brixton residents felt they had been occupied by officers of the Metropolitan Police.

Friday, 10 April 1981 was the first warm day of the year and Police Constable Stephen Margiotta, a twenty-seven-year-old probationary officer with just over one year's experience, was out on regular uniform foot patrol in Brixton. As he approached the junction of Atlantic Road and Coldharbour Lane, a flash of movement caught his eye: a Black youth in a state of distress was heading his way, with three other Black youths also running close behind him.

'The street was busy and through the crowd I could see this person running towards me, he was coming at quite a speed,' PC Margiotta would later recall. 'He was coming straight at me and so I had to stop him. We collided, and as we got up his shirt came off the shoulder and I could see he was bleeding. I was also covered in blood.'

As soon as he got to his feet the youth ran off again. PC Margiotta was joined by a colleague and the pair gave pursuit, catching up with the youth a short time later. When they asked what was wrong, the boy took off his shirt. The officers saw a three- or four-inch wound just below the centre of his back between the shoulder blades. It was bleeding profusely.

It was clear the youth had been stabbed and was in need of serious medical attention. In many other parts of the country, most people finding themselves in a similar situation would have sought out a police officer as someone who could help them. But this was Brixton and relations between the police and the Black community were at rock bottom. So far as the youth was concerned, the police were the enemy. He would no more seek their assistance than he would seek a bucket of petrol to put out a fire.

Instead of allowing the officers to assist, he struggled to get away from them. His actions soon attracted the attention of another group of Black youths who, equally unwilling to believe that the police would do anything to a Black youth other than arrest or detain them, began jostling the officers and telling them to leave him alone. The confrontation became increasingly heated, allowing the stabbed youth to break away once again, running off along Coldharbour Lane towards Lambeth Town Hall.

As a larger crowd began to gather, PC Margiotta tried to explain that the youth who had run off needed urgent medical attention, showing them the blood that was on his own clothing. The crowd began to calm down with some even offering to help with the search. The officer also made a radio call to Brixton police station, alerting more officers to the incident.

In the meantime, the injured youth had made his way into a house containing a number of flats and randomly asked for help. The occupier arranged for a taxi to be called and tried to stop the bleeding using sheets of kitchen roll.

Two more officers, who were on patrol in a Transit van at the time PC Margiotta put out his call, spotted the injured youth being loaded into the taxi and watched it drive off, before quickly catching up with it. One of the officers examined the youth and soon realised that the bubbling in the blood coming out of his chest likely meant the youth's lung had been punctured. They applied a sterile dressing, kept pressure on the wound and called for an ambulance.

A crowd gathered and formed an alternative view of the scene playing out before them. They saw a badly injured Black youth in a taxi who had been on his way to the hospital being detained by several police officers.

The crowd grew larger and more hostile. 'Look, they are killing him,' shouted one. Despite their best efforts to explain, the officers were pushed aside and told 'we will look after our own'. The injured youth was pulled from the taxi and placed in the back of another car to be taken to hospital.

The moment the crowd had appeared and started to push them aside, the officers treating the injured youth had called for back-up, requesting urgent assistance. PC Margiotta was one of a number who responded to the call and found himself going to the aid of his colleagues, running through a forty-strong crowd and having bricks and bottles thrown at him along the way.

Within a few minutes the crowd had grown to more than one hundred and the command was given for a recently arrived police van carrying four officers with three riot shields to deploy and disperse the crowd.

It was then that the police made an error that would see the situation become decidedly worse. Despite the tensions, the misunderstandings and the growing resentment over the way members of the local Black community were being treated by the police, the decision was made that Operation Swamp would continue the next day.

The police clearly set out to provoke. On the morning of 11 April officers were observed physically attacking several unsuspecting young Black men on the street and bombarding them with racial insults. One witness saw police storm into a shop and beat up all the Black people inside, while another described an incident where a Black man was pushed to the ground by police while he was simply standing at his doorstep.

By 5 p.m., the community had had enough of the police's behaviour and decided to resist and retaliate. Bricks were thrown at police vehicles, and young people violently clashed with officers in the streets. As night descended on Brixton, a full-scale conflict erupted. There were widespread fires for two days as Molotov cocktails were thrown. Police fought running battles with local youths but were unable to control the situation.

By the time it was over, 299 police officers and sixty-five members of the public had been injured. More than one hundred vehicles had been set on fire, almost half of them being police cars or vans. Close to 150 buildings had been damaged, twenty-eight of them having been set alight. Although reports suggested that up to five thousand people were involved in the violence, only eighty-two people were arrested.

Just two days later the then Home Secretary, William Whitelaw, appointed the respected judge and barrister Lord Leslie Scarman to 'inquire urgently into the serious disorder in Brixton on 10–12 April 1981 and to report, with the power to make recommendations'.

Beginning in June 1981, the inquiry took oral evidence for twenty days at Lambeth Town Hall before entering a second phase consisting of written evidence and submissions. The final phase involved a hearing at Church House in Westminster which lasted seven days, ending on 9 September.

The report was published on 25 November. In the preface Lord Scarman chose to directly address critics who complained that, as a judge, he would have little knowledge of what life was like for those living in a place like Brixton at the time.

He wrote: 'Public disorder usually arises out of a sense of injustice. A sense of injustice is not limited to people with legal or judicial training, but judges will certainly have experience in uncovering it and have an instinctive understanding of the causes and consequences of injustice. Above all, a judge has a passion for righting injustice. That is his job.'

The general conclusion of the report was that racial disadvantage was an everyday experience for Britain's Black population and that 'urgent action is needed if it is not to become an endemic, ineradicable disease threatening the very survival of our society'.

It added: '"Institutional racism" does not exist in Britain; but racial disadvantage and its nasty associate, racial discrimination, have not yet been eliminated. They poison minds and attitudes; they are, and so long as they remain, will continue to be a potent factor of unrest.'

Scarman said there were 'complex political, social and economic factors' at play which had created a 'predisposition towards violent protest' and that the uprisings had been a 'spontaneous outburst of built-up resentment sparked by particular incidents'.

However, the inquiry was heavily criticised by many campaigning groups and some Brixton residents who felt it was being used to criminalise those involved in the anti-police actions by oversimplifying their aims and motivations.

Much of the report seemed to rely on clichés and stereotypes. For example: 'Without close parental support, with no job to go to and with few recreational facilities available, the young black person makes his life on the streets and in the seedy commercially run clubs of Brixton. There he meets criminals, who appear to have no difficulty in obtaining the benefits of a materialist society.'

Although he found there had been a loss of confidence and mistrust in the police and their methods of policing, he found they were not responsible for the disadvantages faced by the Black community but played a critical role in stirring things up. 'If they neglect consultation and cooperation with the local community, unrest is certain and riot becomes probable.'

Operation Swamp 81 had involved arbitrary roadblocks, the random stopping of pedestrians as they went about their business and the mass detention of groups of young men whose actions were deemed to be suspicious. In all, nearly one thousand people were stopped, 118 arrested and seventy-five charged.

Scarman uncovered that the operation had been authorised despite the lack of any consultation with the local community or even the officers involved in neighbourhood policing in the area. Although liaison arrangements for the police, local authority and representatives of the local community had previously been in place, these had collapsed in the run-up to the uprising.

Among Scarman's many recommendations were changes in police training and the recruitment of more ethnic minorities into the force, even if this meant increasing their numbers at the expense of white recruits. He suggested that introducing positive discrimination was 'a price worth paying if it accelerates the elimination of the unsettling factor of racial disadvantage from the social fabric of the United Kingdom'.

The report also led to the introduction of the Police and Criminal Evidence Act (PACE) of 1984 which clearly defined the powers available to the police to balance these with the rights and freedoms of members of the public.

Scarman reported that the indiscriminate use of the 'sus' laws along with the 'ill-considered, immature and racially prejudiced actions of some officers' had contributed to the unrest. The introduction of PACE meant stops and searches could only be carried out on specific grounds, not mere suspicion. PACE also mandated the recording of police interviews, though, as we shall see later, that supposed safeguard didn't always work in favour of defendants.

Scarman's recommendations also led to the formation of an independent police complaints authority to ensure police were fully accountable for their actions.

Eighteen years later, the Macpherson Report, which was published in the aftermath of the death of Stephen Lawrence, would find that many of Scarman's recommendations had actually been ignored. Unlike Scarman, Macpherson would find that the Metropolitan Police was indeed 'institutionally racist'.

10

My Story: The Shooting of My Mum, Cherry Groce

I was around ten years old when I first became aware that Black people being stopped by the police was a thing that was happening on a regular basis in the area where I lived, but I had absolutely no idea how scary or dangerous such an experience could be.

I turned ten the same year a reggae singer and DJ going by the name of Smiley Culture released a record called 'Police Officer' which became an instant cult hit and hugely popular with me and my friends. It's the supposedly autobiographical tale of how Smiley is driving around, minding his own business, when the police pull him over on suspicion of possession of cannabis. At one point Smiley recreates the conversation between himself and one of the officers, switching seamlessly between his street patois and a typical south London copper's accent.

I was too young to have experienced that situation first hand, but even so, I was street smart enough to get the humour. The whole thing was hilarious but also entirely realistic, especially when Smiley dares to speak back during the interrogation and is told: 'Shut your bloody mouth. We ask. You answer.'

Behind the humour was a deadly serious point about the way the police were treating members of Black communities, not just in Brixton but all across London and far beyond. In the song, Smiley avoids arrest when one of the officers recognises him and offers to let him go in exchange for an autograph.

Most people could only dream of that sort of outcome. Back then, drugs or not, encounters with the police often ended in the back of a police van defending yourself from kicks, punches and heavy blows from wooden truncheons.

During the 1970s carloads of officers would simply pull up alongside a random Black person walking down the street, jump out, give them a good hiding and then drive off leaving a battered and bruised body behind.

At ten I was still young enough to be immune to the full horror of this, but the song definitely made me think that perhaps the image I'd been holding in my head about police officers might not fully reflect the reality.

It all came with a growing sense of disappointment. I'd long been a big fan of all the cop shows on TV at the time: *Kojak*, *Starsky and Hutch*, *Cagney & Lacey* and *CHiPs*. I'd spend hours at home playing out different scenarios where I was leading a team of officers who arrived on the scene, saved the day and locked up all the bad guys. Even though I knew that in reality, it wasn't going to be non-stop car chases and shoot-outs, I liked the idea of being the good guy, the one who went out and helped people, treated them fairly. In my young eyes that's what being in the police should have been all about.

Back then Brixton was portrayed as this incredibly dangerous place where you wouldn't want to be out walking alone after dark. But that wasn't my experience as a child growing up there. It was exciting, it was fun, and it was definitely safe. When I went out,

I never needed to take a key with me because the back door was never locked.

We were in and out of each other's houses and played out in the streets. My mum's friends became my aunties and uncles. The place had a real sense of community spirit. And there was also a sense that we policed ourselves and didn't need any outside assistance.

I was fully aware that my family was poor. We never had very much to speak of and I saw how much my mum had to fight for everything. So that daily struggle was very real to me. I'd see it every day, the struggle to make sure there was food on the table for every meal. But we were still happy. I spent most of my weekends out on my BMX bike, hanging out with friends.

I was a bit aware of racism. I knew some people wanted to treat me differently because of the colour of my skin. And the one lesson I learned from an early age was that if you ever see a gang of white boys up ahead, run. But that wasn't a problem where we were living as the majority of residents were Black. Racism was something that happened in other places, inflicted by other people.

But at that age, those people were never wearing police uniforms. In my eyes they were still the good guys, the ones you would turn to in your moment of need.

All that changed the moment my mum was shot.

I heard an enormous cracking sound, like a massive twig being snapped in half, followed by a loud bang – a gunshot. I leapt to my feet, fully awake and alert. And I saw my mum was down on the floor while this man – who had a gun in his hand – was just shouting at her over and over in a really aggressive way: 'Where's Michael Groce? Michael Groce?'

When my mum spoke back, her voice was weak, as if she were a long way away. 'I can't breathe. I can't feel my legs. I think I'm going to die.'

That totally freaked me out. I could see my mum lying there, in pain and looking so vulnerable, so I just started screaming and shouting at the man with the gun. I was effing and blinding and everything. *What are you doing to my mum? What has he done to my mum?* To be honest, I just wanted to attack him.

And at that moment he turned and pointed his gun towards me. 'Somebody better shut this fucking kid up,' he said, as if I was annoying him. Looking back, I realise there was no remorse from him for what happened. The guy had shot my mum but there was no sense of 'Oh, my God, I've made a terrible mistake'. There was none of that. Instead he came across as being incredibly annoyed that he wasn't standing over the person he'd wanted to find.

Up until then, I had no idea that the man was a police officer. I only cottoned on when my dad told me to calm down. My dad used to be in the army and was working as a security guard. I could see fear on his face and at that moment I started to think, *Oh, my God, this is serious. My dad's scared, this is serious.*

Someone ushered us out of the room, and it was only then that I saw there were thirty or more police officers inside the house, some of them carrying guns and others with dogs. It was as if the house had been invaded, total madness, and for a moment I thought I must still be dreaming. The hardest part was being confused over the fact that it was the police who were doing all of this. They were supposed to be the good guys, the ones I looked up to, but were behaving as if we had done something to them.

I knew my mum was still in the bedroom and I wanted to get back there. I managed to get past one officer and asked: 'What's happened to my mum?' Some part of me had put two and two together and realised that she must have been shot. But the officers in the room said: 'Oh, she just got grazed.'

But I could see blood pouring out of her. I said: 'If she's only got a graze, how come she's bleeding so much?' After that I was quickly rushed out the bedroom and taken to join the rest of the family.

A little later an ambulance arrived and my dad went off to the hospital with Mum, leaving just my sisters and me in the house. The police allowed newspaper reporters and photographers to come into our home and take pictures of us. Despite the fact that none of us could stop crying, they made us line up on the sofa and started snapping away. It was mayhem. We were all crying the whole time, trying to deal with the shock, the combination of anger, confusion, trauma and fear. None of it seemed real.

The next thing I remember were crowds of locals gathering outside the house, demanding to know what on earth was going on. We were asking for news, too, but the liaison officers didn't seem to know much themselves, or at least nothing they were willing to pass on.

At one point they must have put the television on in an attempt to distract us but unthinkingly, they had selected the news channel. Suddenly, I heard the name of our street and I instantly knew they were talking about what had happened. The words on the reporter's lips seemed to be coming out in slow motion as he explained that my mum had died. Mum was gone!

It had been hard enough seeing my mum being taken away in the ambulance but at least I knew she was in good hands. And she'd had the strength to throw a little wave our way as they took her out of sight. I had been holding on to that hope, convincing myself that everything was going to be all right, but now all my hopes had fallen apart, leaving me confused and sinking into a pool of despair.

My mum was my whole world and if she was no longer around, I didn't want to be either. I made a dash for the kitchen, frantically opening and closing drawers, looking for one of the big kitchen knives, pulling it out and pressing the cold, sharp edge against my skin, ready to end it all.

I closed my eyes, took a deep breath and at that moment, one of the liaison officers caught up with me and snatched the knife out of my hand. She tried to reassure me that the story on the news was wrong but I just didn't know if I could trust them any more.

Fortunately, the rumours were incorrect. My mother survived, although the shooting ultimately left her paralysed. But the announcement about her death, then the whispers that she was critically wounded and might die anyway, outraged the community. A crowd assembled outside Brixton police station. They wanted answers but nobody was saying anything.

This scenario is one that plays out too often in these kinds of situations. Emotions are running high, leading to both frustration and anger so it needs incredibly careful handling. But the police weren't doing that. Instead, they were making matters worse by using racist language to provoke the crowd, only increasing the potential for violence.

It had only been four years since the 1981 uprising and memories of those days were still fresh in the minds of many. People felt as if nothing about their situation had improved, and ultimately it all kicked off once again.

I hadn't been around to see any of it, of course. We'd spent the night in the house in Normandy Road, with the bedroom where my mum had been shot closed off and everyone packed into the front room, along with the liaison officers who had been assigned to look after us.

We all spent more time crying than sleeping. I kept asking the officers if they had any updates on my mum's condition but she remained critical the whole time and they were never able to tell me the only words I wanted to hear: that she was going to be OK.

The following morning my friend Stephen McCalla came to visit and insisted on taking me out into the streets to see what had happened in direct response to my mum being shot.

I wasn't sure it was a good idea at first but curiosity soon got the better of me and it was an excuse to get away from the house for a bit as the atmosphere was becoming increasingly oppressive. We hadn't got far before I became aware of the scale of the destruction. There was still nothing to see but the smell of it was hanging in the air in all the roads leading up to the high street.

I'd seen pictures of London during the Blitz and that was what came to mind as we turned that final corner. There were burned-out overturned cars, buildings reduced to empty shells filled with nothing but smoke, bricks and broken bottles strewn across every inch of road and pavement.

I felt grateful that Stephen had insisted I come and witness it but it took many years before I could fully appreciate what it all meant.

This had been no riot, this was an uprising. It may have started as an explosion of anger after rumours circulated that my mum had been killed, but it quickly became something much more. Years of suppression and racism and police brutality had pushed people to breaking point, and this was the only way they could find to express their frustration.

While the press would go on to describe many of those who took part in the events that night as thugs or opportunists – or insist they were only using the disturbances to cover up the looting and pillaging that went on – I knew the truth.

They were standing up for us, showing a united front. They were telling the police that from that moment on, any action against an individual member of the community would elicit a response from the community as a whole.

Had they not done so, we might never have been given the platform we needed to be able to seek justice. And for that, I am forever grateful.

My mum had been the most amazing woman. She had brought up six children almost single-handed by working untold hours as a secretary and a cleaner. She had so much energy. My abiding memory is of her dancing. In particular, I remember one day in 1982 when she came home from Brixton market brandishing her latest purchase – the single 'Someone Loves You Honey' by June Lodge and Prince Mohammed. She put it on the record player and invited us all to dance.

When I went to the hospital to visit Mum a few days after she had been shot, I remember hearing the doctor explaining that she was paralysed from the chest down. She would never walk again. She would never dance again.

The look on her face when she was told the news was absolutely devastating. It was in that moment that I made a promise to myself. Whatever happened from that point onwards, I was going to care for my mum. I said to myself: 'I can't rely on my mum in the way that I did before. Now I've got to be there for her.'

I'd grown up with old-fashioned values. I believed that men were there to look after women. Even though my mum had been fiercely independent and hadn't ever needed any help from anyone, I still believed in those values so if my dad and older brother were not going to step up, I'd have to do it myself, even if I was only eleven years old.

That was the day my childhood came to an end. Looking back, I'm surprised that we were just left on our own to get on with it and find a way to cope with all the madness. Despite everything we had gone through, we just had to find our own way to survive.

After the shooting there was no support of any kind. I was back at school just two weeks later and no teacher ever said anything or asked how I was feeling about it all. I started to have a recurring nightmare that I was the one that had been shot. I also started to resent my father and my brother. They were both off the scene so I felt as if all the male support I should have been able to rely on had been taken away from me.

I would visit my mum every single day after school and sit beside her hospital bed for hours until they told me it was time to leave. For two long years my entire life revolved around just three activities: going to school, visiting my mum and going to sleep.

When my mum was finally discharged from hospital she was rehoused in a bungalow in nearby Gipsy Hill, with me and two of my sisters, Sharon and Lisa. At first she tried to carry on just the same as before. She was still cooking for us all and vacuuming in her wheelchair. But it didn't last long. She was in pain and became increasingly irritable. Every day before I went to school I'd ask her if she would like a cup of tea. One day that same question turned out to be the straw that broke the camel's back. She suddenly lashed out and screamed at me – *why didn't I just go and make it instead of always asking?*

In January 1987, sixteen months after the police raid, Inspector Douglas Lovelock, the officer who fired the shot that hit my mum – and who had sworn and pointed his gun at me – appeared at the Old Bailey, accused of maliciously wounding Cherry Groce.

The operation had been conducted under the false assumption that my brother, Michael, had discharged a weapon at police officers and was now in the house. Though Lovelock strongly denied a suggestion from prosecuting counsel that he needed to be the one to shoot first or else risk being shot himself, he accepted that he had been under intense pressure.

Giving evidence, Lovelock told the hushed courtroom that, in the event of a confrontation, he had been trained to pull the trigger two times: 'Twice – bang, bang, as quickly as that.'

He claimed that his .38 Smith and Wesson revolver had gone off accidentally soon after fellow officers had sledgehammered their way into the house.

Lovelock said he shouted 'Armed police!' as he entered and, seeing no one in the hall, he had levelled his gun in the operational stance. Seeing a door ajar, he kicked it in. 'As the door crashed in, I stepped into the room in the ready position. I was about two foot inside at the very most.'

He went on to describe how a 'dark shape' came upon him which 'seemed almost in the air. I turned towards it and tensed, and the shot had gone off. I was absolutely dumbfounded when it happened. I never had any intention of firing at anybody.'

He was ultimately acquitted of the charges against him. I was angry and upset but my mum just seemed to accept it. Mum said, 'Lee, the police are a force. And we can't beat the force.' I understood where she was coming from, but I also knew I could never accept that attitude. For many years all I could think about was hunting Lovelock down and taking my revenge. I wanted to see him suffer the same way that my mum was suffering.

I didn't just want to kill him – that would have been too simple. I wanted him to end up in a wheelchair in constant pain. I wanted him to have to deal with the consequences of his actions.

My next encounter with the police came when I was thirteen or fourteen years old. I'd been riding on the back of a friend's moped, driving round the streets of Brixton, completely oblivious to the fact it had been stolen. The officer who placed me under arrest called me a monkey. I couldn't believe it. I was so shocked I just burst out laughing. I remember thinking, *This only happens in movies.* But the laughter didn't last. The whole experience hardened me on the inside. I was thinking, *So this is really how you see us?*

By then my attitudes to the police had changed dramatically.

I became more and more political. During Black History Month, I would see plenty of programmes on the telly about the 1981 uprising, but the fact that just a few years later a Black woman had been shot in her home in front of her children was just skimmed over. From that moment on, a little flame ignited within me.

I left school at the age of fifteen, desperate to support both my mother and my sisters, and thought the best way for me to do so was to start selling drugs. I saw myself as more of a businessman than a criminal and justified my actions by telling myself it was just a means to an end. I never referred to myself as a dealer as I never saw myself that way. Most of my clients were rich and had the same accents as members of the royal family. That made it easier to think of what I was doing as a legitimate business.

Trading on the hard-won reputation of my older brother, I soon picked up the nickname Younger Cowboy. It didn't take long for me to see the massive hole in my business plan. There I was dealing drugs because I wanted to provide security and stability for my family but the whole time I was doing that, I was risking being locked up and leaving them with nothing at all. I quit while I was ahead.

By twenty-one, I had a son, Brandon, and a whole bunch of responsibilities. I met my wife Gem when I was twenty-eight, became a father to two little girls, Harmony and Ruby-Lee, and settled down to a simpler way of life. During the day I worked as my mother's official carer and during the evenings I DJed, ran a nightclub and organised events. Then, during the early 2000s, I started working as a black cab driver.

As the years went by, I became increasingly determined to right the wrongs done to my mum, especially as the world seemed to have forgotten her.

In 2010, a friend attended a community celebration of another woman who had died following contact with the police, and afterwards asked me, 'How come your mum's not recognised in that way?' I went back to my mum and told her we needed to do something to bring her story to a wider audience. Mum hated the idea of being in the limelight so initially said no, but I was persistent and kept on bugging her. Eventually she gave in. 'OK, if you want to do something, do something,' she said.

I began work on a play about her life with my aunt, the actor Sutara Gayle (Lorna Gee), but in April 2011 my mum died of kidney failure. She was sixty-three.

That October, *Her Story* had its premiere at the Brixton Ritzy. In 2012, I proposed that a blue plaque be installed outside our family home, which was still owned by Lambeth Council, to further honour my mother's memory. When the council refused, I ignored them and put one up anyway.

After my mother passed away, the pathologist's report identified a connection between the gunshot wound and the kidney failure that resulted in her death, prompting an inquest. However, we couldn't afford legal representation and were denied legal aid. I reached out to my local MP, Chuka Umunna, for help and initiated a petition. By the time we submitted it to 10 Downing Street in April 2014, it had gathered 130,000 signatures. As a result, the family received legal aid. For the first time, I began to see that people who didn't necessarily look like us might still be willing to support us. It made me realise the power of unity and what can be accomplished when people come together.

Just a month before my mother died there had been yet another tragedy within the Black community as the result of the police. It was just the latest in the long, long line of deaths that followed police contact with a Black person, but like the death of Stephen Lawrence, this one resonated with me on a more personal level.

Smiley Culture (real name: David Emmanuel) had been a key part of the soundtrack of my early life with his iconic songs about life on the street shaping my understanding of what it was like to be Black and growing up in south London during the 1980s.

Although Smiley's first two songs had been big hits, with 'Police Officer' in particular reaching number twelve in the charts, his follow-up releases failed to crack the top fifty. Though he would be a huge influence on generations of musicians that followed, his own musical career would be tragically brief.

He made a brief cameo in the David Bowie film *Absolute Beginners* and (ironically, given the exploitative nature of such enterprises) invested in diamond and gold mining with investments spread throughout various African countries.

In an interview with the *Guardian* the year before he died, he said:

Police Officer was a true story – the police used to take my weed. It was better than being arrested and I made that into a hit. With Cockney Translation, I was a black man talking cockney. I integrated cultures even though I didn't understand it at the time. I was invited to meet the Queen, who said she listened to my records in the palace.

Although I paved the way for people like the Streets and Dizzee Rascal, I left the music business because I wasn't rich.

In July 2010 he was arrested and charged with conspiracy to supply cocaine with his trial set for the following March. But a week before the case was due to begin, the police raided his home in order to search for more Class A drugs.

Somehow, during the course of the search, Smiley suffered a single stab wound to the heart which proved almost immediately fatal. There were four police officers in the house with him at the time, but all denied any involvement, claiming the wound had been self-inflicted.

His close friend Asher Senator later said: 'When I first heard, I thought, "He did it." With his arrest and the [upcoming] court case . . . he wasn't in a good place. But when I went to the coroner, I was told that he was stabbed with a precision cut to the heart. That made me think things weren't as straightforward as what we'd been told.'

An inquest returned a verdict of suicide and cleared all the officers of any misconduct. An investigation by the then Independent Police Complaints Commission (IPCC) reached the same conclusion, finding no evidence to justify criminal charges against any of the officers. It did, however, point out a number of flaws in the way the raid on the house had been carried out.

Barrister for the family Leslie Thomas, QC, said: 'Despite the suicide verdict, the jury did find that the way in which Mr Emmanuel was supervised following his arrest materially contributed to his death. In particular, the fact that a single officer was left to supervise Mr Emmanuel while also completing paperwork was felt to be inappropriate.'

As is so often the case when Black people die after contact with the police, these official findings satisfied no one, least of all the remaining members of Smiley's family. There were simply too many unanswered questions.

Back in 1985, only a week after my mum was shot, it felt like history was repeating itself when London exploded into violence once again. We were all still raw and in shock, worried about the future and trying to deal with all the practicalities and logistics of our situation, when trouble flared up on Tottenham's Broadwater Farm estate.

On 5 October, Floyd Jarrett, a young Black man living on the estate with his mother, had been stopped by police and taken into custody at Tottenham police station.

While he was being held, four officers decided to conduct a search of his mother's house. The officers had no search warrant and used Floyd's own keys to let themselves in. They opened the door to find the family watching television, unaware that Floyd was at the police station.

Almost as soon as the officers entered the house, Floyd's mother, forty-nine-year-old Cynthia, collapsed from a heart attack. She was given mouth-to-mouth resuscitation but to no avail – she would never regain consciousness.

The exact circumstances of Cynthia's death remain a matter of dispute. During the subsequent inquest her daughter, Patricia, said she had witnessed her mother falling to the ground after being pushed by one of the officers. The officer denied having done so and the inquest jury ultimately returned a finding that her death was not the result of an intentional action. Following direction from the judge, they accepted that Cynthia may have been pushed but it was more likely to have been accidental than deliberate.

No police officers were ever charged or disciplined in relation to her death.

The day after she suffered her heart attack, a small crowd of Cynthia's friends, family and other residents of Broadwater Farm gathered outside the police station to protest. As had happened the week before, this quickly escalated. Police attempted to clear the streets with a series of baton charges, but the protestors fought back, throwing bricks and petrol bombs into the police lines.

Shots were also fired, with two officers treated for gunshot wounds that first evening. As news of the uprising spread, and more and more people joined in, cars were used to create make-shift barricades and then set on fire. People were settling in for a long engagement.

The main unrest was taking place in the centre of the estate but reports were also coming from nearby of other incidents. As they were considered to be in less immediate danger, police, fire brigade and ambulance crews in these areas lacked the riot gear of those in the heat of the battle.

When the London Fire Brigade responded to reports of a fire in a block at the edge of the estate, they were escorted in by a police unit. As the firefighters approached, they immediately came under attack from a hostile crowd. They withdrew and as they did so, PC Keith Blakelock, one of the officers on escort duty, tripped and fell. Suddenly a mob of around fifty people, armed with machetes, knives and other weapons, surrounded him, stabbing and kicking at his body.

A colleague who attempted to rescue Blakelock was stabbed in the face and neck and had his jaw broken, forcing him to with-draw. When Blakelock's body was recovered, a pathologist found he had at least forty separate wounds, eight of them to his head, and a six-inch-long blade was embedded in his neck, as far as it could go. His attackers had also turned his head to one side and attempted to decapitate him.

The violence eventually petered out over the course of the next day, helped by a spell of heavy rain.

With the police under intense pressure to find who was responsible for the murder of one of their own, it seemed almost inevitable to those of us living in the Black community that their efforts to do so would create yet another miscarriage of justice.

A total of six people were charged with Blakelock's murder: three youths and three adults named Winston Silcott, Engin Raghip and Mark Braithwaite. Once the trial started it quickly emerged that the police had been extremely heavy-handed in their treatment of the suspects.

In the case of the juveniles, not only had they been questioned without a legal guardian being present but they had also been denied food and other comforts. The judge dismissed all the charges against the juveniles due to the inappropriate conditions they had been held in during their interrogation.

Silcott, Raghip and Braithwaite were all found guilty, despite there being no witnesses or forensic evidence linking them to the crime. Instead, the judge and jury had relied on supposed confessions the trio had made during their interrogations, all of which had been captured by hand in a series of police notebooks.

Silcott was especially demonised in the press when it was revealed he had been on bail for another murder at the time that Blakelock was killed. He was given a life sentence with a minimum term of thirty years.

All three continued to proclaim their innocence and were eventually granted a retrial. In November 1991, their convictions were quashed when new tests proved the supposedly contemporaneous notes of the police interrogations, which had been the only real evidence produced against them, had been tampered with.

In a pattern that by now must be becoming horribly familiar, three of the police officers that had conducted the interview with Silcott and the others were charged with perjury. They were all cleared.

As with Brixton, the Broadwater Farm estate suffered from high levels of unemployment and social deprivation, especially among the Black community. The uprising had been the only way they could find to express their frustration.

In the aftermath a lot of time was spent reflecting on

police–community relations across the UK and there were calls for police reform, better community engagement, and more effective strategies to address underlying social issues such as poverty and discrimination.

But despite all these efforts to rebuild bridges, tensions with the community had remained high ever since the 1985 uprising. As a result, the violent death of another young Black man in 2011 – this time shot dead by a police marksman – took many of those in the community right back to square one.

On 4 August 2011, twenty-nine-year-old Mark Duggan was shot dead by police in Tottenham as they attempted to arrest him on suspicion of possession of a firearm. Duggan, who had a couple of minor convictions, had been travelling in a minicab when it was stopped by armed officers. Although accounts of what happened next differ, it seems that Duggan attempted to get out of the cab and flee but was shot twice.

A gun was later recovered from the scene, but it was found approximately ten to twenty feet away from where Duggan was shot. This led to questions about whether Duggan had the gun in his possession at the time he was shot or if he had thrown it away shortly beforehand. In either case, he was unarmed.

(An inquest into Duggan's death concluded in January 2014, with the jury reaching an eight–two majority finding that Duggan was lawfully killed. The jury determined that although Duggan was not holding a gun when he was shot, the police officer had an honest belief that he was acting in self-defence.)

Two nights after the shooting Duggan's relatives and friends, along with a large number of local residents, arranged a march from the Broadwater Farm estate to Tottenham police station, demanding answers about the circumstances of his death.

After a couple of hours, a chief inspector came out of the station and asked the crowd to disperse. Instead, they demanded to speak to someone of higher rank with more knowledge of the situation.

A scuffle broke out and riot police who had been waiting on

standby stormed forward with their shields and batons, causing a number of injuries among the crowd. The response to what was thought of as an unprovoked attack was to set fire to two nearby police cars. Within minutes, Broadwater Farm was again at the centre of a full-blown uprising. The violence also quickly spread to other parts of London and then around the country.

Although Duggan's shooting may have been the spark, this was once again more of an uprising with young people across the country using the only voice available to them to make the wider world aware of the ongoing issues they had with policing, poverty and racial tensions.

A small aside. You may be beginning to notice a pattern of behaviour here. The issues that Black people find themselves dealing with don't start and end with the police. The wider criminal justice system also seems to be doing everything it can to keep them oppressed. And little wonder.

A 2022 study led by barrister Keir Monteith, KC for the University of Manchester found discrimination within the judiciary was particularly directed towards a huge proportion of Black people appearing in court, regardless of whether they were lawyers, defendants or witnesses.

A poll conducted among 373 legal experts revealed that 56 per cent reported observing judges displaying racial bias towards defendants, and 52 per cent had seen instances of discrimination directly influencing judicial decisions.

They cited examples of judges being openly hostile towards Black defendants with one making use of the term 'you people'. There were also multiple instances of Black defendants being given harsher sentences for identical crimes to white defendants.

Writing in the foreword of the report, Professor Leslie Thomas, KC said: 'Judges need to sit up and listen, because it is a myth that Lady Justice is blind to colour. Our judiciary as an institution is just as racist as our police forces, our education system and our health service – this is something that cannot be ignored for any longer.'

Much of the problem relates to representation. At the time of writing there has never been a Supreme Court justice from a BAME background and there are no Black judges in the Court of Appeal. Overall, just 1 per cent of the judiciary are Black. Hailing from a mixed-race background, Linda Dobbs became the first non-white person to be appointed a judge in England and Wales, and that didn't happen until 2004. In the same year, Michael Fuller became the first Black man to lead a police force when he was appointed chief constable of Kent. He remains the only Black man to have had the title (though Neil Basu held an equivalent rank in the Metropolitan Police).

Commenting on the findings of the report, Keir Monteith said: 'Racism in the justice system has to be acknowledged and fought by those at the highest level, but at the moment there is complete and utter silence – and as a consequence, there is no action to combat racial bias. It is impossible to have diversity and inclusion if the system itself unfairly discriminates.'

Recently I attended a training session for officers from MO19, the division of the Metropolitan Police that trains and deploys firearms officers. This was to see whether the anti-racist training that I offer could have an impact but also to help with my own journey and in understanding what differences there are today compared to the way officers were trained at the time my mum was shot.

I asked an officer how they address stereotypes and unconscious biases within MO19 training. In answer to my question, he showed me one of the videos they use, to highlight the outdated Americanised material which he felt could reinforce biases, whether conscious or unconscious.

The footage had been created by an American company and the scenario was that of a shooting in a school. At the start of the simulation, the officer pushes open a door into a school corridor and you see dead white children on the floor. The officer being trained holds a laser gun and the objective is to decide when and who to shoot, if anyone.

The scenario then moved to another room where several white people were standing together and shaking with fear. Then you see a young Black man with a gun in his hand walking up and down in front of them, shouting. At that point I noticed that the hand of the police officer holding the gun – the character you are essentially playing in this scenario – was also Black.

I was deeply shocked. If you are training police officers to see the Black man as the offender, even in crimes where the vast majority of perpetrators are white, then what are you expecting when they go out?

Such incidents happen far too often all across the USA but the vast majority of the perpetrators are white. Of the 151 mass shootings that took place in America between 1982 and September 2024, Black individuals were involved in twenty-six, while Latino individuals were responsible for twelve. The remaining eighty-two shootings were committed by white people.

Shortly before the 2014 inquest into my mum's death we were surprised to learn that West Yorkshire Police had been brought in to investigate as an independent outside force, but the report they had produced had been suppressed.

After more legal action we eventually won the right to have it disclosed. Not surprisingly, the 357-page report was damning. Its author, Assistant Chief Constable John Domaille, had encountered error after error and concluded: 'The raid should not have gone ahead in the manner planned due to the total lack of information . . . grave risks were created both for public and police, which should have been avoided.' These findings were fully accepted by the Metropolitan Police.

Twenty-nine years after the shooting, on 10 July 2014, an inquest jury at Southwark Coroner's Court found that my mum 'was shot by police during a planned, forced entry raid at her home, and her subsequent death was contributed to by failures in the planning and implementation of the raid'. The jury found multiple errors including a lack of a proper briefing for the officers involved. There had also been a failure to conduct any surveillance of the home ahead of the raid or adequately check who was living at the property at the time – which would have revealed that Michael was not there.

We were vindicated. That was the most meaningful tribute I could offer to my mother in her absence and built on what had gone before. Following the shooting incident, an extensive evaluation of the Met Police's firearms policy had already resulted in a ban on detectives carrying guns. In 1993, my mother received a £500,000 settlement – too late to prevent my involvement in drug dealing and not enough money to cover her care until she died eighteen years later.

I told the police that an apology was inadequate. The events of that day shattered the lives of my sisters and me. What I wanted was full accountability for how profoundly our lives had been impacted by their shortcomings. When the Met refused to accept this responsibility, we had no alternative but to go back to court once more.

In 2016, the High Court determined that the Metropolitan Police had a responsibility of care towards Mum's children, with the exception of Michael, who was not present in the house during the incident. As a result, they were required to pay us compensation.

But the issue of justice remained unresolved. The officer who fired the shot that eventually led to my mum's death was able to continue living his life without the consequences we were forced to endure. Neither he nor anyone else had any kind of penalty imposed.

Our legal representatives, Bhatt Murphy, proposed the possibility of 'restorative justice'. This process would involve a meeting with the Metropolitan Police to discuss the effects the shooting had on our lives and explore ways for them to make amends.

To kick-start this process the Met consented to our request to have some level of participation in police training. We wanted to help to create a programme to assist individuals who had been left traumatised due to police errors and we wanted the force to make a donation to the Cherry Groce Foundation, which I established in 2014 to aid community members facing mobility challenges.

Since then, I have served as an unpaid advisor for the police, participating in board meetings, attending graduation ceremonies at the Met's Hendon police college, and delivering a training session on how the police handle complaints.

While I've met some individual officers who are trying to make a difference, I'm not at all impressed with what I've seen of the force as a whole. The system is badly broken.

And I'm not convinced the will is there to fix it. The Met's workforce remains overwhelmingly white and the statistics show that its officers are still many times more likely to use force against Black people than white people. I remember being stunned after asking one graduating officer if their training included negotiation skills. The officer said it did not and instead they were taught to make assumptions and then proceed on the basis of those. I thought back to the assumptions that Lovelock had in his mind when he smashed his way into our Brixton home and fired the shot that ultimately led to my mum's death.

Every day seems to bring a fresh story about the devastating impact that stops and searches of Black people in Britain can have. In May 2020, twenty-three-year-old Jordan Walker-Brown ran away when the police tried to stop him because he had a small amount of cannabis in his possession. As he tried to escape over a wall, he was tasered, causing him to fall and leaving him paralysed from the chest down, just as my mum had been.

I wrote my first book, *The Louder I Will Sing*, because I wanted to share the story of what had happened to my mum and its impact on us as a family. I wanted people to understand the dangers of unconscious bias and then think about the people in their lives, the ones they live near or work with, to think about what can be learned from it all.

Soon after the book came out, a police officer got in touch to tell me he'd been moved to tears after reading it and needed to reach out and let me know. For me, that's the best possible measure of the book's success.

I had been a child when it all happened and my focus since that time had been looking after my mum as best I could. Everything else took second place. It was only after she had gone that I went back over everything with adult eyes, going through the paperwork my mum had kept and all the information from the first inquest.

I needed to unload it all. It was challenging and emotionally draining to write about it, but also therapeutic. There were times when I'd need a day or two to recover from reliving the trauma. I'd need time to find my balance again.

What next? I often wonder, having overcome my own challenges and shared my story in a way that resonates with others, what more I can do to promote balance and contribute to a more equitable society.

A couple of years ago, I found myself dealing with the police after a man on a bicycle rode into the back of my car one morning. I hadn't done anything wrong, and the cyclist immediately apologised, but the officers insisted that I be breathalysed. As they were getting ready to administer the test, a white woman who was passing by came over and stood beside me. 'I'm a witness,' she said. 'I'm not moving.' The officer asked why she felt she needed to be there and she replied, 'I see this every day. All you do is stop young Black men and harass them.'

For me that incident was proof of just how much the world has changed in the last forty years, but also made it clear that there is still a lot to do.

11

The Cardiff Three

I mentioned earlier about being stopped by the police as a teenager. I was arrested, taken to the local police station and placed in an interview room. Right away, I was made to feel that if I didn't speak up, if I tried to keep quiet, then not only would I not get out of the station but that my silence would be held against me, seen as proof that I was guilty.

I felt that unless I spoke up, I was going to be stuck in that room forever, and being stuck in that room for any time at all was just the worst feeling ever. So I had to say something. Anything.

People sometimes question why anyone would admit to something they did not do – they just can't get their head around how that could happen. Let me tell you, you can only understand it if you've been through it. You are effectively coerced into speaking, but as soon as you do, you open yourself up to being manipulated; you lose control.

The classic police interview technique involves asking the same questions over and over, covering incidents from every possible angle. Even if you're entirely innocent, it's easy to get confused and end up with tiny changes in your story each time you relay it. You can end up questioning your own version of events, even your sanity. If someone builds up a vivid enough picture of an alternative scenario in your mind, it's easy to forget where you started with it all.

The reason solicitors always advise their clients to answer 'no comment' to every question – even the seemingly innocent ones confirming someone's name, address or date of birth – is that it eliminates the possibility of messing up the details. Even if you have nothing to hide.

The time I spent in that interview room and the intense pressure I felt came back to me dramatically as I researched the pages that follow, and you will soon understand why.

There's a certain irony to the fact that one of the most outrageous and disturbing acts of racial injustice in recent years took place in an area once known for being the very model of racial harmony. It is a place we have visited twice before in the pages of this book, first to cover the three deaths that occurred during the 1919 uprising and then for the appalling miscarriage of justice that led to the hanging of Mahmood Mattan.

I'm talking, of course, about the Tiger Bay area of Cardiff.

On Valentine's Day 1988, the horrifically mutilated body of twenty-one-year-old prostitute Lynette White was found in a first-floor flat on James Street in Tiger Bay.

The flat where she died was as squalid and as miserable as her death itself. It was not her home, just the place she took clients. It had no heating or lighting and the only furniture was a filthy mattress in a corner of the living room. Lynette rented the flat from her friend and fellow prostitute Leanne Vilday.

Earlier that same week, Lynette's boyfriend and pimp, Stephen 'Pineapple' Miller – so named because of the way his dreadlocks

were always tied up high on top of his head – had approached
Vilday concerned that he had not seen or heard from Lynette in
several days. Vilday tried to get into the flat herself but found it to
be locked and Lynette had the only set of keys.

She eventually made a missing persons report to the police,
who broke into the property on the Sunday evening and immediately discovered Lynette's fully dressed body. She had suffered
at least fifty major stab wounds to her face and chest, as well as
defensive wounds to her hands and wrists. Her throat had been
cut so deeply from ear to ear that the bones of her spine were
exposed.

Whenever the police launch a murder investigation, the first
sixty minutes after a body has been found are by far the most
crucial. Known as the 'golden hour' it's when all the strongest evidence is often found and can be crucial in securing a conviction.
In the case of Lynette, that first hour revealed precious little.

There was no murder weapon at the scene and no clues as to
which client she had been with – the initial assumption being
that a client had been responsible – at the time of her death. With
no leads of any kind emerging from going over the crime scene
with a fine-toothed comb, it was clear the investigation would be
a challenging one.

Though Lynette had her regulars, the docks were also occasionally visited by people from out of town. Officers had to confront
the possibility that, if the killer had been a stranger and they had
managed to get away clean, they might never be found.

The scene was covered in blood and it was highly likely that
whoever attacked her would have got some on themselves as well.
This is quite common at crime scenes when domestic weapons,
such as kitchen knives, are used. They don't have the protective
hilts of military knives meaning that assailants will often cut their
hands in the process of stabbing someone and leave their own
blood at the crime scene. One hundred and fifty separate fingerprints and palm prints were found but with the police only too

aware that dozens of men would have entered and left the flat each week, they offered little hope of identifying a suspect.

But they had to try. A total of 324 men who were known to use local prostitutes, along with others with convictions for robbing prostitutes of their earnings or other violent sexual offences, were identified and interviewed. Thousands of house-to-house enquiries were conducted in the days following the murder. Thirty key suspects were identified and police began to eliminate them one by one.

They also began looking a little closer to home. Once they discovered that Stephen Miller was a pimp and had been living off the money Lynette had earned, another potential motive for murder emerged. Miller had an expensive drug habit and was wholly reliant on Lynette bringing home enough cash to fund it. Friends suggested that the reason Lynette had been missing for a few days before her death was because she was avoiding Stephen.

He became a key suspect and was brought in for questioning the day after the murder. His home and car were also searched but nothing incriminating was found. He gave a statement about his whereabouts at the time of the murder and this seemed to satisfy the police who eliminated him from their enquiries.

And then there was a breakthrough. A total of four separate witnesses came forward to say they had seen a pale, brown-haired man in the vicinity of the flat around the time the murder was thought to have been committed. He was in his mid-thirties with a dishevelled appearance and seemed to have a cut on his hand and blood on his clothing. He was crying and muttering incoherently to himself.

The following month Detective Chief Inspector John Williams, the officer in charge of the case, appeared on *Crimewatch UK* where he presented an e-fit of the suspect and stated that the man had been identified as the prime suspect in the killing. 'This man almost certainly had the blood of the deceased on him,' he said.

In the meantime, the list of thirty suspects had been worked through and all the men named were systematically eliminated until only one remained. Known only as 'Mr X', this suspect had convictions for sex offending and paedophilia. He lived only a short drive from the flat in James Street and admitted to police that he was a frequent user of prostitutes and had paid Lynette for sex in the past. The man also had a history of mental illness, having been classed as a psychopath by his doctor. He was unable to account for his movements on the night of her death. Like the man seen outside the flat in the early hours of the morning in the immediate aftermath of the murder, he was white.

The suspect became all the more significant when, two weeks into the inquiry, the forensic science team revealed that they had found blood at the scene that did not belong to Lynette. DNA evidence was still in its infancy, having only been used in a case for the first time around two years earlier, but it was possible to determine the blood type and sometimes that could help point the way to the guilty person.

The blood type was found to be AB, one of the rarest in the UK and found in only 3 per cent of the population. Mr X also had AB blood.

Numerous interviews with Mr X yielded nothing more but the whole team was convinced that they had their man. A decision was made to try to extract a DNA profile from the blood samples and Mr X was placed under close surveillance for several weeks in the hope he would reveal himself to be the killer.

By now nearly eight months had passed since the murder and the local community was becoming restless. The close-knit nature of Tiger Bay meant that Lynette was widely known and the idea that a stranger – no one living there could ever believe a local could have been responsible – had committed such a vile act was a constant source of discomfort.

Back in those days, DNA tests often took months to complete, so it wasn't until early November that the results came back from the lab. The blood at the scene did not belong to Mr X. The investigation was back at square one.

At this point, the officers leading the investigation seem to have given up. To speculate, it is likely that they believed the killer was someone merely passing through Cardiff docks who would never return to the area and likely never be caught.

But growing pressure from the press and the public meant they could not continue to fail to solve this horrific crime. Someone, somewhere seemingly made the decision that if the true killer was going to remain at large, the next best thing would be to find an individual or group of individuals whom they could pin the whole thing on.

The animosity between the police and members of the Black community that boiled over into deadly violence back in 1919 was still there in the background. How much temptation might there have been for the police to find a few shady characters who they would prefer to keep off the streets and somehow generate enough evidence to get a jury to convict them? They would then be able to kill two birds with one stone.

Prior to Mr X emerging as a suspect, police had been focusing their attention on the close circle of prostitutes and petty criminals that Lynette had considered to be her friends. Their interest in this group had peaked in May when, after a long night on drink and drugs, Leanne Vilday told a group of friends that 'Pineapple' and 'Dullah' had murdered Lynette right in front of her eyes.

Dullah was the nickname of Yusef Abdullahi, another Tiger Bay resident. He had already been interviewed as part of the initial sweep of men in the area and had given the police a solid alibi. At the time Lynette was stabbed, he had been working on a ship, the MV *Coral*, which was some eight miles away from the murder.

When the news got back to the police, they arranged an interview in which Vilday admitted saying those words but claimed that none of what she had said was true. She explained she was angry at Miller because of the way he had treated Lynette, taking up to £90 a day from her and therefore preventing her from ever being able to move away from the cycle of prostitution.

Desperate to find a way of extracting the truth from Vilday, the police decided to try a more unconventional approach to crime solving and hired a hypnotist to place her in a trance so that she could be interrogated on a deeper level. Though such evidence was unlikely to have ever been allowed to go before a court, the interview went ahead and revealed nothing of interest. Despite this, the police were convinced that there must have been some element of truth in her drunken rant.

Though both Miller and Abdullahi had already been eliminated from the inquiry, the police decided to look at them once again, this time a little more closely.

On 10 November 1988, just a day after the DNA results had cleared Mr X of any involvement in the crime, the police finally got the breakthrough they had been waiting for, even though it took the investigation in a whole new direction, and that new direction would be found to be based on fabrication and falsehood.

Violet Perriam worked as a receptionist at a health club in the heart of the docks and as a result knew many members of the local community. In a statement given to detectives she explained that she had been driving her car along James Street at around 1.30 a.m. on 14 February and had seen 'four coloured men' having an argument outside number seven, the same address as the flat where Lynette had been murdered.

She identified two of the men as Rashid Omar and John Actie. Asked whether Stephen Miller was among the group, Perriam said she was certain that he was not. Actie was the cousin of Ronnie Actie, Leanne Vilday's boyfriend, but the pair were not close and never socialised together.

By now the police had four core witnesses whom they were relying on to build a case. In addition to Leanne Vilday they had

Mark Grommek and Paul Atkins, both of them associates of Mr X who lived in the flat immediately above the one where Lynette had been murdered. Finally, there was Angela Psaila, a woman who lived a short distance from the flat and had an IQ of just fifty-five. She claimed to have heard screaming and run across the road, just in time to see Lynette being murdered by a group of men.

Using Perriam's statement as their guide, the police interviewed the four again and again. Each of them had a distrust of the police and plenty of reasons to avoid saying anything that might implicate them in other petty crimes they may have been involved with at the time. As a result, their accounts of their movements and what they saw changed time and time again.

It should have been clear that nothing the four said could be taken as gospel but the police helped to shape and reshape their accounts until they matched how investigators saw events unfolding, with any perceived inadequacies or contradictions smoothed away to present a seamless narrative. In order to achieve this, the police essentially treated their witnesses as if they were suspects, subjecting them to interview after interview and threatening them with prison themselves if they failed to provide the answers they were looking for.

Looking back, it's incredible that such abuses were able to go on and even more remarkable that the so-called investigation was allowed to proceed at all. Take, for example, Mark Grommek. He was told something along the lines of 'if you don't tell us what we want to know you'll be behind bars yourself'.

Several times the officers interviewing had made homophobic statements (he and Atkins were lovers and both had previous convictions, making them susceptible to police pressure tactics) and one would throw furniture around the room while questioning him. At no point was he asked if he would like a solicitor or someone else in the room with him.

In total, he was pulled in for questioning on at least fifty occasions. 'I was at the end of my tether, I really think I was on the verge of a nervous breakdown,' he said later. For the first few interviews he repeatedly stated that he didn't know anything about the murder but then on one especially challenging day, 22 November, he finally cracked. That morning he repeated what he had always previously said about knowing nothing but in the afternoon he began to give a highly detailed account. Not only did he suddenly know all about the circumstances surrounding the murder but he also named the same men now on the police's radar.

Both Grommek and Atkins provided new statements to the police claiming that they had seen a group of men, including Ronnie Actie and Abdullahi, outside the flat.

The same treatment was meted out to the others until the police finally got what they wanted. An official report would later note:

The rough edges of outstanding inconsistencies were in large part either removed or tempered (though not always eliminated) and there were some further fundamental changes to their accounts. By the end of this process, Psaila and Vilday had put themselves in the room at the time White was murdered together with the five men.

Psaila and Vilday said that they had been forced to cut Lynette White's wrists in order to involve and implicate themselves in White's murder and thereby be coerced into silence. Vilday also said that they had been threatened and told that they would be killed if they went to the police. Their combined evidence was that each of the five men had stabbed White.

And so it was that South Wales Police decided that five men – Stephen Miller, Yusef Abdullahi, Tony Paris (a prolific local shoplifter), Ronald Actie and John Actie – had been outside the flat on James Street in the early hours of the morning and had jointly been responsible for Lynette's murder.

There was just one problem: initial eyewitness accounts had identified a single white male as the most likely person responsible for Lynette's death. Now, ten months later, the police were about to accuse five Black men of the crime instead.

The arrests took place between 7 and 9 December. Despite the evidence provided by the four core witnesses, there wasn't much to go on. The police case was that each of the five had taken part in the murder of an innocent white woman as some kind of ritual sacrifice. It was a throwback to the days of scientific racism and played on the idea that Black people (though Yusef was actually mixed race) were savages and capable of behaving in a way that was frankly inhuman.

The first issue the police had to address was the complete and utter lack of evidence to support this theory. There was no forensic evidence of any kind linking any of the men to the flat, let alone to the murder. Had they truly all been in the room together, slashing and stabbing in close proximity, they would all have had traces of Lynette's blood on them. Several of the men had been interviewed as part of the initial sweep in the immediate aftermath of the body being discovered. When Stephen Miller was brought in, he happened to be wearing the same clothes he had worn the previous day, but no traces of blood were seen on him at all. In fact, there was no evidence that any of the suspects had ever been to the flat. No fingerprints, no fibres, no blood and no other scientific evidence. And none of the five had AB blood.

Then there was the fact that several of the men had cast iron alibis, none more so than Yusef, with several witnesses confirming that he was miles away at the time.

But perhaps the biggest issue with the group of suspects the police had assembled was that there was no evidence to suggest they were friends or ever hung out with one another. Even the two cousins almost never spent time together.

Faced with these issues, the police knew there was only one way to get the case to move forward. Someone was going to have to confess.

Stephen Miller seems to have been identified as the weakest link and therefore singled out for the harshest treatment. He was considered highly vulnerable, had the IQ of a twelve-year-old and could not read or write. But the police ignored all of that.

He was kept in a police cell for four days, undergoing nineteen interviews for a total of thirteen hours, during which he was intimidated and threatened repeatedly. Listening back to the tapes, it is clear what is going on. Using a classic good cop/bad cop routine, along with a dose of humiliation, the police slowly convinced him that he witnessed the murder of his girlfriend by the other suspects but, because he could do nothing to stop it, he had blanked out the memory. You can easily hear his distress as the allegations are fired towards him, and then his eventual relief when he understands that if he simply confesses and tells the officers what they want to hear, the torment will be over.

Although reading the exchange on the printed page is a poor substitute for hearing it, you need only a few lines to appreciate just how badly he was being treated:

STEPHEN WAYNE MILLER: They can lock me up for fifty
        billion years, I said I was not there.
DC GREENWOOD: 'Cause you don't wanna be there.
STEPHEN WAYNE MILLER: I was not there.
DC GREENWOOD: You don't wanna be there because if . . .
STEPHEN WAYNE MILLER: I was not there.
DC GREENWOOD: As soon as you say that you're there you
        know you're involved.
STEPHEN WAYNE MILLER: I was not there.
DC GREENWOOD: You know you were involved in it.
STEPHEN WAYNE MILLER: I was not involved and I wasn't
        there.
DC GREENWOOD: Yes you were there.
STEPHEN WAYNE MILLER: I was not there.

The tapes are filled with these kinds of exchanges. Despite having a solicitor present at most of the interviews, there was never any attempt to intervene.

Confessions were and sometimes still are compelling evidence when they reveal information that is unknown to the police and could only have been known by the offender, especially if this information can later be independently verified. But this wasn't the case with Stephen. Nothing he told the police was new, other than the information they fed to him in order to corroborate the story they wanted to tell.

The following morning, the questioning began again and through insidious questioning and the power of suggestion, Stephen became convinced that perhaps the vast quantities of drink and drugs he usually consumed had impacted his memory.

'I am just ... I am just certain that I wasn't there that's all, I am, I am certain I wasn't there but it could ... it could happen, it could have happened.'

Once police managed to open up that tiny chink of admission, they forced it wider and wider until they finally achieved their goal. After denying any form of involvement 307 times, Miller finally confessed. He had been there when Lynette died. He had personally stabbed her at least once and the other four had all taken part as well.

On 11 December 1988, Stephen Miller, Yusef Abdullahi, Anthony Paris, Ronald Actie and John Actie were charged with White's murder and remanded in custody. They would soon become known as the Cardiff Five.

The core four were set to be the key prosecution witnesses in the trial ahead but behind the scenes, cracks were beginning to show. In January, Leanne Vilday wrote a letter to a friend which set out exactly why she had made statements which she knew to be false.

She explained that the police had given her a stark choice – either help create the false narrative that would convict the accused or be charged with murder herself. Having seen the length that the police were prepared to go to in order to create fake evidence to support a bogus prosecution, Vilday was in no doubt the threat was a genuine one.

The trial of the five defendants began on 3 October 1989 before Mr Justice McNeill. The prosecution case was that Lynette had left Stephen Miller after an argument. With no income of his own, meaning he was unable to fund his drug habit, he became increasingly furious. He tracked her down to the flat in James Street, along with his co-accused, intending to teach her a lesson, but things got carried away and Lynette ended up dying.

The main evidence supporting this version of events was the confession that Stephen had made, the accounts of the core four and a few other witnesses the police had gathered together claiming that at various times, other members of the Cardiff Five had confessed to their involvement. However, unlike Stephen's confession, none of them had been captured on tape so their impact was minimal.

But none of it made any sense. With Stephen wholly reliant on Lynette and her reliant on her looks to attract punters, it would make no sense for him to attack let alone kill her, but such was the case put before the jury.

The trial reached its closing stages at the end of February 1990, by which time each of the Cardiff Five had been in prison on remand for more than a year. Mr Justice McNeill had begun drafting his summing up in which he pointed out the weakness of the evidence presented by the prosecution.

'There is a suggestion that the evidence against each of the five defendants has been made up ... there is not a shred of evidence that it happened.'

But he never got to deliver these words to the jury. On the morning of 26 February, the judge died suddenly of a heart attack. The jury was discharged, and a second trial was arranged. This began in May and concluded in November 1990. This meant the Cardiff Five were on remand for almost two years and that their murder trial was, at the time, the longest in British legal history.

Stephen Miller, Yusef Abdullahi and Tony Paris were all convicted of murder while Ronnie and John Actie were both acquitted.

But there was a problem. The prosecution case had been that all five men had acted together. This was what Vilday and the others had said. But Stephen had said that the Actie cousins had been outside of the room during the time the stabbing was taking place. That meant the jury had chosen to believe Stephen's account over and above that of the core four.

There was also an elephant in the room: no one had given much thought to the presence of the AB blood at the murder scene. There could be little doubt that it belonged to someone who had been involved in Lynette's death and Stephen's confession had said nothing about anyone else being present at the time. The matter was simply pushed under the carpet.

The families of the convicted men, now known as the Cardiff Three, refused to take the verdicts lying down and began a grass roots campaign to prove their innocence. This was bolstered in February 1992 when an episode of the BBC's investigative documentary series *Panorama* questioned the objectivity of the police investigation and the credibility of the prosecution witnesses. The suggestion was that a miscarriage of justice had taken place.

After a number of unsuccessful attempts, an appeal for Stephen Miller was heard over four days in December 1992 before the then Lord Chief Justice, Lord Taylor, Mr Justice Laws and Mr Justice Popplewell. Much of the case focused on the interview tapes as it had been clear from the verdict that these were what had influenced the jury the most.

Acting on behalf of Stephen Miller, Michael Mansfield, QC

argued that both judges in the criminal trials had been wrong to allow the jury to hear the recorded confessions as they had been tainted by the officers' 'oppressive' conduct. Rather than a search for the truth the interviews were, he said, an attempt by the police, using any method short of physical violence, to get the stories of Mr Miller and Ms Vilday to match up.

Breaking protocol to remark on the conduct of the police during the hearing, the Lord Chief Justice said: 'We are bound to say that on hearing tape seven, each member of this court was horrified. Miller was bullied and hectored. The officers, particularly Detective Constable Greenwood, were not questioning him so much as shouting at him what they wanted him to say. Short of physical violence, it is hard to conceive of a more hostile and intimidating approach by officers to a suspect.'

He asked for copies of the recordings to be sent to both the chairman of the Royal Commission on Criminal Justice and the Director of Public Prosecutions as an 'example of what we hope we shall never hear again in this court'.

On 10 December the convictions of all three men were declared 'unsafe and unsatisfactory' and the trio were immediately released from prison.

The case of the Cardiff Three has gone on to be cited as one of the most blatant miscarriages of justice of recent times, but not everyone felt that way.

Having a conviction quashed is not the same as being found innocent of a crime. It simply means the conviction has been ruled unsafe. In the immediate aftermath South Wales Police announced they had no plans to reopen their investigation into the murder of Lynette White.

The implication was clear: they had found the people responsible for her death and the men had now been freed on what was considered to be a technicality. Though they were no longer behind bars, the case remained closed.

The years that followed saw widespread criticism of the police handling of the case which, in June 1999, led South Wales Police to conduct a review of the original murder investigation.

Two retired detectives from Lancashire Constabulary, William Hacking and John Thornley, were appointed to ensure independence. At the same time Dr Angela Gallop was brought in to review all the forensic evidence in the case.

The 477-page report the two Lancashire detectives produced was packed with details and criticisms of the handling of the case. It made more than one hundred recommendations including reopening the investigation into the murder and applying the very latest forensic techniques to all the available samples.

They also recommended that a criminal investigation be opened into the conduct of the officers who carried out the original investigation and obtained the statements from the core four and Cardiff Five 'in an effort to ascertain if any criminal offences have been committed. Particular emphasis should be placed on the possible offences of perjury and/or conspiracy to pervert the course of justice.'

While these and other recommendations were being examined, new developments in forensic science meant it had finally become possible to extract a full DNA profile from the 'foreign' AB blood sample that had been found at the murder scene.

At first no match was found on the DNA database so the scientists tried out a new method that looked for DNA of people who may be related to a suspect. A match was found with a fourteen-year-old boy, who was well known to the police, but clearly too young to have been involved as he would not have been born at the time of the murder.

Investigating the boy's family background, the police started looking at his uncle, Jeffrey Gafoor, as a potential suspect. When police went to visit to request a blood sample, he said he was happy to provide one but added: 'I knew Lynette. I have had sex with her ... A week before she was murdered ... In the flat ... the one in which she was murdered.'

Detectives were immediately concerned that he was attempting to provide an excuse for why his DNA might have been found at the flat. He was placed under surveillance while they waited for the results to come back. With hindsight, it had been an incredibly wise decision. The very next day he was spotted purchasing a large quantity of paracetamol. Members of the surveillance team forced entry and discovered he had taken a huge overdose.

On the way to hospital Gafoor said: 'Just for the record, I did kill Lynette White. I've been waiting for this for fifteen years. Whatever happens to me I deserve ... I sincerely hope that I die.' But he lived. Charged with murder, he appeared at Cardiff Crown Court on 4 July 2003 and pleaded guilty. He was sentenced to life imprisonment with a minimum term of thirteen years.

With the actual killer of Lynette White behind bars, senior officers within South Wales Police had to finally admit that their original investigation had been deeply flawed and that some officers might even have broken the law in their eagerness to pursue what turned out to be a group of entirely innocent men.

Over the course of the following year, approximately thirty individuals were taken into custody in relation to the investigation, with nineteen of them being either active or retired police officers. In 2007, three of those who had testified on behalf of the prosecution in the initial murder trial were found guilty of lying under oath and received an eighteen-month prison sentence.

By 2011, eight former officers faced charges of conspiring to obstruct justice. This led to what became the largest trial for police corruption in the history of British criminal law. In 2012, an additional four officers were scheduled to face similar charges. However, in November 2011, the trial fell apart when the defence argued that essential documents, which they were entitled to review, had been destroyed.

As a direct consequence of this, the judge determined that the defendants were unable to receive an impartial trial, leading to their acquittal. In January 2012, the missing documents reappeared. They were still in their original box.

In February 2015, Theresa May, then Home Secretary, announced an inquiry into the collapse of the police corruption trial, to be conducted by Richard Horwell, QC. May dismissed demands for a full public inquiry, but stated: 'There remain unanswered questions regarding why no individuals were held accountable for this grave miscarriage of justice.' Horwell's report was not published until 2017 but immediately revealed the failings that denied justice to the Cardiff Three. While he understood that the accused were convinced the collapse of the trial against the fifteen officers was the result of corruption and their colleagues attempting to protect them, this conclusion had 'not been supported by the evidence'.

Rather, a mixture of human error, poor training, inexperience and a general lack of common sense had been responsible. None of this came as much of a surprise. When a force can arrest and prosecute five Black men for murder when all the evidence points towards a single white suspect, you don't end up with a huge amount of faith in how competent they will be, even when investigating themselves.

Quite rightly, Mr Horwell described what happened as an 'embarrassment on a national scale'.

By now you'll be picking up on several common themes associated with the cases of injustice featured in this book. One of the more prominent ones highlighted by the Cardiff Three is that the police officers involved are rarely held accountable for their actions.

Lovelock, the man who shot my mother, was acquitted in court despite it later emerging that the raid had been botched from the start. Ridgewell, the officer who 'fitted up' the Oval Four and others, was later arrested and jailed but for crimes that had nothing to do with his corrupt practices.

Journalist Tom Mangold, who covered the Cardiff Three case for the BBC, said in 2012 it was 'one of the biggest on-going scandals in British criminal justice'.

Even if you get an apology and full admission that the injustice was influenced by prejudicial attitudes of the officers involved, it's rare for those officers themselves to face any punishment. And with so few officers being held to account, it is little wonder that others feel emboldened to act with impunity.

Whether they fail to investigate a case properly, treat victims as if they were offenders or choose to rely on the accounts of those who are white rather than those who are Black, the end result is the same: a lack of transparency, non-existent accountability and zero justice for those who need it most.

Another prominent theme can be summed up by the legal maxim, 'Justice delayed is justice denied.' It was first coined by British Prime Minister William Gladstone in 1868 and repeated by Martin Luther King Jr in his 1963 *Letter From Birmingham Jail*. It means that if you are wronged and fail to get justice in a timely fashion, then it's just as bad as not getting any justice at all. But time and time again in this book, both in the cases we have covered up to this point and the ones that will follow, we see that obtaining any form of justice can take many years, and even several decades.

Too many individuals and their families are having to live with the consequences of injustice for far too long and the level of drive and energy needed to constantly battle against the odds is often too much for many.

Research by the Institute of Race Relations suggests there are around five racist murders each year in England and Wales but most pass by relatively unnoticed. But for one such murder in 1993, the tenacity, courage and sheer persistence of the parents of the victim would ensure that the case is still being discussed more than three decades later.

12

Stephen Lawrence

In early 1991 Rolan Adams was fifteen and just about to take his GCSEs. He was a talented musician, while both he and his younger brother Nathan were gifted footballers.

On Friday, 21 February, Rolan and Nathan had played a game of table tennis at a youth centre in Thamesmead before heading off to catch a bus home to Abbey Wood. As they waited, a gang of up to fifteen white youths saw and chased them. Some of the gang members were shouting racist abuse and one of them pulled out a butterfly knife and stabbed Rolan in the throat. He started to run and told Nathan to do the same and in the process the pair became separated. When Nathan returned to the bus stop a few moments later, his found his brother bleeding to death in the middle of the road.

This was not the first racist attack to take place in the area. Several other young Black and Asian boys had been left needing hospital treatment in the months leading up to the attack on Rolan. The problem had become increasing acute since 1989 when the British National Party (BNP) relocated its headquarters to a building in nearby Welling.

The gang responsible for the attack on Nathan and Rolan had been among those regularly targeting the local Black community and the failure of the police to effectively deal with the issue meant they had become bolder. They even named themselves the Nazi Turn Outs.

As the attackers were well known, it did not take long for the police to track them down and make a series of arrests, but rather than remanding them all in custody while further investigations were carried out, the court chose to bail them. As a result, gang members continued to harass members of the local community.

From the outset, both the police and the CPS refused to acknowledge that Rolan's murder was driven by racial motives. They downplayed this aspect and instead incorrectly labelled it as a territorial dispute. This issue has long plagued victims of racially motivated crimes, as the police and other public agencies often fail to acknowledge the racial motivations and intents of those responsible. They ultimately perpetuated the racist stereotype of assuming that Rolan and Nathan, as Black boys, could not be wholly innocent. It was an attitude we would see play out once more with the Stephen Lawrence murder.

The main witness in the case was Nathan but he was treated in a way that suggested the police thought he was actually involved in the crime, not a victim. Although he had also been attacked during the incident, nobody was ever arrested as a result. In the following weeks, he was stopped and searched in the street on multiple occasions. At other times he was taken into custody and charged with various crimes. At one point he was told that he was banned from visiting Thamesmead.

Of the white youths taken into custody for the murder of Rolan, only Mark Thornborrow ended up facing murder charges. Although the prosecution attempted to remove racial elements from Rolan's murder during the court case, the judge presiding

over the case concluded that the murder was racially driven and
sentenced Mark Thornborrow accordingly. This marked the first
time the state officially acknowledged Rolan Adams's murder was
in fact a racially motivated attack.

I had met Rolan a couple of times, though I was too young to
remember much about him. My mum was friends with some of his
family and he and his wider family would sometimes come to visit.
As a result, his death resonated with me even more deeply than
many others. But two years later, the murder of another young
Black man would go on to have far greater impact, not just for me
but for the country as a whole.

I still remember exactly where I was when I first heard the news
about the murder of Stephen Lawrence. A whole group of us were
at my mate Martin's house in Kennington when we learned that
an eighteen-year-old Black boy had been stabbed to death by some
white teenagers in Eltham the previous night.

For me it almost seemed as though we were going back in
time – surely this sort of thing just didn't happen any more. But
there were other reasons this death resonated. Stephen was exactly
the same age as me and the random way in which he had been
targeted – simply because of the colour of his skin – meant that it
could have been any one of us, any of my friends.

In the years after my mum had been shot, I had taken great
strength from growing up in a strong Black community. My
school had a majority of Black students and the white pupils that
were there knew that racism was entirely unacceptable – that was
something we had helped them to understand over time – so that
became another safe environment for me.

So the fact that some white boys could just turn around and kill
one of us just seemed so wrong. I felt that I wanted to go there and
find the people responsible and teach them a lesson they would
never forget. I was saying to my friends, *We need to go down there,*

we need to find them. I felt we were being disrespected as a people and that we could not let them get away with it. Thankfully my friends talked me out of going there right away.

Instead, I was one of many who sat back and watched the events unfold, unaware of just how massive the impact of that one murder would come to be.

The last day of Stephen Lawrence's life contained little to make it stand out from any other. He had spent the morning at Blackheath Bluecoat School, where he was studying for his A levels with ambitions to become an architect. After speaking with one of his teachers about his coursework, he spent the afternoon in Lewisham looking around the shops before heading over to the house of his uncle in Plumstead. There he was joined by his best friend, Duwayne Brooks, and the two played *Street Fighter II* until it was time to head home.

Stephen's mother, Doreen, had been away from home for a few days attending a course so he was keen to get back in time to speak to her. His father, Neville, was out of work at the time and had been feeling a bit down that morning so he also wanted to check up on him.

The first bus they caught followed a longer route that would have got them home too late, so they decided to get off at Well Hall Road in Eltham, to wait for a bus that would get them back sooner. Stephen stepped across the road to see if the bus they wanted was on its way. It was about 10.30 p.m. and the pair were in high spirits, chatting and practising dance moves.

Around this time, Duwayne saw a group of up to six white youths on the other side of the road. He called out to ask if Stephen could see the bus yet. One of the white youths heard him and called out in reply, 'What, what nigger?' The members of the white group quickly crossed the road and within moments Stephen was surrounded.

Duwayne began running and told Stephen to follow him, but wasn't sure if he was going to. He would later recall: 'Everything flashed in my head. Why hasn't he run? What's he still doing there? Maybe he has run. I hope he has run. All these things were flashing in my head in that split second before I turned round to make sure he was behind me . . . I was sure he was running but couldn't bring myself to turn around. I was too scared. I started to cry . . . Then my legs went to jelly.'

There were three people waiting at the bus stop, all of whom witnessed what happened next. They would describe the attack as sudden and brief, but none of them were later able to recognise any of the men involved. Stephen sustained stab wounds on each side of his chest, both penetrating five inches deep. After breaking away from his assailants, he managed to run more than one hundred yards alongside Duwayne before falling to the ground.

Duwayne then found a phone box and rang 999 asking for an ambulance, and he gave the address of the phone box not knowing it was incorrect. Duwayne sounded so manic that the operator worried he was having some kind of breakdown. Instead of sending an ambulance, they decided to send a police car first, to make sure he was not dangerous.

Duwayne tried to stop one of the many passing cars but they simply drove on. But a white couple called Mr and Mrs Taaffe who were out walking did offer their assistance. An off-duty police officer stopped his car and covered Stephen with a blanket. Then Louise Taaffe comforted him with what may have been the last words Stephen was to hear. She put her hand on Stephen's face and spoke softly into his ear. 'You are loved, you are loved,' she told him.

The first two duty police officers to arrive checked his vital signs but not the full extent of his injuries. The first inspector 'simply took it for granted that someone junior was appropriately in charge of Stephen'.

Extraordinarily, no log or record was made of the event. Officers did not even conduct house-to-house enquiries in and around the area where the youths had escaped. They thought it was too late to wake up local residents. Duwayne tried to explain what he had seen and told the police that Stephen had been hit over the head. But Duwayne didn't know that his friend had actually been stabbed, the blade entering his shoulder and travelling downwards, puncturing his lung.

Stephen was wearing lots of layers and it was dark, so the stab wounds were not visible let alone obvious. The wounds were only discovered when the paramedics arrived around fifteen minutes later, but by then it was too late.

From the start, the officers were not buying the story of the gang of five white boys who had made racist remarks, stabbed Stephen then run off. They didn't believe these two Black boys had simply been waiting for a bus. As far as they were concerned, the attack was more likely to be the result of a drug deal gone wrong or a fight over territory.

At the Lawrence family home, Doreen had just arrived back from her course and there was a knock at the front door. It was their neighbour and his son who told them there had been an incident on Well Hall Road and that Stephen might have been hurt.

Stephen's parents called 999 but couldn't get any answers so they jumped into their car and headed to the scene. By this time everyone had cleared away so they headed to the hospital where they found Duwayne in a state of shock and almost unable to speak, despite Doreen repeatedly asking him what had happened.

At 11.12 p.m., they were all informed that Stephen had been pronounced dead.

Utterly distraught, Doreen and Neville would go home to tell their two remaining children what had happened, but Duwayne would spend the night at Plumstead police station, being questioned again and again about the events of the evening. At one point, the officers asked him whether he was completely sure that the assailants had used the n-word in the lead-up to the attack. Could that simply be Stephen's nickname?

Within twenty-four hours of the murder, police received no less than twenty-six anonymous tip-offs providing the names of five youths who were thought to have been responsible for the murder. Some tips came in by phone, some were made in person. The same list of names was also sent to Plumstead police station and placed in a phone box close to the scene of the stabbing. The names were Neil Acourt, David Norris, Jamie Acourt, Gary Dobson and Luke Knight.

Despite this, the police decided not to arrest the suspects but instead place them under surveillance. The officer in charge of the case at the time would later say he was unaware that he could have arrested the boys on the basis of information alone (i.e., them being named as suspects) rather than actual evidence of crime.

It was just the start of what would turn out to be a hugely bungled investigation. Even the surveillance operation that was set up proved to be a failure. There was a delay because the officers assigned to the task refused to work at the weekend. By the time the operation got underway, there were a number of issues with the cameras and a lack of communication between the different teams involved.

Early on, Jamie Acourt was seen leaving his home with a large black bin liner. Instead of following him to see what he was getting rid of, the surveillance team chose to stay in place. He later returned, minus the bag. With hindsight, it seems highly likely that this contained some of the clothes that he and the others had on during the night of the murder, but because the items have never been recovered, it is simply not possible to say.

In the meantime Doreen and Neville had family liaison officers assigned to them. Usually these officers are there to provide support and form a crucial link between the investigation and the victims. However, it did not take long for the Lawrence family to realise the liaison officer appeared to be intent on gathering information. The line of questioning they were pursuing seemed to be all about Stephen's alleged connections to crime and the underworld. It felt as though the police were trying to support their own narrative about Stephen being a gang member.

Neville told the officers to leave after just a few days and never return. The family had not had any previous dealings with the police and trusted the authorities to do the right thing in their time of need. They were left bitterly disappointed.

Five days after the murder hundreds of people attended a vigil to demand that something be done to protect others like Stephen but still no arrests were made.

It was around this time that Nelson Mandela arrived in the UK as part of a short state visit. The Anti-Nazi League arranged for him to have a meeting with the Lawrence family. The aftermath of the meeting was televised with Mandela explaining how in South Africa, Black lives were cheap and that he was incredibly surprised and saddened to see that the same thing now seemed to be happening in the UK.

The following day, despite there being no other developments in the case other than a wave of publicity in the light of Mandela's visit, the police arrested all the prime suspects. They carried out searches of their houses and took away a number of items. However, as more than two weeks had elapsed since the murder, the suspects would have had plenty of time to rid themselves of anything incriminating. During their interviews, all five refused to say anything except for 'no comment'.

The only one who needed to provide more of an explanation for his whereabouts was Gary Dobson. Another witness had placed him at the house of Neil and Jamie late in the evening of the murder, though Dobson had initially said he had spent the evening at home. He then changed his story. While he claimed to have spent the whole evening at home, he now recalled that he had visited the Acourts shortly before midnight in order to borrow a Bob Marley CD which he wanted to listen to. It was a pathetic attempt to portray himself as someone who could not possibly be in any way racist simply because he listened to reggae music.

Dobson also made the mistake of claiming that he did not know David Norris at all. But police found a picture of him and Norris standing together and smiling directly outside the Acourt house, exactly one week before the murder.

In early May, a protest took place against the BNP who many claimed were stirring up further racial hatred in the area. Concerned the protest might end in violence, the Lawrence family decided not to attend but among those who did was Duwayne Brooks. He would eventually be pictured helping to turn over a car. It did little to help rid himself of the police allegations that he was involved in violence.

The next day, the story was covered in the *Daily Mail* not only with a picture of Duwayne but also with one of the Lawrence family, implying that they had been at the event. Neville was outraged and called up the editor, Paul Dacre, who he knew a little, having been involved in doing some plastering at his house a few years earlier.

Dacre apologised, claiming he did not realise that Stephen was Neville's son. He then offered the couple the chance to put the record straight with an exclusive story for the *Mail*. It would be a connection that would become even more important in the years that followed.

On 29 July came a devastating blow – the Crown Prosecution Service deemed that there was insufficient evidence to bring the prosecution. The five suspects were off the hook.

Appalled, the family decided to bring a private prosecution, which anyone is able to do. A huge fundraising campaign was launched to cover the considerable costs and many of the lawyers on the case agreed to work for free.

Private prosecutions are rare and this would be the first ever in connection with a racially motivated crime, but the family were determined to get justice. There was one massive gamble that they were taking, however. In the event that the private prosecution failed, the suspects could never be tried again due to the law of double jeopardy which prevented people being tried more than once for the same crime, even if new evidence against them were presented. If the case against them was thrown out, they would be forever free of the possibility of facing justice.

The police were still involved in the investigation, despite having no part in the prosecution. In order to bolster the case they had decided to plant a secret camera in Dobson's flat. It quickly captured the five suspects talking about their hatred of Black people, praising Enoch Powell, graphically describing how they would like to torture and kill as many Black people as possible, and playing around with knives.

One particularly shocking piece of footage showed Neil Acourt wielding a knife using a strange overarm strike, as if he were bowling a cricket ball. It was significant because it was the movement that Duwyane Brooks had mistaken for a strike to Stephen's head with a cosh, but was actually the exact move that would have caused the wound to Stephen's shoulder that ultimately led to his death.

Although the deeply disturbing footage provided compelling evidence of the character of the five, none of it provided any direct link to the murder of Stephen.

Almost from the start, the prosecution started to fall apart. Duwayne Brooks should have been the main witness but this was undermined by a statement given by one of the police officers who claimed that immediately following an identification parade, Duwayne had expressed uncertainty about the people he had picked out.

Duwayne's credibility had been further undermined after he had been charged for his part in the BNP protest where a car had been turned over, though the case was thrown out by the judge. (Duwayne's presence had come to light as a result of intelligence passed on by Peter Francis, one of three undercover officers who had been tasked to spy on the Lawrence family.) His evidence was deemed unreliable, depriving the prosecution of a major part of its case and forcing it to withdraw.

This means the jury never got to see the secret camera footage. All the defendants were allowed to go free. Upon hearing the news, Doreen Lawrence collapsed.

An inquest into Stephen's death was held on 13 February 1997. The five suspects attended but all of them claimed the right of silence and provided no information whatsoever.

However, the inquest verdict was that Stephen Lawrence was unlawfully killed in a completely unprovoked racist attack by five white youths. The inquest jury had no power to accuse the suspects of murder, but they had come as close as possible to doing so. The next day the then Commissioner of the Metropolitan Police had lunch with Paul Dacre, editor of the *Daily Mail*. He explained that the five were undoubtedly guilty but that the police had simply not managed to find the evidence to prove this.

The next day, at least in part because of his friendship with Neville Lawrence and sympathy for his plight, Paul Dacre decided to run one of the most compelling and shocking front pages in British newspaper history. It featured images of all five suspects in the death of Stephen underneath the headline MURDERERS. A short sub-headline stated that the paper believed these men had got away with murder and invited them to sue the paper if the claim was not true. Although the parents of the five made a huge fuss, no legal action was ever taken.

The general election in May that year saw a Labour government come to power. While the Conservatives had paid little attention to the Lawrence case, the new Home Secretary Jack Straw brought new life to the proceedings. The first thing he did was set up a meeting with the family – something his predecessor had never done. He also arranged for a former High Court judge to open a public inquiry into the circumstances of Stephen's death. Finally there was a chance for the family to get answers as to exactly what had gone wrong.

Launched in March 1998 the Macpherson Inquiry made some truly shocking discoveries including that not only was no first aid administered to Stephen by police, the first aid kit was not even taken out of the car. Although all of the officers on the scene had passed first aid courses, none of them knew the ABC – 'airways, breathing, circulation'; they literally didn't know the first thing about first aid.

Once again the five prime suspects were called to give evidence to the inquiry and once again they refused to give any information. As they strutted out of the hearing, the crowd became hostile and it seemed like the whole event might descend into violence. Each one was walking with a deliberate gangster swagger and wearing dark glasses as if they were movie stars on the red carpet. Knowing they had refused to meaningfully engage in the inquiry had got many people's backs up and they played to this, holding out their hands and gesturing for anyone who felt up to it to have a go.

I was there that day, part of that crowd. I wanted to be there because I was always mindful of the fact that people came out to support us after my mum had been shot. I was too young to join in back then, but this was a different story; I was old enough now. Whenever the opportunity came along for me to support others, I would, because that's what had been done for my mum and family back in 1985.

Fighting broke out, hot drinks and empty bottles were hurled at the five, staining their bright white shirts, and at least one, David Norris, exchanged both insults and punches with some of the demonstrators before being shoved into a white police van and driven away at high speed.

Doreen and Neville were forced to make an appearance and appeal for calm.

Before they left the five released a handwritten statement headed 'On behalf of all five of us'. It read:

In 1993 we were all arrested for the murder of Steven Lawrence, which we all vehemently deny.

We do sympathise with Mr and Mrs Lawrence and the tragic

loss of their son. We understand their quest to discover what ·
happened to their son and why no one has been convicted of
his murder.

We have no knowledge of this murder, we were not involved, we did not kill Steven Lawrence.

The fact that, after so many years, they had not even noticed that
they were spelling his name wrongly spoke volumes about them.

In 1999, the Macpherson Report was released. It concluded
that the investigation had been hindered by a mix of professional
incompetence, institutional racism and poor leadership.

The report spanned 389 pages and made seventy recommendations aimed at demonstrating a policy of 'zero tolerance' towards
racism in society. These suggestions included initiatives to change
police attitudes and enhance accountability within the civil service, NHS, judiciary and other public institutions. Among the
most significant of the proposed changes was the elimination of
the 'double jeopardy' rule, which prevented a person from being
tried for the same offence more than once.

Sir William Macpherson had enough evidence to be convinced
that the Metropolitan Police was institutionally racist. He defined
this as:

> The collective failure of an organisation to provide an appro-
> priate and professional service to people because of their colour,
> culture, or ethnic origin.
>
> It can be seen or detected in processes, attitudes and be-
> haviour which amount to discrimination through unwitting
> prejudice, ignorance, thoughtlessness and racist stereotyping
> which disadvantage minority ethnic people.

In addition to the recommendation to scrap double jeopardy, the
report led to an equally important but lesser reported change in
the law. The introduction of the Race Relations Amendment Act

in 2000 required public bodies to actively work towards equality. This crucial piece of legislation made it compulsory for entities such as police forces, local councils and government departments to demonstrate their commitment to fair and equal treatment for all individuals.

By 2006 a series of significant advances in forensic science enabled the Metropolitan Police to revisit a previously unresolved case, leading to the conviction of the individuals responsible for the death of ten-year-old Damilola Taylor, who was originally from Nigeria. The initial investigation had overlooked crucial DNA evidence, which later played a key role in securing the convictions. Inspired by this approach, Scotland Yard's new Lawrence team collaborated with LGC Forensics to perform a thorough review of the cold case.

Gradually, after months of rigorous testing, intriguing evidence came to light. Technicians discovered minuscule blood flakes in the bag containing Gary Dobson's jacket. The DNA extracted from these flakes corresponded to that of Stephen Lawrence. This was supported by the presence of fibres transferred from the victim's clothing.

The most significant discovery was a tiny droplet of blood embedded in the fabric of the jacket's collar. Once more, the DNA matched with Stephen Lawrence's. It could only have come from being freshly splashed at the crime scene itself.

Edward Jarman, the scientist responsible for retrieving the DNA, said that it was only observable under a microscope and represented the tiniest blood evidence ever utilised to initiate a prosecution. The defence claimed that the stain resulted from contamination due to mishandling of the exhibits over the years. However, extensive testimony from witnesses, detailing how the items had been transported, managed and stored, provided sufficient counter-evidence. Gary Dobson and David Norris were convicted on 3 January 2012.

Though the pair had been found guilty based on what seemed

to be minimal evidence – described by the defence as not even enough to fill a teaspoon – it was the quality of this evidence, not the quantity, that ultimately mattered most.

In June 2023, following an investigation by the BBC, details emerged of a possible sixth suspect in the murder case.

When giving his original statement to the investigation, Duwayne Brooks had described an attacker resembling Matthew White to the police, but White was initially treated as a witness rather than a suspect. It was not until 2000 and then again in 2013 that White was considered a suspect and was interviewed by detectives and eventually charged.

However, the charges were dropped after the CPS decided there was not sufficient evidence to move forward with a prosecution.

White, who had been a drug user at the time of Stephen Lawrence's murder and went on to become a drug addict, died in 2021 at the age of fifty. Throughout his life he worked only occasionally, sometimes as a scaffolder and sometimes as a gardener. He accumulated a significant criminal record for theft and other offences and had served time in prison. Shortly before he died, White was convicted of assaulting a Black shop worker who had caught him attempting to shoplift.

His body had not been found for several days after his death, meaning a cause could not be determined. However, a police investigation found no suspicious circumstances. White was later reported to have been suffering from a range of health problems linked to his drug use. He was also said to have been suicidal and had once overdosed by accident.

There is no doubt that his passing closes one chapter in this tragic saga for the family, but with three of the original five suspects still to face the full force of the law, the battle for justice goes on.

*

Years after Stephen's murder I was introduced to Neville Lawrence at an event hosted by *The Voice* newspaper and we instantly connected and have stayed in touch ever since. It was in part because of the suffering we had endured, along with our joint protracted battles for justice, but also something more personal.

Stephen and I had been the same age and that, along with the shared surname, almost made it feel as though we were from the same family.

His death had an impact on me in other ways too. My mum had always been a big reader and one book I remember her poring over during the last years of her life was by David Icke, the footballer turned conspiracy theorist, called *And the Truth Shall Set You Free*. After she died I found her copy and saw that she had a newspaper clipping about the Stephen Lawrence case tucked inside.

In that clipping, someone had spoken about the importance of allowing the truth to emerge if you want to be free of past trauma. Once we finally had our victory in my mum's case I had those same words added to her gravestone.

I knew that sentiment was close to her heart and when I finally felt we had delivered on what she wanted, I wanted to make sure it was acknowledged.

13

Dalian Atkinson

Shortly after 1 a.m. on the morning of 15 August 2016, West Mercia Police received a 999 call from a woman living in Telford who was worried about the welfare of one of her neighbours.

She told the call handlers that a few minutes earlier, a car had pulled up outside the house of an elderly man who lived alone and that the driver, a young Black man, had got out of the vehicle and gone up to the property, shouting loudly and angrily punching and kicking at the front door. She explained the young man had shouted something along the lines of 'You'd better let me in, or you're dead.' Soon afterwards, the door had opened and the young man had vanished inside. 'So I'm a little worried,' the woman said.

She knew the neighbour's surname was Atkinson but couldn't remember his first name. The call handler said they would send someone round to investigate.

The neighbour was Ernest Atkinson, an eighty-five-year-old retired church deacon, and the young man hammering at the door was his son Dalian, a former professional footballer who had once had the world at his feet. Within the space of ninety minutes, he would be dead at the hands of the police.

Dalian Atkinson had been born in Shrewsbury, Shropshire, in 1968, and first showed promise as a footballer during his primary school days. By his mid-teens he had enrolled at Ipswich Town's academy and soon turned professional, gaining prominence after scoring a hat-trick against Middlesbrough at the age of nineteen.

His profile rose when he joined Sheffield Wednesday and he then went on to become the first ever Black player to sign with Spanish club Real Sociedad. However, he is best known for his 1991 £1.6 million record signing with Aston Villa.

There, his ability to run fast with the ball at his feet meant his goals were often spectacular. In a match against Wimbledon in 1992 he picked up the ball in his own half and made it past half a dozen players before chipping it over the head of the goalkeeper and into the back of the net. It was later voted *Match of the Day*'s Goal of the Season.

By then Dalian was earning £3,000 per week and being tipped as a future England star, destined for even greater extremes of wealth and success. But a combination of persistent injuries and problems arising from his personal life conspired to prevent him from reaching his full potential.

In the years that followed he scored a further twenty Premier League goals for the side, but his star began quite quickly to fade. When he missed a summer tour to South Africa for what he described as 'family reasons' the club imposed a fine, leading to simmering resentment.

Off the pitch, he encountered financial troubles, including bankruptcy proceedings, as well as three driving bans. In 1995, a single mother alleged that he was the father of her child and had refused to provide financial support.

Parting ways with Villa, he moved through a series of smaller and smaller clubs before ending his career in South Korea and

Saudi Arabia. He then returned to Shropshire and set up a sports consultancy called Players Come First, but life outside football proved to be a struggle.

Over the decade that followed, his problems multiplied as he began to experience a series of health conditions. He was suffering from high blood pressure and both his heart and his kidneys were beginning to fail, the latter meaning he would require regular sessions of dialysis.

These mounting physical challenges were also pushing his mental health to the brink and this was made all the worse by the build-up of toxins in his body which began to affect his behaviour. By early August 2016 he was starting to crumble and, unbeknown to anyone else, on the verge of a full-blown psychotic episode.

On Sunday, 14 August, the pain was becoming too much. Dalian began prophesying his own death, telling his partner he believed he would either be killed by the NHS or the police. He told her the 'world is sock-shaped' and described himself as the messiah. That evening, while the pair were staying at the house of a friend, Dalian once more proclaimed that he was the messiah and insisted on driving to the house where his father lived. Realising something was seriously wrong, the others tried to stop him but he ignored them, getting to his father's house just after 1 a.m.

On arrival, he pounded on the front door and pleaded with his father to let him in, to which Ernest eventually relented. Once inside, Dalian told his father how much he loved him then asked why it was that the rest of the family were trying to murder him.

According to Ernest, Dalian seemed incredibly angry and, in particular, angry at himself. He shouted at him: 'I'm alive. I'm the messiah and I've come to kill you.' By now the neighbours were getting increasingly concerned. One called the land line but Dalian answered instead of his father and again said he was the messiah.

It was around this time that the 999 call to the police was made.

*

The first two officers on the scene were Police Constable Benjamin Monk, a twelve-year veteran of the force, and PC Mary Ellen Bettley-Smith who had joined up little more than a year earlier and was still in her probationary period.

As they approached the address they heard shouting, one voice much louder than the other. Monk went forward and knocked on the door. After a few moments, Dalian appeared.

Bettley-Smith reported: 'When he initially came out of the door, I was very taken aback at just how angry he was. Immediately, my threat level went through the roof . . . I felt terrified.'

Monk had a similar impression, recalling that his 'face was one of utter rage' when he opened the door. 'It was surreal, he'd got the biggest wildest eyes I'd ever seen, they were protruding from his head. That was the anger simply coming from this man's face. The bloke was towering above me, absolutely towering. His shoulders literally filled the frame of the door.'

As Dalian continued to advance, he repeated his claim that he was the messiah. Monk was doing his best to calm Dalian down but he became increasingly petrified and convinced that he could not outrun or overpower this man, so he decided to deploy his Taser. But Monk also had other considerations on his mind.

'It was my belief there was no way I could match Mr Atkinson in any sense, he was too big and intimidating. I was no match for him. If I got injured . . . then Ellie would be completely vulnerable and anything could happen to her. This could escalate out of control unless it was dealt with properly.'

In addition to being crewed together, Monk and Bettley-Smith had also been lovers for the best part of a year (which they had failed to mention to their bosses) and his desire to protect his girlfriend and not be humiliated in front of her was found to be a factor in the subsequent events.

Monk pulled his Taser out of its holster, shouting a series of warnings and then activating the red laser sight which can in itself often result in a rapid de-escalation. Monk had drawn his Taser on four previous occasions during the course of his career and that alone had been enough to resolve the situation. That didn't happen in this case and as Dalian took another step towards him, Monk fired, hitting his target right in the centre of his body.

But Dalian kept on coming. The Taser had struck its target but seemed to be having no effect at all. Monk reloaded and fired a second time, but again the device seemed to have no effect. Dalian moved back to the doorway of his father's house, smashing a glass pane of the door with his fist in an effort to get back inside.

In the meantime, Bettley-Smith had activated her emergency button, sending out an automated call for all available units to make their way to her location to provide urgent back-up. Monk heard one unit replying that they were six minutes away from them.

Dalian now advanced on Monk again, his pace quickening. 'You can put a hundred thousand volts through me, I'm the fucking messiah – your Taser won't work and now I'm going to take you to the gates of hell.'

Monk ran backwards, loading his third and final Taser cartridge. 'I genuinely thought we had had it. I remember just thinking, "We're done for." He was very, very scary and the device which I thought might work for me, hadn't worked. I was terrified.'

As Dalian advanced, Monk fired again. 'He stopped moving towards me and seemed to stop where he was. He fell to the floor.'

A Taser delivers nineteen electrical pulses per second, with an average current of two milliamps. In operation, it creates an electric field, which stimulates nerve cells. This forces them to send out an electrical impulse, causing the muscles to contract at random. In most people, this loss of muscle control leads them to stiffen up and fall to the ground immediately while experiencing extreme pain.

On its default setting, the phase lasts five seconds, but it is possible to manually override that by simply holding down the trigger. During the incident, Monk held down the trigger of his Taser for a total of thirty-three seconds.

As he continued to discharge the Taser, he called out to Bettley-Smith to 'fucking hit him'. She pulled out her extendable baton and struck Dalian across the lower legs at least three times.

Once Monk let go of the trigger, he noticed that Dalian was plucking at his clothes, seemingly trying to remove the barbs and wires that a Taser uses to deliver its shocks. He appeared to be trying to shift into a position where he was going to be able to right himself and sit up.

An eyewitness account from a neighbour, which was read in court, explains what happened next: 'The male officer immediately gave him a couple of light kicks to the torso area using the top of his right foot ... The officer's leg went straight back and snapped forwards as though he was kicking a football.' The neighbour initially thought the kick was to Dalian's chest, but 'given the strength of the impact it looked as though the kick bounced off the chest and hit him in the chin, because [I] saw the black male's head snap back'.

More officers arrived on the scene. By now Dalian was on his right-hand side in a foetal position with officers sitting directly on top of him as they tried to get him into handcuffs. The eyewitness later stated that he could hear 'a clear breathing difficulty as if he couldn't get any air into his lungs' and that he was 'shocked at how loud it was'. In between all of this, Bettley-Smith was seen to deliver further blows to Dalian's legs with her baton.

Dalian was unresponsive but breathing unaided when the ambulance left Meadow Close at 2.04 a.m. for the six-minute drive to hospital. He had been placed in the ambulance on a trolley with his hands handcuffed behind his back, as Monk believed he could still be a threat. Soon afterwards he went into respiratory arrest.

Once in hospital, at 2.10 a.m., efforts to revive him included a medical crash team being called, as Atkinson's heart had by now stopped. It was noted by medics that he was 'cold to the touch' with his pupils showing no reaction.

Despite thirty minutes of intensive efforts to resuscitate him, he was pronounced dead at 2.45 a.m.

Back at the scene, officers were conducting house-to-house enquiries and taking statements from those who had witnessed the moments immediately before and after Dalian had been tasered.

One witness reported hearing Monk shout 'Keep your head down' before seeing him stamp on Dalian's head at a time when he was clearly not resisting. Another recalled that Monk had simply begun 'kicking the shit' out of Dalian.

One of the back-up officers arrived at the scene to find Monk standing above Dalian with his right foot resting on top of his head, as if he were some kind of trophy.

When Monk himself was interviewed he claimed he had been aiming for Dalian's shoulder and that the level of force he used was only a four on a scale of ten. He also claimed only one kick had been delivered.

The autopsy confirmed Dalian had been kicked at least twice and that the level of force was so great it had left the imprint of Monk's bootlaces on Dalian's forehead.

In the aftermath of Dalian's death, West Mercia Police made a mandatory referral to the IPCC who began their own investigation that same day. The force also suspended PC Monk and PC Bettley-Smith while the circumstances of Dalian's death were being examined.

Two days later the IPCC released a statement saying that, after looking at evidence they had gathered so far, both Monk and Bettley-Smith would be interviewed under caution and face a full criminal investigation.

As I learned first hand after my mother was shot, the wheels of justice move incredibly slowly whenever the police are accused of wrongdoing. The Independent Office for Police Conduct (IOPC), in particular, are notorious for the length of their investigations, which often see officers placed on what is known as 'gardening leave' for years at a time while misconduct is investigated. Complex cases where criminal charges are involved generally take far longer.

In October 2018 the IOPC submitted their evidence to the CPS and asked them to consider criminal charges against the two main officers involved. But the CPS decided not enough investigation had been carried out, requesting an expert report from an additional pathologist along with a number of other enquiries.

As a result, it wasn't until November 2019 that the CPS finally announced they had given the go-ahead for a charge of murder against Monk, along with an alternative charge of manslaughter. They also authorised charges of assault causing actual bodily harm against Bettley-Smith.

Contrast this with the death of George Floyd, who was killed in May 2020. The trial of the officer responsible, Derek Chauvin, began in March 2021, less than a year later.

Monk and Bettley-Smith were originally due to face trial in September 2020, but delays as a result of the COVID-19 pandemic meant proceedings did not begin until April 2021.

As the trial got underway, the jury noticed that Monk did not appear to be calling any witnesses to testify about his good character. They sent a note to the judge asking for clarification on this matter and were instructed to concentrate solely on the evidence presented to them. The reasons soon became clear. The prosecutor informed the court that in 1997, Monk had been cautioned for theft while working as an employee at Woolworths. In 1999 he had received a further caution after being found drunk.

Although he was required to do so, Monk failed to mention either caution while applying to join the police in 2001 and the discrepancy was not picked up until 2010 when Monk underwent another vetting process.

Monk was charged with gross misconduct and made to face a police disciplinary hearing which might have led to him being dismissed from the force. He was subsequently found guilty of the disciplinary charge, which was the equivalent of 'discreditable conduct', but rather than being dismissed, he was handed a final written warning.

Police officers in England and Wales are legally allowed to use only 'reasonable force' when they are making an arrest, preventing a crime taking place or defending themselves from attack. The UK is also a signatory to the European Convention on Human Rights which allows 'the use of force which is no more than absolutely necessary'. By striking Dalian at a time when he was no longer a threat, Monk had broken the law.

Giving evidence, a forensic pathologist stated that although his various underlying health conditions meant that Dalian was at higher risk, he might still have been alive had it not been for the kicks to the head and blasts from the Taser delivered by Monk. They also stated that the poor level of care after Dalian fell unconscious, such as keeping him in handcuffs throughout the journey to the hospital, contributed to his death.

Monk was found not guilty of murder but guilty of manslaughter. The same jury failed to reach a verdict on Bettley-Smith's assault charge.

On 29 June, Monk returned to court for sentencing. The judge told him:

> The obvious aggravating factor is that you committed this offence whilst on duty as a police officer. The police play a central and important role in upholding the rule of law in our society. The public entrust powers to the police which they expect to be used for the common good of society. It is not an easy job and the police have to go to dangerous situations.
>
> The sentence must reflect the importance of maintaining public confidence in our police. You have let yourself and the force down. Although they were difficult, you failed to act appropriately in the circumstances as they developed and you used a degree of force in delivering two kicks to the head which was excessive and which were a cause of Mr Atkinson's death.

Judge Melbourne Inman, QC told Monk it ought to have been obvious to him that the force used was excessive. He was sentenced to eight years in prison. It was the first time in more than thirty years that a serving police officer had been found guilty of manslaughter during the course of their duties.

The following September, Bettley-Smith faced a retrial over the assault charge. Although she was cleared, she subsequently faced a disciplinary panel in March 2023.

The tribunal found that her first three strikes against Dalian, prior to any kicks being landed, were 'lawful' but that her decision to use her baton to strike him three further times, despite back-up having arrived, 'did breach professional standards for use of force'. Although she had been found guilty of gross misconduct, Bettley-Smith was not dismissed and remains a serving officer with the force at the time of writing.

Far from taking comfort from the end of the criminal proceedings, Dalian's family could only express their frustration that no allowances seemed to have been made for his obviously fragile mental state, that a lesser charge had been applied to the officer responsible for his death and perhaps most of all, that it had all taken so long.

In a statement to the press they said:

We are hugely relieved that the whole country now knows the truth about how Dalian died.

While it has been hard for us not to be able to talk about the details of Dalian's death, it has been even harder to sit through this trial and to hear PC Monk try to justify the force he used.

On the night he died, Dalian was vulnerable and unwell and needed medical attention. He instead received violence, and died with PC Monk's bootlace prints bruised onto his forehead. [. . .]

The fact that this case has taken nearly five years to get to trial is completely unacceptable, especially when you consider that PC Monk's identity was known to the prosecuting authorities from day one. [. . .]

Dalian's footballing talent led him to achieve great things in his life. Our sincere hope is that now that the truth about his death is known, and justice has been done, we can start to remember him not for the manner in which he died, but for the way in which he lived.

As in my own case, spending four decades pursuing justice after my mother was shot, having the police admit their part in this kind of death is another important step in allowing any family involved in such a tragedy to start the healing process.

In September 2021 a new chief constable, Pippa Mills, took charge of the West Mercia force. One of her first tasks was to write a letter of apology to Dalian's family.

'A police uniform does not grant officers immunity to behave unlawfully or to abuse their powers. Ben Monk's conduct was in direct contradiction to the standards and behaviour of the policing service, and understandably undermined public confidence.'

The letter accepted that Monk had used a level of force that was 'unreasonable' with the kicks to Dalian's head directly contributing to his death. It also accepted that Monk had breached his right to life, protected under the European Convention on Human Rights.

Mills added: 'I cannot imagine the immense pain you have felt and how the significant delays with the trial have also added to your burden of grief. You have demonstrated great strength and dignity throughout the past five years.'

The chief constable promised that lessons would be learned as a result of the death, saying: 'I am deeply sorry for the devastating impact the actions of a West Mercia officer has caused you and I extend my deepest condolences.'

Kate Maynard, the solicitor for Dalian's family, said the official apology was 'welcomed and overdue'. She added: 'The chief constable's acknowledgement that a police uniform does not grant immunity is especially pertinent in a year that has seen other terrible examples of deadly police violence ... it is hoped that this will serve as a deterrent, and also embolden those who seek police accountability.'

The death of Dalian Atkinson is important for other reasons.

Research conducted on behalf of the charity Inquest, which helps bereaved families whose loved ones have died following contact with the police or other parts of the state, found that, compared to white people, Black people are seven times more likely to die if they are restrained.

Previous studies have also found that Black people are significantly more likely to die in police custody than whites, but the level of racial disproportionality was found to be much higher than had previously been made public, thanks to new data sources uncovered by the charity.

Its report also found that the current system for investigating such deaths fails to provide justice for Black families and ignores the notion that racism has ever played a part in such tragedies. According to the report, there has never been a case in which an officer has ever been found to have acted in a discriminatory or racist way following a Black person dying after contact with the police.

As recently as 2021 the government has insisted that evidence to show Black people were dying in greater numbers than white people after police contact does not exist, but Inquest found that deaths following restraint can be placed into one of two sets of official data, meaning the true number of deaths was previously hidden from the public.

A specific sub-set of official statistics focused on deaths that occurred in custody involving the use of restraint. However, other deaths were categorised differently, under a section labelled 'other'. This category included fatalities that occurred after police contact but did not technically happen while the individual was under arrest or detained in a cell.

One notable case missing from the official tally of deaths following restraint is that of Dalian Atkinson. Because he was never under arrest, he was never technically in custody when he died, allowing the police to keep his name out of the official records.

The same criteria can be applied to many other cases including that of Cynthia Jarrett and, of course, my mum, both of whom died without ever having been officially detained as neither was suspected of having committed any offence.

The key part of the report says:

> From IOPC data obtained by Inquest between 2012/13 to 2020/21, there have been 119 deaths involving restraint recorded by the IOPC 'in or following police custody' or recorded as 'other deaths following police contact'. Of these 23 were of Black people, 86 were white, five were Asian and four were mixed race.
>
> Assuming constant demographic profiles over the period considered, Black people are 6.4 times more likely to die than the proportion of the population they represent. For white people the comparable figure is just 0.84.

The report's title – 'I Can't Breathe' – is a reference to the final words spoken by George Floyd as he was slowly suffocated to death by a white police officer, who knelt on his neck for a total of nine minutes. They were also the words my mother used in the moments after she was shot. I may have only been eleven at the time, but they are seared in my memory for ever.

The figures for deaths in custody are only part of the racial disproportionality that Black people face in the UK.

In 2022, the National Police Chiefs' Council (NPCC) released its Race Action Plan, a set of recommendations aimed at 'improving policing for Black people'.

It had been commissioned in the wake of the death of George Floyd and the mass Black Lives Matter protests that took place across America, the UK and beyond. The introduction of the report makes a bold admission: 'We accept that policing still contains racism, discrimination and bias. We are ashamed of those truths, we apologise for them and we are determined to change them.'

Later, it lays out the bare facts, showing both the scale of the problem and just how much work still needs to be done.

The official statistics for England and Wales, which are published by the Home Office and based on police-recorded data, regularly show that we use our powers on Black people disproportionately often compared with white people. Last year, we stopped and searched Black people at a rate that was seven times higher than it was for white people. The rate at which we used force was five times higher for people we perceived to be Black. We discharged or drew Taser on Black people at a rate that was six times higher.

Other sources portray a similar picture. The Crime Survey for England and Wales, which extrapolates data from face-to-face interviews with around thirty-five thousand people each year, notes that Black people are far more likely than white people to find themselves under arrest or in police custody, even after adjusting the data to allow for other explanatory factors.

Worryingly, the NPCC report found significant gaps in police knowledge. For example, the use of some powers, such as Section 163 of the Road Traffic Act – which allows police officers to direct any vehicle being driven on a road to stop even if there is no suspicion that a criminal offence has been committed – is not routinely monitored. This means it is impossible for the police to say whether such powers are being used disproportionately on the Black population.

Following the release of the report, Andy George, president of the National Black Police Association, told the *Guardian* that he had been shocked by the figures and believed stereotyping of the Black population was to blame, at least in part.

> The lack of a diverse workforce means officers and staff are less likely to have personal connections to Black communities, which leads to them having a biased view of people they come into contact with.
>
> This can impact decision making, with officers more likely to view Black people as bigger, stronger and more dangerous due to their lack of exposure to Black communities.

Indeed, a common thread in many such cases is that the officers involved recall an 'exaggerated perception of the physical threat posed by the victims', which remains even when the people in crisis have called the police themselves.

We can see this clearly in the accounts Monk and Bettley-Smith gave of their encounter with Dalian, in which they both made a point of calling attention to his size and how this made him extremely terrifying. In reality, Monk was actually an inch taller than Dalian (who may have only looked bigger because he was standing on a step when he opened the door).

Writing for the academic website *The Conversation*, a few days after the conclusion of the court case, Yvette Russell, an academic at the University of Bristol Law School, said:

> A common way disproportionate and deadly violence against black men has been justified and excused throughout history is by invoking exactly these tropes that Monk relies on in his defence: that black men are enraged, hulking, out of control, inhuman. Research into the disproportionate rate of deaths in custody and following police contact of black and brown people shows that these types of stereotypes are frequently used to justify the use of force, including of weaponry and untested or sanctioned restraint techniques.

The other reason the Dalian Atkinson case is important has once again to do with accountability. Although ten police officers have faced murder or manslaughter charges since 1990, in every instance the case has either collapsed or the officers concerned have been acquitted. Dalian's case was the only exception.

Going further back to David Oluwale, we can recall the prosecution decided not to charge the two officers connected with his death with murder but instead chose manslaughter. In the event, the jury rejected these charges and convicted the men of several counts of assault. That was in 1972. The research by Inquest shows precious little has changed since then.

Deborah Coles, executive director of Inquest, said:

For too long, the government and IOPC have ignored the extent of racial disproportionality in deaths in their own official data and failed to publish these stark figures.

They have chosen to focus on a limited dataset, which obscures the reality for Black people. This has excluded numerous contentious and high-profile cases from the official statistics. Rendering these figures and this reality invisible perpetuates the problem and frustrates the opportunities for change.

Also connected to Dalian's case are the concerns about the way Tasers are used and, once again, their disproportionate use on members of the Black community. Initially, only specialist firearms officers were issued with the weapons but since 2007 they have been increasingly deployed to a wider group and many forces now routinely issue them to every front-line officer.

Black individuals facing arrest are three times more likely to have a Taser used on them than their white counterparts. This can't be blamed on the Taser itself so the conclusion is that there is an underlying prejudice in the way officers use it. These weapons are capable of producing fifty-thousand-volt shocks which incapacitate a person by locking all their muscles. The effect is also extremely painful but is supposed to only last a few seconds. However, a particularly concerning study found that many officers increasingly consider Tasers as a tool of compliance, which, combined with stereotyping, means they are far more likely to be used against Black individuals who officers may fear will prove to be more difficult to 'control'. There is evidence that this can lead to the Taser being discharged for longer than the recommended three-second burst, as was the case with Dalian. This can lead to other problems. Although it is regularly referred to as a 'less lethal weapon' and therefore one which 'saves lives', a 2018 report by Amnesty International found that across England and Wales, police Tasers had been implicated in at least eighteen fatal incidents since 2003, when they were first deployed in the UK.

Some of the others who have died had heart conditions – like Dalian – which may have increased their chances of having a fatal reaction, but Tasers can cause life-threatening and debilitating injuries in an indirect way, even in the fit and healthy.

Another factor which dictates the likelihood of police using a Taser on someone is their mental health state. Research shows that 67 per cent of people who have been on the receiving end of a Taser discharge suffer from some form of mental illness. The shocking state of mental health in modern day Britain has been widely documented but what is less known is the disproportionate number of Black people whose lives are marred as a result. Black men are seventeen times more likely than white men to suffer from some form of psychotic illness which means that, like Dalian, they face an even greater risk when being confronted by officers with Tasers.

In 2014, officers from Staffordshire Police were called to a flat in Newcastle-under-Lyme where a man had reportedly become paranoid after snorting a large quantity of cocaine. He had barricaded himself in a room and the sergeant who arrived at the scene told the police control room that the man – thirty-four-year-old father of two Adrian McDonald – seemed to be rambling and subject to delusion. But instead of treating McDonald as if he were going through a mental health crisis, the police broke the door down and sent in a police dog which bit him. The officers followed up with a Taser and then placed McDonald in the back of their van where he repeatedly stated that he was unable to breathe and then lost consciousness.

The officers did not call an ambulance until nine minutes later, and McDonald was pronounced dead at the scene.

A subsequent IPCC investigation concluded that the use of Tasers and a dog to subdue McDonald was 'reasonable', but directed Staffordshire Police to bring charges of misconduct against two officers for their failure to care for McDonald when he complained he could not breathe.

In the disciplinary hearing the officers were cleared of gross misconduct, which could have led to them losing their jobs, and were instead found guilty of the lesser charge of misconduct due to the fact they had not checked on McDonald promptly enough. However, in 2018 the officers succeeded in appealing this decision and a tribunal cleared them on the basis that there had been a 'misunderstanding' during the original three-day hearing. The written warnings that had been issued to them were erased from their records.

It is not that these deaths in police custody have prompted no action. The circumstances of these deaths and the multiple shortcomings in the way they were dealt with have been serious enough to have produced far-reaching recommendations from external reviews and coroners concluding that 'unlawful', 'excessive' or 'disproportionate' force was used, leading to changes in police guidance and the law. These include police vans in London being fitted with CCTV in 2015, front-line officers in the Metropolitan Police having to wear cameras from 2016, and a law restricting the use of force in mental health units in 2022.

But what is missing is real accountability. Despite these changes, aside from the case of Dalian Atkinson, no death of a Black person in custody has resulted in any kind of conviction, dismissal for gross misconduct or other action. The officers have held on to their jobs and, in some cases, risen up the ranks.

The over-policing and under-protection of members of the Black community shows no signs of being resolved any time soon, especially when the ethnic make-up of police forces themselves continues to be so far removed from the communities they operate in.

In response to the significant public outrage after the kidnapping, rape and murder of Sarah Everard by a serving Metropolitan Police officer, along with other deeply concerning events, the Metropolitan Police Service appointed Baroness Louise Casey to conduct an independent examination of its culture and behavioural standards.

This review started in February 2022 and concluded in March 2023 with the release of the final report and recommendations. Although the review had a broad focus, it had much to say about the state of race relations within the police, both in regard to the relations between the police and minority communities but also the way that ethnic minority officers are treated.

One of the elements I found most striking about the Casey Report is the way it shows that the kind of issues which are at the heart of the problems between the police and the Black community – blatant discrimination, unfair treatment, white privilege and so on – are equally present within the ranks of the police themselves.

The horrific experiences of some of the first few Black people to join the police, such as Norwell Roberts and Leroy Logan, have been well documented, but it's terrifying to read just how little has changed since then.

According to Baroness Casey's report:

There are people in the Met with racist attitudes, and Black, Asian and ethnic minority officers and staff are more likely to experience racism, discrimination and bullying at their hands. Discrimination is often ignored, and complaints are likely to be turned against Black, Asian and ethnic minority officers. Many do not think it is worth reporting. Black officers are 81 per cent more likely to be in the misconduct system than their White counterparts. The organisation has failed to significantly improve the recruitment and retention of Black officers at all levels. This is particularly true of Black and ethnic minority women.

Forces around the country have been making efforts to improve the ethnic diversity of their workforces and the Met is now roughly on a par with urban forces across England and Wales, but there is still a long, long way to go.

As the report notes, if current rates of recruitment remain the same, it will take at least thirty years before the ethnic mix of the Met comes anywhere close to matching the ethnic mix of London itself.

The misconduct system also suffers with bias and nearly half of all Black officers and staff and a third of Asian officers and staff told a survey conducted on behalf of the review that they had personally experienced racism while at work.

Meanwhile Black Londoners in particular remain over-policed. They are more likely to be stopped and searched, handcuffed, batoned and Tasered, are over-represented in many serious crimes, and when they are victims of crime, they are less satisfied with the service they receive than other Londoners. There is now generational mistrust of the police among Black Londoners. Stop and search is currently deployed by the Met at the cost of legitimacy, trust and, therefore, consent.

The Macpherson Report was supposed to usher in change, but twenty-two years later Parliament's Home Affairs Committee found that, while the policing of racist crimes had improved, 'persistent, deep rooted and unjustified racial disparities' remained in a number of key areas.

In an interview with the *Telegraph* in January 2023, His Majesty's Inspector Matt Parr, who oversees the evaluation of London's police force, said he had encountered anecdotal evidence suggesting that the Metropolitan Police was hiring individuals who lacked basic literacy skills in English, claiming the force had deliberately lowered its standards to better reflect the community it serves.

However, Mr Parr later communicated to the Casey Review that he had no proof of any lowering of standards. He also noted that such perceptions create additional divisions between ethnic minority officers and their colleagues. The report stated:

> The Met misses opportunities such as this to rebut this narrative and defend its Black, Asian and ethnic minority recruits.
>
> This has translated into a myth that is repeated in the organisation, so much so that officers at different ranks in the organisation felt comfortable repeating it in the company of their colleagues who are from a Black, Asian and ethnic minority background, officers and members of the Review team.
>
> It is going to be a huge challenge for the Met to reflect the diversity of the communities it serves.

One of the key recommendations of the 1999 Macpherson Report was that police chiefs across the country should take action to ensure their forces better reflected the communities they served by matching the percentage of ethnic minority officers to that of the populations they policed. Forces were given ten years to achieve this aim – and every single one of them failed to do so.

In the years since, while the target remains some way off, the situation does appear to have improved significantly, although only when the figures are taken at face value. Between 2007 and

2018, the number of officers from Black, Asian and minority ethnic (BAME) backgrounds grew by 43 per cent, even though the overall number of police officers decreased over this period. Whereas BAME officers made up just 3.9 per cent of the workforce in 2007, this increased to 6.5 per cent in 2018. As of March 2023, 8 per cent of UK officers identify as BAME – the highest proportion since records began.

But the overall figures hide a more disturbing trend – the number of Black officers in England and Wales was found to have risen by 140 between 2010 and 2020, from 1,446 to 1,586, representing just 1.3 per cent of all officers.

A study by the Police Foundation published in 2020 said: 'The main driver of increasing police officer ethnic diversity since 2007 has been the recruitment of Asian and mixed ethnicity officers, especially men, while black representation has barely increased.'

The importance of the distinction between Black and BAME cannot be overstated. While there is a clearly an issue with diversity within the police and the relationship between police and the BAME community, everything you have read in this book up until this point only drives home the fact that these problems are particularly acute within Black communities.

Research from West Midlands Police revealed that Black individuals are nearly four times more likely to be stopped and searched within the force area compared to white individuals. For Asian individuals, the likelihood is two and a half times greater.

The analysis also highlighted a disproportionately high use of force, accounting for 19 per cent of incidents involving Black individuals, compared to their 6 per cent representation in the 2011 census.

The WMP study concluded: 'The data shows use of force is disproportionate on the black community rather than the wider BAME community. The force cannot satisfactorily account for this and this warrants further assessment.'

In some regions, Black people are up to nine times more likely to be stopped and searched than other ethnic groups.

These discrepancies have been noted by the likes of Dr Victor Olisa, the former head of diversity with the Met. In an interview with Sky News in June 2020 he said:

> Today there is a growing practice – as often posted on social media and according to anecdotal information I hear from accounts of police training – of officers handcuffing young black boys who have not been arrested and are not resisting or showing any signs of aggression, before they start searching them.
>
> This happens while white friends who are with them are searched without being handcuffed.
>
> This is a worrying development of a practice that seems to reinforce the stereotype that conflates blackness with dangerousness.

In May 2020, the IOPC announced it was investigating nine separate incidents involving excessive use of force against Black men by WMP. The following month, it announced a similar inquiry into use-of-force allegations involving Black men in London.

Analysis of this IOPC data showed that over the previous decade 8 per cent of all deaths in police custody in the UK were of Black people, despite the fact that, at the time, they made up just 3 per cent of the population.

The origins of the acronym BAME go back to the 1970s, when different ethnic groups banded together to fight racism under the universal term of 'Black'. Initially met with hostility, the idea slowly gained traction and BAME is now widely used. However, it is highly unlikely to be used by members of the communities themselves. Already by the 1990s, its use was being challenged – by British Asians in particular – who argued it gave undue prominence to those from Afro-Caribbean backgrounds.

The use of a single collective term makes it easy to obscure the shortcomings. By labelling all non-white people as BAME, forces need only to recruit a handful of Asian or mixed race employees to be able to say they are dramatically improving the racial diversity of their workforce and moving closer to becoming fully representative of the communities they serve, even if no Black officers have been recruited.

According to Home Office data, five of the nation's police forces – Durham, North Yorkshire, Warwickshire, Dyfed-Powys and North Wales – had only one Black officer each as of March 2019.

The figures showed that twenty-six of the forty-three police forces in England and Wales had fewer than ten Black officers on their books. These same twenty-six had just 111 officers who identified as Black or Black British, among 46,162 in total.

Even in the Met – the largest and most diverse force in the country and currently home to half of all the ethnic minority officers serving in the UK – those falling under the BAME banner are more likely to be Asian, mixed race or 'other' than they are to be Black. At present, 14 per cent of the force is BAME. The figure compares well with the 3 per cent of ethnic minority officers who were employed by the Met in 1999 but even the current figure is a long way shy of the 19 per cent target that had been set for 2022. Around 30 per cent of those being recruited are from ethnic minority backgrounds, but the Met admits there are issues with retaining them.

In January 2020 Chief Constable Ian Hopkins, then NPCC lead for workforce diversity, said:

The proportion of black, Asian and ethnic minority officers and staff is at its highest ever level but we recognise we have been far too slow to increase diversity and we know there is still a long way to go so that policing is truly reflective of the communities we serve.

While there is a growing diversity in junior ranks, significant challenges persist at the senior levels. For instance, the Metropolitan Police lacks Black officers in senior roles. In all police forces, only 4 per cent of those at the chief inspector level or higher are from Black, Asian and minority ethnic backgrounds, in contrast to 8 per cent among constables.

Data from the Home Office in 2019 revealed that there was just one Black chief officer nationwide. Although this figure had risen to ten by late 2024, none of them are chief constables.

Those who advance in their careers often encounter significant difficulties. Superintendent Robyn Williams, among the highest-ranking Black female officers in the Met, was added to the sex offenders' register for five years after being convicted of possessing an indecent image sent to her phone. The Met Black Police Association criticised the decision to prosecute her, calling it a prime example of institutional racism.

Those members of the Black community who decide the best way to change the situation is to do so from the inside face many hurdles. Despite an increase in the level of recruitment targeted at the BAME community, many experience difficulties during the assessment process.

Data provided by the College of Policing shows that while the overall pass rate for the Met Day One assessment centre for new recruits is 63 per cent, the picture changes dramatically when race is taken into account. While 71 per cent of white candidates pass, only 51 per cent of BAME candidates do.

The 2019 Home Office data also found that while 23 per cent of recruits to the Met described themselves as having come from BAME backgrounds, the voluntary resignation rate stood at 26 per cent compared to 17 per cent for those who identified as white. In addition, some 2.6 per cent of those officers described

as BAME were dismissed following disciplinary hearings compared with 1.2 per cent of the white officers facing the same
hearings.

According to Dr Olisa, a Black person choosing to join the
police faces a number of challenges: 'The journey for many
black officers ... is comparable to them running a 400-metre
steeplechase alongside their white colleagues who are running
a 4 × 100-metre sprint relay. Consequently, black officers never
realise their potential, because the hurdles they must overcome
grinds them down and saps away their energy.'

Writing anonymously in the *Guardian*, one Black female Met
officer outlined her experiences, noting that despite her regularly
being the target of abuse from members of the Black community
while out on patrol, her white supervisors seemed entirely unaware
of the negative emotional impact this had on her. She added that
she had also been the victim of racist comments made by other
officers.

Sergeant Tola Munro, when president of the National Black
Police Association, confirmed such experiences were commonplace and deter many from joining in the first place. In January
2020 he told the *Guardian*: 'There is a distrust of policing within
black communities, particularly among Caribbean communities.
Why would you look at policing when you run the risk of discrimination from some of your colleagues?'

Based on current hiring and departure trends, along with pro-
jected increases in officer numbers, the Met is expected to raise
its representation of Black, Asian and ethnic minority officers to
only 22 per cent by the year 2055. Achieving a higher percentage
would necessitate a substantial rise in the recruitment of officers
from these backgrounds.

To attain a situation where 46 per cent of officers come from
Black, Asian and ethnic minority communities within the next
decade, the Met would need to immediately raise the recruitment percentage of these groups to 50 per cent. It would then be

necessary to recruit an additional 3 per cent of officers from these backgrounds each year until they constitute over 80 per cent of all new recruits. This level and pace of recruitment has never been achieved.

14

Joint Enterprise

It was 5.13 p.m. on Thursday, 12 May 2016 when a CCTV camera monitoring traffic running across Princess Road in Manchester's Moss Side picked up the image of eighteen-year-old Abdul Wahab Hafidah weaving through the vehicles as he ran as fast as his legs would carry him. Close behind him were two other teenagers, one on foot, the other on a bicycle. Hafidah was allegedly a member of a street gang known as the Rusholme Cripz and was supposedly being chased because earlier that day he had deliberately entered the territory of a rival gang known as AO (Active Only) with what would later be described as 'hostile intent'.

But he had been spotted, and now he was literally running for his life. As his pursuers drew closer, Hafidah became increasingly desperate, grasping at the door handles of cars passing by. He then pulled out a knife and turned to face the two men chasing him.

The sight of the blade stopped them in their tracks for a moment, but they were soon joined by seven other members of AO. Knowing that despite being armed he was totally outnumbered, Hafidah turned and continued running, this time along Moss Lane East.

For a second time he tried to open the door of a passing vehicle, then ran across the street, only to be struck by a glancing blow from a Vauxhall Corsa. But this was no accident – the driver of the Corsa was yet another AO member and while the impact caused only relatively minor injuries, it was enough to force Hafidah to slow right down.

A minute later, close to the junction of Denhill Road and Moss Lane East, the pursuers closed the gap. Hafidah was knocked to the ground and then subjected to a flurry of kicks and punches. He gave up trying to defend himself and simply curled up into a ball as the blows rained down.

Several passers-by shouted and screamed at the attackers to leave the boy alone and all but two ran away. The eyewitnesses watched in horror as one of the pair that were continuing the attack pulled out a knife, leaned over and repeatedly thrust it down towards Hafidah's throat. Only then did the last two attackers run off in the same direction as the others.

The bystanders moved in, trying to staunch the flow of blood. With his last few breaths, Hafidah asked them to let his family know that he loved them. By the time the paramedics arrived he had slipped into unconsciousness. He lasted two days in the intensive care unit of the Manchester Royal Infirmary before dying of his injuries. A post-mortem found that he had suffered two fatal stab wounds to the neck.

A lengthy police investigation would conclude that the man who struck the fatal blow was a nineteen-year-old by the name of Devonte Cantrill and he was subsequently charged with and convicted of murder, receiving a mandatory life sentence with a minimum term of twenty-three years.

Although this is a book about racial injustice, there seems little doubt that Cantrill, who is Black, was guilty as charged and absolutely deserved to be punished for the brutal crime he committed.

But this chapter focuses less on him and more on the fate of the six others who were convicted of the same murder at the same time, along with a further four convicted of manslaughter.

How can eleven people be convicted of a stabbing committed by only one of them? The answer is a 160-year-old English law known as 'joint enterprise' which states that those who 'aid, abet, counsel, or procure the commission of [an offence] shall be liable to be tried, indicted, and punished as a principal offender'. What this means in practice is that if one person commits a murder, and a second person was there at the time and potentially aware that a murder had been planned, yet they did not do anything to stop it happening (or actually encouraged it), they may be charged with and ultimately convicted of the murder.

Historically, joint enterprise was introduced to deal with duels, enabling the authorities to prosecute not only the duellers themselves but also their seconds, supporters and even any doctors who treated the wounded at the scene.

The law has been controversial ever since it was used in the 1952 case of Derek Bentley, already referenced earlier in this book. Bentley and his best friend Christopher Craig were caught red handed by police officers while attempting to rob a factory in Croydon. While one of the officers held on to Bentley, Craig fired a shot at PC Sidney Miles, killing him. According to the evidence given during the Old Bailey trial, moments before the shot had been fired Bentley had yelled out to Craig, 'Let him have it.' It was never clear whether this was a plea to hand over the gun to PC Miles or a demand that he pull the trigger. Either way, under the joint enterprise rules, both were charged and convicted of murder.

But that's where the case becomes morally questionable. The death penalty was still in place so, in principle, both men faced the gallows. But Craig, who had fired the fatal shot, was sixteen at the time and the rules meant no one under the age of eighteen could be executed, so his sentence was commuted to life imprisonment. Bentley, despite not being the one with the gun, was nineteen and therefore old enough to die. In 1998, forty-five years after he was executed, Bentley would receive a pardon.

In the case of Abdul Hafidah, the six other teenagers found guilty of murder alongside Devonte Cantrill included Nathaniel Jermaine Williams, the seventeen-year-old driver of the Corsa which had struck Hafidah as he ran away from the other AO gang members. Williams remained in his vehicle throughout the incident. Another was eighteen-year-old Reano Walters. Mobile footage shot immediately after the fatal blow was struck shows he was at least twenty metres away from the victim at the time.

With ages ranging from fourteen to twenty, the six youths convicted of murder alongside Cantrill received life sentences with minimum terms of between sixteen and twenty years.

There have been other cases where the convictions seem to defy all logic, including that of a fifteen-year-old boy who was registered blind but convicted of murder because he was present among a group of youths that kicked a man to death. Or the case of a couple who were involved in a brawl but then left the scene long before other members of their group later returned with weapons and killed one of the participants. Despite having had no involvement at all in the second fight, the pair were also convicted of murder.

Despite such extreme examples, there are plenty of cases where joint enterprise not only makes sense but is sometimes the only way to secure a conviction that delivers justice. If, for example, two people are holding down a rival gang member so that a third member of their team can stab the person, then it makes perfect sense for all of them to be equally culpable in the death that follows.

One of the most famous cases of racial injustice in British history – the murder of Stephen Lawrence – would never have achieved any kind of resolution without it. The only two men to have been convicted in connection with Stephen's death, Gary Dobson and David Norris, were prosecuted under the joint enterprise doctrine.

The fact that such laws would apply to the case was recognised from an early stage and appears clearly in the Macpherson Report, which states during its description of the facts surrounding the case:

> The group of white murderers then disappeared down Dickson Road. We refer to them as a group of murderers because that is exactly what they were; young men bent on violence of this sort rarely act on their own. They are cowards and need the support of at least a small group in order to bolster their actions. There is little doubt that all of them would have been held to be responsible for the murder had they been in court together with viable evidence against them. This murder has the hallmarks of a joint enterprise.

By applying the law, the prosecution never had to prove which individual member of the gang of white boys that surrounded Stephen that evening was carrying a knife or dealt the fatal blow. Simply by choosing to take part in the initial assault, they were all equally guilty of contributing to the tragic final outcome.

But the law is also deeply flawed. Not only are there cases in which people who are entirely innocent find themselves caught up in its net, but there are also times when the legislation is not applied despite everything suggesting it should be.

A good example of this is the murder of Rolan Adams, just two years before the Stephen Lawrence case. He was attacked by a group of up to fifteen white youths, one of whom stabbed him in the throat. Although one member of the gang was subsequently charged and convicted of the murder, none of the others were accused of murder, instead facing only charges of violent disorder.

Then there's the fact that the majority of murders, especially those that involve the kind of violence seen in a gang fight, are never straightforward. One defendant might throw a punch or a kick at a rival but have no intention of causing life-threatening injuries and no idea that some other member of his or her gang might be intending to use a knife to deadly effect.

However, in the context of this book, perhaps the most disturbing aspect of joint enterprise is that academic research shows it is disproportionately applied to defendants from the Black community.

Black and mixed-race people are already hugely over-represented throughout the criminal justice system but even when this was taken as a baseline, the number of Black and mixed-race individuals convicted under joint enterprise remained three times higher than it should have been, according to a study by criminologists from Cambridge University.

In England and Wales, most homicides, like the majority of all crimes, are committed by white individuals, who constitute 86 per cent of the population. However, the Cambridge study's findings on joint enterprise reveal distinct patterns that have been echoed by other researchers. A study by the Prison Reform Trust analysed sixty-one joint enterprise cases involving 157 defendants and found that among those whose ethnicity was identified, about two-thirds were from ethnic minority backgrounds, with over 40 per cent being Black. Nearly two-thirds of these defendants were below the age of twenty-five.

Research from Manchester Metropolitan University also highlights similar disparities. Ethnic minority prisoners involved in joint enterprise tend to be younger at the time of conviction compared to their white peers, face charges alongside more co-defendants, and receive longer sentences.

In the Moss Side case, all individuals convicted were either Black or mixed race. The families of those convicted believe that racial factors may have influenced the convictions. 'The jury made up their mind as soon as they saw them,' said the aunt of Devonte Neish, who was found guilty of manslaughter. 'They saw Black boys from Moss Side, they heard "gangs", and that was it.'

Concerns about racial bias have led to a campaign to reform

this aspect of the law, led by a pressure group called Jengba (Joint Enterprise Not Guilty By Association), which represents the friends and family of nearly one thousand people who have been imprisoned after being convicted of joint enterprise.

There is little available information about how common such convictions are as the available statistics make no distinction between a joint enterprise murder and other homicides, but academic studies suggest they account for between 15 and 20 per cent of all murder cases.

In response to the growing concerns, and following a legal challenge from campaigners, the Crown Prosecution Service initiated a six-month pilot programme to track racial bias in prosecutions. The analysis involved examining case files from February to August 2023, and reviewed 190 cases and 680 defendants across six CPS regions: London North, Mersey-Cheshire, North East, North West, West Midlands, and Yorkshire and Humberside.

The findings revealed that 57 per cent of those prosecuted were from minority ethnic groups. While white people account for 81.7 per cent of the general population, they represented only 38.9 per cent of the defendants. Black people, who comprise 4 per cent of the population, constituted 30 per cent of those charged. Therefore, Black people were found to be 15.7 times more likely than white to face prosecution under joint enterprise laws. Asian people, representing 9 per cent of the population, accounted for 14 per cent of joint enterprise cases, making them almost four times more likely to be prosecuted compared to white.

The data also indicates that joint enterprise legal actions have a disproportionate impact. Nearly 93 per cent of those charged in joint enterprise cases were male. Individuals aged fourteen to seventeen represented 14 per cent of cases, while those aged eighteen to twenty-four constituted 40 per cent. Additionally, 5 per cent of defendants had a disability.

Becky Clarke, a senior lecturer at Manchester Metropolitan University who has spent her career researching the criminal justice system, told the *Guardian* that the report only served to confirm previously held concerns that a significantly higher number of people from Black and minority ethnic backgrounds were being convicted through joint enterprise.

In February 2016, a decision by the Supreme Court seemed to introduce a tougher criterion for convictions under joint enterprise. In the case of *R v Jogee*, the court determined that merely predicting a crime like murder might happen was insufficient grounds to convict a secondary party. Instead, the prosecution needed to demonstrate that the accused had the intention for the crime to occur.

During the prosecution of the Moss Side case, however, evidence such as the presence of a hammer during the pursuit and the suggestion that a different defendant, aside from Cantrill, might have carried a knife, was used to argue that the defendants must have anticipated the use of deadly weapons. If the defendants could have reasonably predicted that the confrontation would end with someone being stabbed but nonetheless chose to take part in the chase, the prosecution argued, they were surely just as responsible as the person holding the knife.

But some defendants argued that the only reason they ran towards the commotion was to see what was going on, not to get involved. Others, some of whom had been captured on CCTV towards the front of the mob as the chase crossed Princess Road, admitted being there but said they had dispersed from the area before the fight itself had begun and played no part in it. Cordell Austin said he had joined the chase purely to make sure the younger boys in the group were safe. He was the only one of the defendants to be acquitted.

A few of the defendants were acquainted with Hafidah and felt both intimidated and hostile towards him. Local youth workers had expressed concerns about his behaviour; they wanted to safeguard him yet also recognised that he had been involved in extremely violent acts against others.

Immediately before the pursuit began, the members of the group were socialising in a park near Westwood Street. Hafidah was hiding nearby and, as per the courtroom accounts from multiple defendants, started hurling stones at one of their vehicles. His actions were likely influenced by the fact he had been drinking heavily.

It could be argued that the chase itself was entirely spontaneous, with each participant experiencing the events from a different point of view and therefore having a different understanding of what was taking place, and what the intentions were if and when Hafidah was captured. It's likely that one or two wanted to fight him, that others were just curious and that only one of the group truly had the intention to use the knife they were carrying to stab him. But having established that the defendants were all members of a gang, it made it much easier for the prosecutors to support the claim that they all had murder in mind, no matter how limited their involvement was in the actual killing.

Although Hafidah's body showed he had been injured dozens of times as a result of the punches and kicks that rained down on him, the pathologist concluded that none of them had been serious enough to contribute towards his death.

When a woman yelled at the group to stop attacking Hafidah, only Devonte Cantrill ignored her and carried on. He had been the last to arrive at the scene and only he had chosen to wear gloves, along with a mask to cover his face. While the others attacked with their hands and feet, Devonte was the only one there wielding a weapon.

In August 2023, the human rights campaign group Liberty delivered its submission to the Criminal Cases Review Commission (CCRC) in support of the application made earlier that year by three of those involved in the Moss Side case, Durrell Goodall, Reano Walters and Nathaniel 'Jay' Williams, arguing their murder convictions were the result of institutional racism within Greater Manchester Police and within the wider criminal justice system.

The submission noted that the suggestion that young Black people are actually members of gangs is excessively used, compared to cases involving white defendants. Liberty further stated that doing so amounted to a breach of the human rights of the defendants as it painted them as being engaged in criminal activity during their private lives despite a lack of supporting evidence.

In particular, Liberty argued that conflating involvement in drill or rap music as proof of gang membership was not only racially prejudicial but could only be the result of an ignorance of the reality of youth culture.

The CCRC said they could not give a timescale for considering or deciding the case and it remains under review at the time of writing.

Sometimes we only recognise the most overt miscarriages of justice. We all pay attention when someone dies in police custody and we get outraged by the statistics about racial bias in stop and search, but issues such as joint enterprise pass a lot of people by.

When you hear about someone being stabbed to death and that there were ten people on the scene, your first instinct is that they should all be locked up, but you need a greater understanding of the context. It might seem like a good thing to have taken all those people off the streets and charged them with the same offence, but we all know how easy it is to find yourself in the wrong place at the wrong time. And we all know how impossible it is to know the true intentions of those around you.

In a world where so many of our actions can be caught on CCTV cameras, mobile phones or smart doorbells, the technology isn't always good enough to provide a complete picture. It's an element that might change in the future, but even the best technology in the world has its limitations when it comes to defeating bias in the criminal justice system.

15

Artificial Intelligence and the Future

The blockbuster film *Minority Report*, directed by Stephen Spielberg and starring Tom Cruise, is set in the year 2054 and centres around the work of a specialised police department that aims to identify crimes before they can happen.

The unit, known as Precrime, makes use of information provided by a trio of psychics and its officers then go out and arrest people before they have a chance to offend. Although it is accepted that at the time of their arrest, these people would be entirely innocent, the proven reliability of the visions the psychics provide are deemed good enough for the officers to be sure that at some point in the future, they would commit crimes.

It all sounded a bit far-fetched back in 2002 when the film was released and would have been even more unbelievable back in 1956 when the story on which the film was based was first published.

When it came to creating his vision of the future, Spielberg wasn't just pulling ideas out of thin air – he put together a team of scientists, technicians and visionaries to ensure that as far as possible, much of what was seen on screen would soon come to pass. Which is why the film accurately predicted things like flexible displays, voice activation and wearable technology. The film also showcased self-driving cars, personalised digital advertisements and the ability to use gestures rather than buttons or a screen to control devices.

Minority Report went on to inspire many more creations. According to its production designer, more than one hundred patents have been issued for ideas that first appeared in the film.

As for the main storyline, although today's police don't yet make use of psychics, they have embraced the idea of using technology to try to predict future crimes. They are also using the power of artificial intelligence to boost the chances of catching those who are yet to be apprehended.

But regardless of whether we're talking about predictive policing algorithms or the increasing use of live facial recognition, the implications for racial injustice are significant. Because all such technologies have been found to be racially biased. Their use has proved to be just another way that Black people are being unfairly treated within the criminal justice system.

While many developers were inspired by the ideas featured in the film, the real driver that led to the uptake of predictive policing technology was the 2008 global recession. Police departments across the US and beyond suddenly faced huge budget cuts. They desperately needed to find ways to reduce their spending.

The manufacturers of these products told forces that using data in this way would help the police to make sensible, data-driven decisions about where to allocate their precious resources. They would be able to do more with less. There were other benefits too. By taking human bias out of the equation and relying instead on mathematics and algorithms, they would become both more efficient and fairer. After all, computers operate on pure logic so the colour of a person's skin should have no bearing on whatever predictions are made.

Around the same time, huge government grants became available in the USA for those forces eager to develop smart solutions to policing problems. And so it was that in 2009 the Los Angeles Police Department received $3 million in order to set up the first trials of predictive policing. The idea was for the software to predict the location where a crime was likely to happen next and for the force to deploy extra officers to that place in order to act as a deterrent.

By 2011 *Time* magazine had listed predictive policing as one of the fifty best inventions of the year and described how officers in Santa Cruz, California were 'getting ahead of the bad guys by figuring out where crimes will be committed before they take place'.

Such systems work by feeding computers with data about the time, location and nature of past crimes. As more data is entered, the algorithm 'learns' more about where and when crimes have taken place in the past and uses this to determine the most likely location of the next one.

In theory, this knowledge allows police forces to focus resources on the areas they are needed most. In a very basic example, if the predictive policing software finds that a series of incidents that appear to be random actually occur in the same general areas when looking back over many years, then putting additional officers in those locations can dramatically reduce levels of offending.

This was the case for the Richmond Police Department operating in Virginia. New Year's Eve would always see an increased number of firearms discharges which seemed to be random, but using AI the force was able to anticipate the location, time and nature of future occurrences. Placing officers at those locations resulted in a 47 per cent decrease in incidents of random gunfire discharges and a 246 per cent rise in the number of weapons seized.

Other early results seemed to confirm the effectiveness of the system. In 2012, when its trial was six months old, the LAPD reported that the number of burglaries had fallen by 25 per cent compared to the previous year thanks to the use of predictive policing. Similar results were reported from other forces including those in Seattle and Atlanta.

But when independent researchers looked at the statistics themselves, as opposed to relying on the information being fed to them directly from the forces, they almost always found no significant difference between levels of crime in the districts that were making use of predictive policing and those that were not.

In addition to basic historical statistics, the systems now use weather data, information on population density, the location of businesses, schools and the timing of social events to assist with predictions. In principle this makes sense – certain crimes have been proven to be less likely on cold or rainy days while activities such as anti-social behaviour or car theft are more likely to occur in the hours after a major event such as a football match.

However, a key problem with all such systems is that it is impossible to assess the true impact they are having. They don't provide detail of a specific future crime, just suggest a location where it is mathematically possible that a crime may occur.

If officers follow the guidance provided by the software and add a patrol, how can you ever be sure whether they actually prevented a crime or not? One 2016 report on this very issue found the advantage of predictive policing software compared to best-practice policing was 'incremental at best'.

Even in the few short years that predictive policing has been around, it has quickly become more sophisticated. With more and more data available to them, the latest systems not only predict where crime may occur but also predict, profile and assess the risk that certain individuals may become involved in criminality. These systems are also being used to help make decisions about whether people should be prosecuted or placed into rehab programmes and how long prison sentences or probation should be. Those impacted by these systems may not even be aware they are in use.

In New Orleans in 2018 it emerged that the city's police force had been using this kind of data to compile lists of people likely to be involved in shootings, and then targeting the at-risk individuals for intervention. When this fact became public, the programme had been in place for six years without the knowledge of the city's mayor. It was terminated immediately.

No surprise, then, that racial justice organisations and civil liberties groups are extremely wary. They contend that predictive policing reinforces racial prejudice in a new and dangerous way, lending it the legitimacy of a branch of science.

Any such system is only as good as the data that you can enter and as you know from everything you have read up until this point, the criminal justice system in the UK (and in many other places such as the US) is deeply racially biased.

As a result, crime prediction software actually reflects that same bias. A 2016 study into the use of a popular system called PredPol in Oakland, California, found that supplying the algorithm with historic data on drug crimes resulted in additional patrols being sent to areas that were already heavily policed. As a result, Black people became twice as likely to be targeted by the software as white people, despite similar rates of drug use.

One of the researchers, William Isaac, noted the system 'is predicting future policing, not future crime'.

Attempts to address these problems have so far proved ineffective. Rather than using arrest data, which is known to be biased, some developers have switched to using data based on victim reports only, but this data has also been found to be skewed.

Researchers who built their own algorithm using victim data found that in areas where crime was low, only a fifth of predictions were accurate while in areas where crime was high, the system predicted far more crime was taking place than was the reality.

A key issue is that Black people get reported for crimes more often than white people, if you make allowances for the representations in populations, which leads to areas with large Black populations receiving far more predictions than they should.

The level of trust between victims and the police is another factor. It means that if you are living in a community with a historically racially biased force – for example, living on the Broadwater Farm estate in north London – that will impact on whether or not people report crime. If they tend not to, that can lead to predictive tools underestimating the level of crime in some areas, meaning they fail to get the right number of patrols which makes it easier for the criminals who are living in that area to continue operating.

At least fourteen police forces in the UK are known to have used or considered predictive policing technologies.

A 2021 inquiry by Parliament's Justice and Home Affairs Select Committee urged the government to create an oversight body and certification system for artificial intelligence tools, warning they could 'undermine human rights'. The government rejected most of the Committee's suggestions, saying they were 'not persuaded by the arguments'. It all goes back to the problems of the 1970s when the moral panic about mugging first began. When Black people started to be associated with the crime, police poured more resources into catching those responsible by increasing the number of patrols and proactive operations within areas with large Black populations.

The result was that the offenders in those places, who would only ever be a small minority of the population, then became more likely to be apprehended. This, in turn, made it seem as if the operation was successful and even more resources were invested. The true end result was increased tension and ever falling levels of satisfaction.

Back in 2019 researchers from the Royal United Services Institute warned of the same problem occurring with the ever-widening use of predictive policing, after being commissioned to look into the issues by the government's Centre for Data Ethics and Innovation.

Interviewed as part of this research, a police officer said that young Black males are more frequently subjected to stop and search procedures than their white counterparts, chiefly because of inherent human prejudice. This prejudice is then reflected in the data sets, leading to biased outcomes when those data sets are applied.

Another officer explained that police departments often allocate significant resources to specific areas, resulting in a 'self-fulfilling prophecy'. This is not necessarily due to officer discrimination, but rather because increased policing leads to more crime being detected. When the researchers examined the workings of predictive crime mapping, they found that algorithms which have been trained using historical police data can replicate – and in some instances even amplify – whatever biases are already present within the data, leading to the under- or over-policing of certain communities. There is also a danger of 'automation bias', favouring the output of analytical tools over police officers' own judgement and other important factors and considerations.

Civil rights groups such as the NAACP have repeatedly called on legislators to properly evaluate and regulate the use of both predictive policing and the kind of artificial intelligence that powers facial recognition systems.

The growth of the Black Lives Matter movement, in particular, has led to increased scrutiny of this kind of technology. In 2016 the American Civil Liberties Union launched its Community Control Over Police Surveillance campaign which hands control of the use of many types of surveillance technology to local officials rather than police forces.

Pressure from such groups and widening concerns about potential bias are part of the reason why the LAPD and several other large forces stopped using PredPol in early 2020, though they also admit that further testing found that the technology did not lead to a reduction in crime. The company behind PredPol insists the software works as it should and any shortcomings are the result of human error.

The European Parliament is looking at taking an even more radical approach and banning the use of predictive policing completely.

The police have also tried to make use of other forms of crime prediction that rely less on technology but have every bit as much potential for bias.

In 2011, following the uprising in Tottenham, the Metropolitan Police set up the Gangs Matrix, a database containing the personal data of persons supposed to be in a gang and likely to commit violence. Names could be listed even if a person had never committed any offence, simply because they lived in a certain area or had friends who were known to the police.

Details of who was on the Matrix were kept secret from individuals, but the information could be shared with third parties. This saw instances of people being excluded from school and evicted from their homes. In some cases, individuals were stripped of welfare benefits, threatened with deportation or told their children were being taken into care.

The one fact we do know, thanks to data released as a result of a review carried out by the London Mayor's Office for Policing and Crime, is that 80 per cent of those named on the Matrix were Black. It meant people were being profiled and identified as criminals from an early age with a complete absence of evidence. The police were effectively saying, *Look, here is a young Black boy and we think he's going to be a future problem so we'll keep an eye out and we'll come back for you.*

People had no chance. The secrecy surrounding the identity of those whose names were on the Matrix made everyone paranoid. Children were killing other children because they were worried that they might be members of rival gangs. But you could end up on the Matrix just because you were seen to say hello to someone in a different area to you, or because you lived in the same block as someone, even if you didn't know them at all. It was all so loose that it was crazy.

The police had created a problem and then made it seem that they were also offering the solution.

In February 2024 the Matrix was decommissioned. The Met Police said they were doing so due to concerns about its proportionality.

In recent years there have been concerns about another new technology increasingly used by police forces across the world: facial recognition.

In January 2020, Robert Williams arrived at his home in Farmington Hills, Michigan to find police officers from Detroit waiting for him. He was immediately arrested and detained for thirty hours on suspicion of stealing high-end watches worth thousands of dollars. Williams had become the first person in the world to be wrongfully arrested on the basis of facial recognition technology. Surveillance footage of the crime had been obtained by the police and run through their software, which found a match to a picture on an old driver's licence belonging to Willliams.

Williams is Black and numerous studies have shown that this kind of software is significantly less reliable for Black people as the algorithms have difficulty distinguishing between facial features in those with darker skin tones.

In the UK the first force to begin making use of facial recognition technology was South Wales Police – the same force responsible for policing the 1919 unrest in Cardiff (albeit under a different name), for the false prosecution of Mahmood Mattan and for the epic miscarriage of justice that saw members of the Cardiff Three spending years behind bars.

Liberty took the force to court on the grounds that the tech will make racism within the police worse. South Wales Police was forced to halt its trials as a result, but these have since re-started after independent reviews claimed the technology was not discriminatory.

Katy Watts of Liberty said: 'Facial recognition doesn't make people safer, it entrenches patterns of discrimination and sows division. History shows us that surveillance technology will always be disproportionately used on communities of colour and, and at a time when racism in UK policing has rightly been highlighted, it is unjustifiable to use a technology that will make this even worse.'

While there has yet to be a similar case of wrongful arrest in the UK at the time of writing, the potential is there, and many civil rights and campaigning groups are concerned that it is only a matter of time.

My final issue with all of this is: all predictive policing software, as well as that involved in facial recognition, is in the hands of private companies. As each firm involved in the business wants to keep the details of how their specific algorithms work secret in order to retain their market advantage, such information is not available anywhere. This means no one can determine exactly how decisions about where to allocate police resources, who to arrest or who might be at risk of a violent attack are actually made.

When decisions are made using such flawed systems, the level of trust within the Black community only stands to fall further still. And that's not a future any of us wants to see.

16

Towards an Anti-Racist Society

There is no such thing as race.

Biologically, race does not exist and yet the concept of it has become so powerful that it shapes our lives and influences our experiences in a multitude of ways, no matter which classification you happen to fall into.

We have seen throughout this book that historically, racist views were considered normal in culture, media, institutions and social systems and used to varying degrees to justify the unfair treatment and oppression of some people based purely on biological markers or physical traits such as skin colour or facial features.

But these so-called differences between the humanoid inhabitants of this planet are really not so different at all. Look around you at the vast diversity of flora and fauna and marvel at how two specimens can have vastly different characteristics, to the degree that they seem poles apart, and yet they are fundamentally the same.

Rather than a biological fact, race is merely a social construct that developed over time in order to make it easier for societies to separate themselves from one another by creating boundaries that implied that anyone outside of these boundaries was in some way 'inferior'. This kind of thinking shaped the attitudes that created the issues we are still dealing with today.

These ideas are far from new. More than a century ago, American sociologist and Black civil rights activist W. E. B. Du Bois – who attended the first Pan-African Conference in London in 1900 – raised worries about the misuse of race as a biological justification for differences he viewed as largely social and cultural among various human populations. To Du Bois, race was little more than a badge. Only now are scientists coming to the same conclusions.

But this fails to address the significant real-world impact of race, particularly in societies shaped by colonialism and slavery.

Racism has been described as the most aggressive cancer humanity has ever known and if we are going to defeat it, we have to do much more than simply not be racist. We need to be actively anti-racist.

Being anti-racist involves recognising and challenging the policies, practices and attitudes that sustain racial inequalities. This starts with a thorough understanding of the history and contemporary realities of racism and the ways racial bias presents itself within society. You then need to examine your own beliefs and behaviours by reflecting on your past actions and being willing to address and change personal prejudice.

The next step is to actively challenge racism whenever it occurs, regardless of the context. This might mean calling out anyone who behaves in a racist way or giving support to organisations that promote anti-racist causes. It might mean going on protests and supporting political movements that advocate for policies that support racial equality.

Being anti-racist means actively supporting marginalised

communities and amplifying their voices. It means listening to what the members of the Black community are saying and helping to dismantle any barriers to equality.

For members of groups such as the police, it means members challenging institutional racism by working to change policies and practices that reinforce racial stereotypes. It means recognising that the same issues also exist in other areas of society, such as education, healthcare, housing and criminal justice. Only by acknowledging these issues are all around us can we begin to address them.

No one is born with in-built racist or anti-racist attitudes. It is learned behaviour. The greatest proof of this came through an experiment conducted by a white schoolteacher named Jane Elliott who taught eight- and nine-year-olds in a small town in Iowa, USA.

On 5 April 1968, the day after the assassination of Martin Luther King, eager for her pupils – all of whom were also white – to understand the impact of racism first hand, she split the class up into groups: those with blue eyes and those with brown eyes. She then told them that brown-eyed children were superior to blue-eyed ones, a claim she justified by explaining that intelligence was linked to melanin levels and the more you had, the darker your eyes would be.

The brown-eyed children were then allowed to go to lunch early and have a longer break between lessons. They were allowed to drink directly from the water fountain while the blue-eyed children had to use cups.

The change was almost instant. The brown-eyed children became more confident, some to the point of arrogance. They made it clear that they considered those with blue eyes to be inferior. When a series of numeracy and literacy tests were carried out later that day, the brown-eyed pupils did well while the blue-eyed ones tended to make lots of silly mistakes and become despondent.

The brown-eyed children soon began hurling insults at the

blue-eyed ones, fights even broke out. The only thing that had changed was the mindset, but the blue-eyed children quickly became more subservient and timid, including the ones who had previously been loud and extroverted.

The following week, Elliott reversed the experiment, explaining that new research showed it was the blue-eyed children who were superior. Although many of the blue-eyed children turned the tables, their actions were never as extreme as those seen in the brown-eyed children, most likely the result of having lived through that kind of discrimination.

The concepts of racism and anti-racism are defined not by one's identity but by one's actions. To be anti-racist is to recognise that tackling racism is a collective responsibility, requiring each of us to contribute to its eradication.

It's important to recognise that being anti-racist is an ongoing commitment and not a one-time action. It requires sustained effort and dedication to create meaningful change.

Living an anti-racist lifestyle involves a conscious commitment. It means actively choosing it as a way of living. To embody anti-racism, you must be ready to live with discomfort and prioritise bravery, empathy and openness.

Achieving an anti-racist society is the goal, and I recognise that it's a big goal but it's worthy of pursuit all the same. We might not all see the fruits of our labour in our time, but trust people will benefit from what you do.

We need to understand that racism is at the core of so many of the issues we are facing. If racism didn't exist, we wouldn't be having these discussions. It's racism alone that is giving life to the prejudice and causing all the damage. We need to recognise that and be more empathetic to one another.

The more of us that can embrace these principles, the faster we can move towards the goal of having an anti-racist society with justice and equality for all.

If such a world had existed at the turn of the twentieth century,

Charles Wotten would never have been thrown off a pier in Liverpool and left to drown. Mahmood Mattan would never have been hanged, David Oluwale would not have been hounded to death, the Mangrove Nine and the Oval Four would never have entered the criminal justice system.

In such a world, the likes of Sean Rigg and Dalian Atkinson would have received the help they so badly needed. None of the Cardiff Five would have spent a day in jail and Stephen Lawrence would be known only for his work in the field of architecture, not his untimely death.

And of course, in a truly anti-racist world, my mum would have lived a life free from pain and sorrow. She would now be gracefully approaching her late seventies, obsessed with her grandchildren and great-grandchildren, always laughing, always smiling, strong and independent, still dancing up a storm at every possible opportunity.

Afterword

Winston Churchill once said, 'Those who fail to learn from history are doomed to repeat it.'

It has been almost forty years since my mother was shot in a botched police raid. My quest for justice provided a first-hand experience of how deep-rooted racism is within policing, devastating the lives of individuals, impacting communities and creating a negative ripple effect throughout society. In that time, I've been increasingly determined to ensure that the lessons of the past are learned.

The stories in this book sadly show that the same mistakes have been repeated time and again. The tendency to repeat patterns is hardwired into human nature and conscious effort is required to overcome this.

We all need to be vigilant to avoid taking two steps back for every step we take forward. In July 2025, several works from the *Windrush Untold Stories* exhibition – a collection of portraits (including one of myself) and recollections from the last seventy years, installed in Windrush Square in Brixton – were slashed and covered with paint.

Police were quick to announce that they did not believe the incident was racially motivated, but without providing any context for this statement, all they did was raise the hackles of the Black community, in the exact same way as they did when they claimed the murder of Stephen Lawrence had not been racially motivated.

I fully understand what they were trying to do, but better to say nothing at all than to release a knee-jerk, out-of-context remark that suggests nothing has changed.

A week later we saw it again, following a misconduct hearing that saw two police officers dismissed for gross misconduct, and a third given a final written warning, over their involvement in the December 2020 strip search of a fifteen-year-old Black girl, known as Child Q. She had been stripped at school while on her period, without the presence of an appropriate adult, and the action sparked understandable outrage.

The hearing 'did not find that the officers were influenced by Child Q's race' but the report did include an apology for the impact the incident had on the Black community. You can't have it both ways, and failing to understand the potential impact of such words speaks of a lack of empathy.

The Louder I Will Sing was very much about my personal redemption. The book came out shortly after the death of George Floyd and coincided with the rise of the Black Lives Matter movement and raising public awareness about the exact same issues I had experienced.

I began to see that if I really wanted to bring about cultural change in the police, I needed to understand the issues from a wider perspective, and that's when I started working on this book.

Delving back in time and digging deep into the stories of others who have also suffered as a result of racial injustice has broadened my understanding, added new context and prompted ideas for pathways to progress. I don't have all the answers, and no single approach is going to resolve it all – this has to be approached from multiple angles – but it's all part of the solution.

Since the publication of *The Louder I Will Sing*, I have increasingly devoted my time to delivering the Lee Lawrence Leadership Programme, Encounter, Repair, Transform, working with senior leaders and new recruits at the Metropolitan Police Service with the aim of shifting their beliefs, practices and actions. The goal is to effect cultural change, so that in the future, officers of all ranks adapt their behaviour and mindset to be consistent with the stated goals of the police. The programme, based on the principles of restorative justice, explores the history of policing as well as the force's relationship with the Black community.

In late 2024 my skillset reached a new level when I graduated from the Meyler Campbell Clear Leaders business coaching programme. I was awarded a scholarship based on the work I do advocating for racial justice and police reform with schools via the Cherry Groce Foundation, which enabled me to participate in this highly regarded programme.

I can now apply non-directed coaching in my training sessions, a style of communicating with people which is predominately facilitative, enabling the individual to learn and discover for themselves rather than simply being told.

Through my work, I have also learned the true power of restorative justice. Studies show it reduces re-offending and makes victims feel far better. But we also know it's more likely to be offered to white offenders than Black ones, meaning it is not being applied where it is needed most.

When we talk about the impact of some of these issues on the Black community, the word 'community' can often be interpreted as a term of exclusion. But if you break it down, it's really about common unity. If you believe that the world should be equal, that racial injustice is a real thing, then you are part of my community, no matter your race, religion, sex or geographical location.

To truly start the process of healing, we need to be able to acknowledge what has happened in the past. We need to have empathy, to understand that a large proportion of our society has not been treated fairly. Only then can those people feel seen.

My greatest hope is that, having read this book and gained an understanding of how we got to where we are, you will have arrived at a brand-new starting point from which to effect change.

Let's all move forward from here.

Acknowledgements

First and foremost, I want to acknowledge my mum, Cherry. I dedicate this book to her memory and to my children, Brandon, Harmony and Ruby-Lee, for whom I hope the world becomes a better place.

I would also like to acknowledge the work of the Cherry Groce Foundation, United Friends Family Campaign (UFFC) and the charity Inquest.

There are so many people doing important work in this field that a separate book would be needed just to name them all. But if I had to select a few they would include my cousin Nana Meduty Kwaku Bonsu, for his uncompromising stance against racism and his lifelong commitment to the Pan-African movement; Marcia Riggs, for her tenacity in seeking justice for her brother, Sean, and her steadfast capacity to show up for others; and Stafford Scott, for his tireless community activism and dedication to improving race relations.

I'd also like to thank Tony Thompson for his advice and assistance in the crafting of this book.

Finally I'd like to make special mention of Sir David Adjaye, the architect and designer of my mum's memorial in Brixton; everyone at Bhatt Murphy and in particular Raju Bhatt, who has always given me good advice; and Nigel Pearce, a Metropolitan Police sergeant who has done outstanding work around community relations and is a fine example of the attributes we should expect from a police officer.

I would also like to acknowledge my A-Team – Dionne Lawrence, Kaleb Hailu and Petra Mendes – who have been unwavering in their support. They are the backbone of my work: loyal, dependable and united by our shared belief that the Purpose Outweighs the Challenge.

Sources and Further Reading

Introduction

Akala, *Natives: Race and Class in the Ruins of Empire* (London: Two Roads, 2019)

Ethnicity Facts and Figures Service, 'Police workforce'

IOPC, 'Deaths During or Following Police Contact: Statistics for England and Wales 2019/20'

The Lammy Review: An Independent Review into the Treatment of, and Outcomes for, Black, Asian and Minority Ethnic Individuals in the Criminal Justice System'

Lawrence, Lee: 'Redefining Justice', TedX, November 2019; *The Louder I Will Sing* (London: Sphere, 2020)

Mohdin, Aamna and Amelia Gentleman, 'UK failing to address systemic racism against black people, warn UN experts', *Guardian*, 27 January 2023

National Police Chiefs' Council, 'Police Race Action Plan: Improving Policing for Black People', 2022

Sanghera, Sathnam, *Empireland: How Imperialism Has Shaped Modern Britain* (London: Viking, 2021)

Shah, Vikas, 'A conversation with Sathnam Sanghera on how imperialism has shaped modern Britain', Thought Economics, 19 October 2023

UNHCR: A/HRC/54/67/Add.1: Visit to the United Kingdom of Great Britain and Northern Ireland – Report of the Working Group of Experts on People of Africa Descent – Advance unedited version, UNHCR, 5 October 2023; 'Systemic racism within UK criminal justice system a serious concern: UN human rights experts', UN News, 27 January 2023

'Black men seven times more likely to die following police restraint but racism not being addressed', Inquest, 20 February 2023

1: Origins

Bilby, Kenneth M., *True-Born Maroons* (Gainesville: University Press of Florida, 2008)

Brown, Colin, 'The Black heroes of Trafalgar', *Independent*, 19 October 2005

Costello, Ray: *Liverpool Black Pioneers* (Liverpool: Bluecoat Press, 2007); *Black Salt: Seafarers of African Descent on British Ships* (Liverpool: Liverpool University Press, 2012)

Crymble, Adam and Emma Azid, 'Black Lives, British Justice: Black People in London Criminal Justice Records, 1720–1841', *Journal of Slavery and Data Preservation*, 2:2 (2021), pp. 1–11.

Fryer, Peter, *Staying Power: The History of Black People in Britain* (London: Pluto, 1984)

Garvey, Marcus: *Philosophy and Opinions of Marcus Garvey*, 2 vols (New York: Universal 1923–25); *Selected Writings and Speeches of Marcus Garvey* (Mineola: Dover, 2004)

Gerzina, Gretchen, *Black London: Life Before Emancipation* (New Brunswick: Rutgers University Press, 1995)

Grant, Colin, *Negro with a Hat: The Rise and Fall of Marcus Garvey* (London: Vintage, 2010)

Johns, Steven, 'The British West Indies Regiment mutiny, 1918', Libcom, 7 August 2013

Moody, Harold: *Youth and Race* (London: British Christian Endeavour Union, 1936); *Freedom for All Men* (London: Livingstone Press, 1943); *The Colour Bar* (London: New Mildmay Press, 1945)

Richards, Elizabeth, 'The First Pan-African Conference', Black History Month, 4 July 2020

Vaughan, David A., *Negro Victory: The Life Story of Dr Harold Moody* (London: Independent Press, 1950)

Wambu, Onyekachi (ed.), *Empire Windrush* (London: Orion, 2023)

'An African exhibition at the Crystal Palace', *The Times*, 11 May 1895

'The African Diaspora', The Proceedings of the Old Bailey

'The Battersea mayoralty: Interview with Mr Archer', *South Western Star*, 7 November 1913

'British West Indies Regiment', National Army Museum

'Nelson, Trafalgar and Those who Served', The National Archives

'Remembering London's first ever Black mayor', *South London Press & Mercury*, October 2020

'The Story of the British West Indies Regiment in the First World War', Imperial War Museum

2: Charles Wotten

Hawthorn, Jeremy, '1919 – The Murder of Charles Wootton', *Nerve*, 12 (summer 2008)

Mahamdallie, Hassan, 'Muslim working class struggles', *International Socialism*, 113 (2007)

Mahoney, Michael, 'Raising awareness of the "Race Riots" in Liverpool', The National Archives, 12 June 2019

Pankhurst, Richard, 'An early Somali autobiography', *Africa*, 32:2 (1977), pp. 159–76

Pascoe, Silu Pascoe, 'The Race Riots of 1919 in Liverpool and Cardiff', Bristol Radical History Group, 21 August 2024

Shepley, Nick, *The Story of Cardiff* (Stroud: History Press, 2014)

Sullivan, Chris, 'Lost Cities: How Cardiff's thriving mulitcultural hub was crushed', *Byline Times*, 5 August 2020

'Black in Time: The 1919 Race Riots', Westminster Students Union, 17 October 2022

'Cardiff morals', *South Wales Daily News*, 20 July 1918

'Chief Constable's report on the death of Charles Wotten', HO 45/11017/377969, The National Archives, Kew

'Drowned Negro', *Liverpool Echo*, 10 June 1919

'Lessons from the Glasgow Race Riots: 1919–2019', Black History Month Scotland, 23 January 2019

'Racism reared its head in our post-war capital', WalesOnline, 28 March 2013

3: Next Generation

Constantine, Learie: *Cricket and I* (London: P Allan, 1933); *Cricket in the Sun* (London: Stanley Paul, 1947); 'Why I Did Not Play for Lancashire', *Liverpool Echo*, 7 August 1954

Easton, Hosea, *A Treatise on the Intellectual Character, and Civil and Political Condition of the Colored People of the U. States and the Prejudice Exercised Towards Them* (Boston: Isaac Knapp, 1837)

James, C. L. R., *Beyond a Boundary* (London: Hutchinson, 1963)

Noble, Kenneth B., 'Issue of racism erupts in Simpson trial', *New York Times*, 14 January 1995

Pearson, Harry, *Connie: The Marvellous Life of Learie Constantine* (London: Little, Brown, 2017)

Williamson, Martin, 'We won't have niggers in this hotel', ESPNCricinfo, 26 January 2008

'Coloured Subjects (Discrimination)', Hansard, 392, 23 September 1943

'Learie Constantine was "humiliated"', *Evening News*, 28 June 1944

Judgment: *Constantine v Imperial Hotels Ltd*, High Court of Justice, King's Bench Division, 28 June 1944

4: Mahmood Mattan

Bennetto, Jason, 'Racial hatred that led to a "legalised lynching"', *Independent*, 25 February 1998

Dobson, Roger, 'So who is the real killer of Tiger Bay?', *Independent on Sunday*, 5 October 1997

Dodd, Vikram, 'Met officer investigated after black boy, 16, stopped six times in five months', *Guardian*, 6 February 2024

Fahiya, Daniella, 'South Wales Police apologise 70 years after hanging injustice', BBC News, 2 September 2022

Khan, Stephen, 'Tormented life and death of man in black', *Observer*, 3 August 2003

Mahalingam, Udit, 'South Wales Police finally apologise for Mahmood Mattan conviction – "far too late", says family', The Justice Gap, 7 September 2022

Mansfield, Michael, *The Power in the People: How We Can Change the World* (London: Monoray, 2023)

Midgley, Carol, 'Injustice casts a lifelong shadow', *The Times*, 7 June 2001

Mohamed, Nadifa, *The Fortune Men* (London: Viking, 2021)

Phillips, Chris, *Hanged for the Word If: The Murder of Lily Volpert and the Execution of Mahmood Hussein Mattan* (independently published, 2020)

Sinclair, Neil M. C., *The Tiger Bay Story* (Cardiff: Butetown History & Arts Centre, 1993)

'On murder charge', *Portsmouth Evening News*, 17 March 1952

Mattan: Injustice of a Hanged Man, podcast series, BBC Radio Wales, 2022

Papers relating to Mattan's trial at The National Archives, Kew: ASSI 84/135, DPP 2/2145, HO 594/52

5: Kelso Cochrane

Aldred, Joe, 'From Kelso Cochrane to Brexit', Movement for Justice & Reconciliation, 2019

Berg, Sanchia: 'Kelso Cochrane: trying to unlock the secrets of a 64-year-old racist murder', BBC News, 21 August 2023; 'Police knew murder suspect intended to kill a black man', BBC News, 13 July 2024

Boyce Davies, Carole (ed.), *Claudia Jones: Beyond Containment. Autobiographical Reflections, Essays, and Poems* (Banbury: Ayebia Clarke, 2011)

Eales, Colin, 'Witness to violence', *Kensington News and West London Times*, 5 September 1958

Humphries, Steve and Pamela Gordon, *Forbidden Britain: Our Secret Past 1900–1960* (London: BBC Books, 1994)

Loffhagen, Emma, 'The forgotten racial history of Notting Hill Carnival', *Evening Standard*, 23 August 2024

Nasar, Saima, 'The Mother of Notting Hill Carnival: Claudia Jones', Department of History, University of Bristol

Olden, Mark: 'White riot: the week Notting Hill exploded', *Independent*, 29 August 2008; *Murder in Notting Hill* (Winchester: Zero Books, 2011); 'Profile: Patrick Digby, the sailor who became the prime suspect for Kelso Cochrane's murder', *Telegraph*, 7 September 2011

Olende, Ken: 'The Notting Hill riot and a carnival of defiance', *Socialist Worker*, 19 August 2008; 'Who killed Kelso Cochrane?', *Socialist Worker*, 4 October 2011

Pilkington, Edward, *Beyond the Mother Country: West Indians and the Notting Hill White Riots* (London: I.B. Tauris, 1988)

Salmon, Mr Justice, sentencing remarks drawn from *The Times, Portsmouth Evening News* and *Birmingham Daily Post*, 16 September 1958

Traini, Robert, 'Race-hate murder', *Daily Herald*, 18 May 1959

Travis, Alan, 'After 44 years secret papers reveal truth about five nights of violence in Notting Hill', *Guardian*, 24 August 2002

Willcocks, Rachel, 'The When We Worked at Raleigh project celebrates the lives of the factory's Black British Caribbean workers', Left Lion, 10 July 2020

Williams, Sydney, 'My 44-hour ordeal in murder quiz', *Daily Herald*, 21 May 1959

'Beating back Mosley in Notting Hill, 1958 – Baker Baron', Libcom, 10 September 2006

'Black History Month: Nottingham Riots (1958)', *Royal Gazette*, 4 February 2016

'Cochrane killer is still free', *Kensington News and West London Times*, 3 June 1960

'Coloured people "have lost confidence"', *The Times*, 19 May 1959

'Crowds clamber over tombstones', *Leicester Evening Mail*, 6 June 1959

'Gang victim led double life', *The People*, 24 May 1959

'Heckling at "White Defence" rally', *The Times*, 25 May 1959

'Kelso Cochrane', Unsolved Murders (unsolved.murders.co.uk)

'Landlord Rachman gets rich on racial tension', *Sunday Times*, 2 October 2011

'London racial outburst due to many factors', *The Times*, 3 September 1958

'Murder in Notting Hill', *Daily Express*, 18 May 1959

'Murder in Notting Hill', Our Migration Story (ourmigrationstory.org.uk)

'Political and community activism', Georgepowe.net

'Race hate not murder motive', *Sunderland Daily Echo and Shipping Gazette*, 18 May 1959

'Racial riots at Notting Hill between 31 August and 3 September 1958', MEPO 2/9838, The National Archives, Kew

'Thousands mass at Kelso grave', *Shields Daily News*, 6 June 1959

6: David Oluwale

Aspden, Kester: 'Legacy of hate', *Guardian*, 30 May 2007; *The Hounding of David Oluwale* (London: Vintage, 2008); 'The long hours: remembering David Oluwale', *The Critic*, 15 October 2020

Farrar, Max, 'David Oluwale's Life and Death', Remember Oluwale (rememberoluwale.org)

IOPC, 'The circumstances of Sean Rigg's death, and the history of the IPCC and IOPC involvement', background statement, September 2023

Mayoux, Chloe, 'Olive Morris and the British Black Panthers', Layers of London (www.layersoflondon.org)

Phillips, Caryl, *Foreigners: Three English Lives* (London: Vintage, 2008)

Phillips, Ron, 'The death of one lame darkie', *Race Today*, January 1972

Robinson, Paul, 'Son of whistleblowing police cadet speaks movingly at David Oluwale memorial event in Leeds', *Yorkshire Evening Post*, 20 April 2019

Wilby, Neil: 'Remembering Oluwale: "an indelible, black mark on Leeds police"', The Justice Gap, 29 April 2014; 'David Oluwale: a scandal that stains the history of the grand old city of Leeds', Neil Wilby Media, 9 June 2016

'A blue plaque for David Oluwale', Leeds Beckett University, 2022

'Detentions under the Mental Health Act', Ethnicity Facts and Figures Service, 16 August 2024

'Jury asked to say whether police sergeant is old-fashioned bobby or bully boy', *The Times*, 23 November 1971

'Nigerian diplomat (arrest)', Hansard, vol. 791, 17 November 1969

'Olive Morris – a tragically short life dedicated to struggle', *Socialist Worker*, 18 September 2020

'Police "hounded man to his death"', *Daily Express*, 9 November 1971

'Police sergeant "had a job to do"', *Birmingham Daily Post*, 24 November 1971

'Sean Rigg: Police watchdog issue unprecedented apology to family, 15 years on from Brixton custody death', 8 September 2023

'Thousands battle in violent race riot', *The Mail (Adelaide)*, 23 July 1949

'Vagrant "was built like miniature Mr Universe"', *Nottingham Guardian*, 19 November 1971

7: The Mangrove Nine

Alibhai-Brown, Yasmin, 'Race: The Voices of Britain', *Independent*, 11 May 2000

Ashley John-Baptiste, Ashley, 'The Mangrove Nine: echoes of Black Lives Matter from 50 years ago', BBC News

Bunce, Robin and Paul Field: 'Mangrove Nine: the court challenge against police racism in Notting Hill', *Guardian*, 29 November 2010; *Darcus Howe: A Political Biography* (London: Bloomsbury, 2015)

Busby, Margaret, 'Frank Crichlow obituary', *Observer*, 26 September 2010

Crichlow, Frank and Hassan Mahamdallie, 'Frank Crichlow: sanding tall against racism', *Socialist Worker*, 1 November 2010

du Sautoy, Alex, 'The Mangrove Nine and the history of English juries', 6KBW blog, 11 February 2021

Field, Paul, 'The real guerrillas', *Jacobin*, 14 April 2017

Howe, Darcus: *The Road Made to Walk on Carnival Day: The Battle for the West Indian Carnival in Britain* (editor; London: Race Today, 1977); *From Bobby to Babylon: Blacks and the British Police* (London: Race Today, 1988)

Iglikowski-Broad, Vicky and Rowena Hillel, 'Rights, resistance and racism: the story of the Mangrove Nine', The National Archives, 21 October 2015

Langen, Nicholas Reed, 'Mangrove Nine: when Black power took on the British establishment', 29 November 2019

McQueen, Steve (dir.), *Mangrove*, first broadcast BBC One, 15 November 2020

Randall, Dave, 'Steve McQueen's *Mangrove*: anti-racist struggle takes to the stage of British history', Counterfire, 16 November 2020

Shah, Subi, 'Darcus Howe: "All I want to do is mobilize the people to stand up for their rights"', *New Internationalist*, 30 December 2013

Taylor, Diane, '"It was like a family": remembering the Mangrove, Notting Hill's Caribbean haven', *Guardian*, 15 September 2018

Thompson, Ife, 'The Mangrove 9 and the radical lawyering tradition', Verso Books, 20 November 2020

Waters, Rob, *Thinking Black: Britain, 1964–1985* (Berkeley: University of California Press, 2018)

'J. Edgar Hoover: Black Panther greatest threat to US security', UPI Archives, 16 July 1969

'Mangrove Nine protest', The National Archives

8: The Oval Four

Bull, Clive, 'The man cleared of a serious crime 43 years later . . . thanks to a call to LBC', LBC, 1 February 2018

Campbell, Duncan: '"It shattered me": Winston Trew on his decades-long fight to clear his name', *Observer*, 13 October

2019; '"Oval Four" men jailed in 1972 cleared by court of appeal in London', *Guardian*, 5 December 2019; '"Stockwell Six": two men could have convictions overturned', *Guardian*, 14 December 2020; 'A real *Line of Duty*: the London police officer who "went bent"', *Guardian*, 1 May 2021

Charone, Barbara, 'Eric Clapton: farther on up the road', *Sounds*, October 1976

Crowe, Cameron, 'Playboy interview: David Bowie', *Playboy*, September 1976

Cuthbertson, Peter, 'The growing number of prolific criminals and the increased concentration of crime: A case for more prison places', Civitas, February 2018

Dearden, Lizzie, 'Oval Four: Black men arrested by corrupt police officer could be cleared 50 years after being jailed', *Independent*, 14 October 2019

Foot, Matt, 'Corrupt cops', *London Review of Books*, 46:3 (8 February 2024)

Hall, Stuart, *Policing the Crisis: Mugging, the State and Law and Order* (London: Macmillan, 1978)

Hattenstone, Simon, '"I just went bent": how Britain's most corrupt cop ruined countless lives', *Guardian*, 25 January 2024

MacGuill, Dan, 'Did Eric Clapton once unleash a racist rant onstage?', Snopes, 4 December 2020

Morton, Becky, 'Reform drops three candidates over offensive comments', BBC News, 29 June 2024

Pendlebury, Richard, 'Britain's most bent copper', *Daily Mail*, 9 July 2021

Satchwell, Graham and Winston Trew, *Rot at the Core: The Serious Crimes of a Detective Sergeant* (Stroud: History Press, 2021)

Stubbs, David, 'Eric Clapton & Enoch Powell to Morrissey: race in British music since '76', *The Quietus*, 9 August 2016

Thomas, Lee, 'Eric Clapton's abhorrent racist outburst', *Far Out*, 22 June 2024

Trew, Winston, 'Mehmet and Peterkin: 40 years of systemic failings', The Justice Gap, 21 January 2024

'8 Key Facts About Violence', Youth Endowment Fund report, 2024

'American-style "mugging"', Cheshire Observer, 4 August 1972

'Boy (16) gets 20 years', Coventry Evening Telegraph, 19 March 1973

'If the muggers don't get you ...', Freedom, 34:32 (11 August 1973)

'Man dies after mugging terror', Coventry Evening Telegraph, 16 August 1972

'Mr Kingsley Read', Hansard, vol. 914, 28 June 1976

'Night of the mugger', Daily Mirror, 17 August 1972

Report of court proceedings, Daily Express, 26 September 1972

'Rock Against Racism at 40', New York University, 2 May 2019

'Stockwell Six: Three men have 1972 convictions quashed by Court of Appeal', BBC News, 6 July 2021

'Surrey "mailbag thief" jailed in 1976 overturns conviction', BBC News, 17 January 2018

9: New Cross Fire and Beyond

Mansfield, Michael, Memoirs of a Radical Lawyer (London: Bloomsbury, 2010)

McQueen, Steve (dir.), Uprising, first broadcast BBC One, 20–22 July 2021

O'Neill, Padraig, 'Remembering the Battle of Lewisham', Tribune, 12 August 2023

Peplolw, Simon, Race and Riots in Thatcher's Britain (Manchester: Manchester University Press, 2019)

Saunders, Sarah, 'Remembering the New Cross Fire. 40 years on', Anti-Racist Cumbria, 16 January 2021

Scarman, Lord (George Scarman), The Scarman Report (London: Penguin, 1982)

Thatcher, Margaret, 'TV interview for Granada *World in Action*', Margaret Thatcher Foundation, 27 January 1978

Walker, Peter, '"I couldn't have done anything else" – Brixton riots policeman tells his story', *Guardian*, 2 April 2011

White, Nadine, 'Black People's Day of Action: inside the 1981 New Cross Fire march that brought Britain to a standstill', *HuffPost*, 2 March 2020

'Inquiry into the 1981 Brixton Disturbances (Scarman Inquiry): Evidence and Papers', HO 266, The National Archives, Kew

'Q&A: The Scarman Report', BBC News, 27 April 2004

'Scarman Report', Hansard, vol. 14, 10 December 1981

'What was the "Battle of Lewisham"?', Goldsmiths, University of London

10: My Story: The Shooting of My Mum, Cherry Groce

Basu, Neil, *Turmoil: The Official Autobiography. 30 Years of Policing, Politics and Prejudice* (London: Aurum, 2025)

Hamilton, Davina, 'Asher Senator and the late Smiley Culture: partners in rhyme', *The Voice*, 9 October 2016

Lawrence, Lee, *The Louder I Will Sing* (London: Sphere, 2020)

Monteith, Keir and others, 'Racial Bias and the Bench: A response to the Judicial Diversity and Inclusion Strategy (2020–2025)', University of Manchester, November 2022

Scott, Stafford, 'The police say they support Black Lives Matter. Tell that to people in Tottenham', *Guardian*, 17 June 2020

Siddique, Haroon, 'Mark Duggan police shooting: can forensic tech cast doubt on official report?', *Guardian*, 10 June 2020

Simpson, Dave, 'From pop star to chiropractor: musicians' post-musical careers', *Guardian*, 23 September 2010

Smiley Culture, 'Police Officer', from *The Original Smiley Culture* (1986)

Thomas, Leslie, 'Smiley Culture inquest jury return suicide verdict', Garden Court Chambers, 3 July 2013

'Cynthia Jarrett', Inquest (history.inquest.org.uk)

'Diversity of the judiciary: Legal professions, new appointments and current post-holders – 2025 Statistics', Ministry of Justice, 23 July 2025

'Dorothy "Cherry" Groce inquest finds police failures contributed to her death', *Guardian*, 10 July 2014

'"Dreadful" moment relived by Lovelock', *Dundee Courier*, 10 January 1987

'Jordan Walker-Brown: Tasered, hospitalised but determined to seek justice!', Bhatt Murphy, 24 June 2020

'Jury concludes multiple police failures led to 1985 shooting of Cherry Groce', Inquest, 10 July 2014

'Mark Duggan death: timeline of events', BBC News, 27 October 2015

'New report uncovers "institutional racism" in the justice system', University of Manchester, 18 October 2022

'Number of mass shootings in the United States between 1982 and September 2024, by shooter's race or ethnicity', Statista, May 2025

'Smiley Culture death: no crime committed, says IPCC', BBC News, 29 November 2011

11: The Cardiff Three

Fox, Charlie, 'What price justice? The story of the Cardiff 3', The Justice Gap, 16 December 2011

Howell, Richard, 'Mouncher Investigation Report', House of Commons, 18 July 2017

King, Martin Luther, Jr, 'Letter from Birmingham Jail' in *Why We Can't Wait* (New York: Harper & Row, 1964)

Mangold, Tom, 'An injustice that won't go away', *Independent*, 11 August 2012

Sekar, Satish: *Fitted In: The Cardiff 3 and the Lynette White Inquiry* (The Fitted-In Project, 1998); *The Cardiff Five:*

Innocent Beyond Any Doubt (2nd edn; Hook: Waterside Press, 2017)

'"Cardiff Three" police will not be disciplined', *Independent*, 22 December 1992

'Cardiff murder appeal man "beaten over head verbally"', *Guardian*, 19 December 1992

'Evidence in Lynette White case to be re-examined', WalesOnline, 28 October 2008

'Home Secretary announces investigation into collapsed police trial', Home Office, 26 February 2015

'Justice Denied: The Greatest Scandal?', *Panorama*, first broadcast BBC One, 13 August 2012

'No Justice for Cardiff Three: a summary of the Horwell Report', Gold Jennings, 2 August 2017

Crimewatch UK, BBC One, 17 March 1988

12: Stephen Lawrence

Brooks, Duwayne, *Steve and Me: My Friendship with Stephen Lawrence and the Search for Justice* (London: BrooksBooks, 2006)

Casciani, Dominic, 'Stephen Lawrence: The long road to justice', BBC News, 3 January 2012

Evans, Rob and Paul Lewis, 'Police "smear" campaign targeted Stephen Lawrence's friends and family', *Guardian*, 24 June 2013

Halliday, Josh, 'For father of Rolan Adams, murdered in 1991, anger and pain are undimmed', *Guardian*, 21 April 2018

Harper, Tom, *Broken Yard: The Fall of the Metropolitan Police* (London: Biteback, 2022)

Macpherson, Sir William, 'The Stephen Lawrence Inquiry: Report of an Inquiry of Sir William Macpherson of Cluny', February 1999. Available via gov.uk

Rielly, Bethany, 'The cop who spied on grief: why did the

British state secretly monitor Black families seeking justice?',
New Internationalist, 28 August 2024

'Inquiry into the matters arising from the death of Stephen
Lawrence: records', NT, The National Archives, Kew

'Stephen Lawrence murder: the persecution of Duwayne
Brooks', *Socialist Worker*, 10 January 2012

'Violence erupts at Lawrence inquiry', BBC News, 30 June
1998

13: Dalian Atkinson

Banner, David, 'Atkinson murder accused says he was
"absolutely terrified"', *Shropshire Star*, 20 May 2021

Dodd, Vikram: 'Police chiefs admit failures on diversity 21 years
after pledge', *Guardian*, 27 January 2020; 'Dalian Atkinson's
head was kicked like a football by police officer, murder
trial told', *Guardian*, 4 May 2021; 'Dalian Atkinson's family
says five-year wait for trial was "unacceptable"', *Guardian*,
23 June 2021; 'Dalian Atkinson killing: officer was kept
on despite gross misconduct', *Guardian* 28 June 2021;
'Met police seek judicial review over senior black officer's
reinstatement', *Guardian*, 2 August 2021; 'Black people seven
times more likely to die after police restraint in Britain,
figures show', *Guardian*, 19 February 2023

Evans, Martin Evans, 'Met Police recruit "functionally illiterate
in English" in attempt to improve diversity', *Telegraph*, 26
January 2023

Hales, Gavin, 'A Diversity Uplift?', Police Foundation report,
January 2020

Hamilton, Fiona, 'Policeman who tasered and kicked Dalian
Atkinson "feared for himself and girlfriend"', *The Times*, 2
June 2021

Jackson, Carl, 'Jury fails to reach verdict over cop accused of
assaulting Dalian Atkinson', BirminghamLive, 24 June 2021

Lee, Joseph, 'Dalian Atkinson: police apologise for killing black ex-footballer', BBC News, 27 December 2021

Logan, Leroy, *Closing Ranks: My Life as a Cop* (London: SPCK, 2020)

Mahon, Leah, 'Dalian Atkinson trial: former footballer died only an hour after being Tasered, court hears', *The Voice*, 17 May 2021

PA Media, 'Dalian Atkinson "not in his right mind" when he was tasered, according to his father', Sky Sports, 6 May 2021

Patel, Sima, 'How getting struck by a TASER affects the human body', ABC News, 29 May 2018

Prasad, Raekha, '"How do I heal?": The long wait for justice after a black man died in custody', *Guardian*, 18 June 2024

Qasim, Wail, 'Dalian Atkinson was black and mentally ill – we shouldn't be surprised he was Tasered to death', *Independent*, 17 August 2016

Quinn, Ben, 'Dalian Atkinson: officer told ex-footballer "keep your head down", murder trial hears', *Guardian*, 6 May 2021

Ringrose, Isabel, 'Police were "kicking the shit" out of Dalian Atkinson before his death, jury hears', *Socialist Worker*, 4 May 2021

Roberts, Norwell, *I am Norwell Roberts* (London: Two Roads, 2022)

Russell, Yvette, 'Dalian Atkinson: manslaughter conviction for PC but "justice" for police violence remains elusive', *The Conversation*, 29 June 2013

Speare-Cole, Rebecca, 'Black Police Association accuses Met of "institutional racism" over prosecution of officer for child abuse video', *Evening Standard*, 27 November 2019

Vernalls, Richard, 'Police officers "colluded" after Dalian Atkinson was Tasered, murder jury told', *Evening Standard*, 5 May 2021

'Baroness Casey Review: Final Report. An Independent review into the standards of behaviour and internal culture of the

Metropolitan Police Service', March 2023. Available via met.police.uk

'Black men seven times more likely to die following police restraint but racism not being addressed', Inquest, 20 February 2023

'Dalian Atkinson: murder-accused PC was absolutely petrified', BBC News, 20 May 2021

'Dalian Atkinson: Police officer found guilty of manslaughter', Inquest, 23 June 2021

'Evaluation of the online assessment process for police recruitment', College of Policing, April 2021

I Can't Breathe: Race, Death & British Policing, Inquest report, February 2023

'Inquest concludes Adrian McDonald died of stress of incident following police dog bits and Taser use as well as effects of cocaine', Inquest, 28 November 2018

'IOPC investigating six allegations of excessive use of force against black men in Birmingham', Police Professional, 28 May 2020

'PC Benjamin Monk jailed for eight years for killing footballer Dalian Atkinson', Police Professional, 29 June 2021

'PC feared he was "going to die" during Dalian Atkinson encounter, court told', Police Professional, 2 June 2021

'Police Race Action Plan: Improving Policing for Black People', National Police Chiefs' Council, 2022

'Police workforce', Ethnicity Facts and Figures Service, gov.uk

'Racism won't change until black people no longer seen as police "property" – former Met diversity chief', Sky News, 17 June 2020

'*Regina v Benjamin Monk*: Sentencing remarks of His Honour Judge Melbourne Inman, QC, Recorder of Birmingham', Judiciary of England and Wales. Available via judiaciary.uk

'Review of IOPC cases involving the use of Taser 2015–2020', IOPC, August 2021

'Stop and Search and Use of Force', West Midlands Police paper, 16 June 2020

'UK: Public should "resist drum-beat of calls for all police to carry a Taser', Amnesty International UK, 13 December 2018

'West Mercia Police officer given final written warning for excessive force on Dalian Atkinson', IOPC, 17 March 2023

'West Mercia Police officer sentenced for manslaughter of Dalian Atkinson', IOPC, 29 June 2021

14: Joint Enterprise

Begum, Shahida, 'Liberty intervention on CCRC referral on human rights implications of "gang" evidence in joint enterprise cases', Garden Court Chambers, 23 August 2023

Conn, David, 'Human rights group backs Manchester men who say racism led to murder convictions', *Guardian*, 23 August 2023

Hattenstone, Simon, 'Most people prosecuted under joint enterprise from minority ethnic background', *Guardian*, 30 September 2023

Stopes, Harry, 'How do 11 people go to jail for one murder?', *Guardian*, 9 March 2018

'Bentley, Derek', Criminal Cases Review Commission, 9 September 2024

'Crown Prosecution Service Joint Enterprise Pilot: Data Analysis', CPS, 29 September 2023

15: Artificial Intelligence and the Future

Babuta, Alexander and Marion Oswald, 'Data Analytics and Algorithmic Bias in Policing', RUSI briefing paper, 2019

Bailey, Stephanie, '*War Inna Babylon: The Community's Struggle for Justice Truth and Rights*', Art Papers, 2021

Colbert, Max, 'Lack of transparency over police forces' covert use of predictive policing software raises concerns about human rights abuses', *Byline Times*, 28 March 2023

Dick, Philip K., 'The Minority Report', in *Selected Stories of Philip K. Dick* (New York: Pantheon, 2002)

Fairs, Marcus, '*Minority Report* made today's technology possible', Dezeen, 6 November 2015

Grossman, Lev and others, 'The 50 best inventions', *Time*, 28 November 2011

Heaven, Will Douglas, 'Predictive policing is still racist – whatever data it uses', MIT Technology Review, 5 February 2021

Hvistendahl, Mara, 'Can "predictive policing" prevent crime before it happens?', *Science*, 28 September 2016

Lum, Kristian and William Isaac, 'To predict and serve?', *Significance Magazine*, October 2016

Pearsall, Beth, 'Predictive policing: the future of law enforcement?', *NIJ Journal*, 266 (2010)

Powers, Sara, 'Detroit police to change use of facial recognition technology after man wrongfully arrested for shoplifting', CBS News, 1 July 2024

Saunders, Jessica, Priscilla Hunt and John S. Hollywood, 'Predictions put into practice: a quasi-experimental evaluation of Chicago's predictive policing pilot', *Journal of Experimental Criminology*, 12 (2016)

Scott, Stafford: 'The Met's Gangs Matrix is racist policing in its purest form', *Guardian*, 12 January 2019; *War Inna Babylon* lecture series, available via YouTube

Vargas, Aitana, 'Reporting on the long shadow of the LAPD's data-driven policing programs', USC Center for Health Journalism, 29 August 2023

'Artificial Intelligence Act: MEPS adopt landmark law', European Parliament, 13 March 2024

'Gangs violence matrix', Metropolitan Police. Available via met. police.uk

'Liberty responds to release of research into facial recognition technology', Liberty, 5 April 2023

'Program Profile: Predictive Policing Model in Los Angeles, Calif.', National Institute of Justice, 28 November 2022

'Use of police technologies and tools' in 'The Macpherson Report: Twenty-two Years On', Home Affairs Committee. Available via parliament.uk

16: Towards an Anti-Racist Society

Du Bois, W. E. B.: *The Souls of Black Folk* (Chicago: A. C. McClurg & Co., 1903); *Dusk of Dawn* (New York: Harcourt Brace, 1940)

Elliott, Jane, *A Collar in My Pocket: The Blue Eyes Brown Eyes Exercise* (independently published, 2016)

Madden Al-Shabbaz, Abu-Bakr, 'Black History Toolkit', via Spotify

Onwuachi-Willig, Angela, 'Race and racial identity are social constructs', *New York Times*, 6 September 2016

Index